Regional Intervention Politics in Africa

This book analyses regional interventions in African conflict spaces by engaging with political discourse theory.

Interventions are a performance of agency, but what happens if interventions are performed by forces that scholars have hardly ever considered as relevant agents in this regard? Based on a study of regional politics towards the crises in Burundi and Zimbabwe, the book analyses how these interventions shaped and changed the emerging regional interveners. The book engages political discourse theory, proposing an understanding of intervention as a field, in which multiple and heterogeneous interpretations of the violence, the crisis, and the future post-conflict order 'meet'. It is not hard to imagine that this encounter is not harmonious per se but full of frictions. By making use of political discourse theory as a grammar for studying the complexity of an intervention, the focus is directed to the emerging subjectivities of regional interveners. This enables a view of regional interventions that neither reduces their subjectivity to universalist categories associated with 'liberal peace' nor overenthusiastically embraces them as the solution to all problems.

This book will be of interest to students of international intervention, discourse theory, African politics, war and conflict studies, security studies and IR.

Stefanie Wodrig is a research fellow at the University of Kiel, Germany, and has a PhD in Political Science.

Routledge Studies in Intervention and Statebuilding
Series Editors: Aidan Hehir and Nicolas Lemay-Hébert
Founding Editor: David Chandler

Mediation and Liberal Peacebuilding
Peace from the ashes of war?
Edited by Mikael Eriksson and Roland Kostić

Semantics of Statebuilding
Language, meanings and sovereignty
Edited by Nicolas Lemay-Hébert, Nicholas Onuf, Vojin Rakić and Petar Bojanić

Humanitarian Crises, Intervention and Security
A framework for evidence-based programming
Edited by Liesbet Heyse, Andrej Zwitter, Rafael Wittek and Joost Herman

Internal Security and Statebuilding
Aligning agencies and functions
B.K. Greener and W.J. Fish

The EU and Member State Building
European foreign policy in the Western Balkans
Edited by Soeren Keil and Zeynep Arkan

Security and Hybridity after Armed Conflict
The dynamics of security provision in post-civil war states
Rens C. Willems

International Intervention and Statemaking
How exception became the norm
Selver B. Sahin

Rethinking Democracy Promotion in International Relations
The rise of the social
Jessica Schmidt

The Politics of International Intervention
The tyranny of peace
Edited by Mandy Turner and Florian P. Kühn

The Practice of Humanitarian Intervention
Aid workers, agencies and institutions in the Democratic Republic of the Congo
Kai Koddenbrock

Peace Figuration after International Intervention
Intentions, events and consequences of liberal peacebuilding
Gëzim Visoka

Regional Intervention Politics in Africa
Crisis, hegemony, and the transformation of subjectivity
Stefanie Wodrig

Regional Intervention Politics in Africa

Crisis, Hegemony, and the Transformation of Subjectivity

Stefanie Wodrig

LONDON AND NEW YORK

First published 2017
by Routledge
2 Park Square, Milton Park, Abingdon, Oxon OX14 4RN

and by Routledge
711 Third Avenue, New York, NY 10017

Routledge is an imprint of the Taylor & Francis Group, an informa business

© 2017 Stefanie Wodrig

The right of Stefanie Wodrig to be identified as author of this work has been asserted by her in accordance with sections 77 and 78 of the Copyright, Designs and Patents Act 1988.

All rights reserved. No part of this book may be reprinted or reproduced or utilised in any form or by any electronic, mechanical, or other means, now known or hereafter invented, including photocopying and recording, or in any information storage or retrieval system, without permission in writing from the publishers.

Trademark notice: Product or corporate names may be trademarks or registered trademarks, and are used only for identification and explanation without intent to infringe.

British Library Cataloguing in Publication Data
A catalogue record for this book is available from the British Library

Library of Congress Cataloging in Publication Data
Names: Wodrig, Stefanie, author.
Title: Regional intervention politics in Africa : crisis, hegemony, and the transformation of subjectivity / Stefanie Wodrig.
Description: Abingdon, Oxon ; New York, NY : Routledge, 2017. | Series: Routledge studies in intervention and statebuilding | Includes bibliographical references and index.
Identifiers: LCCN 2016044282| ISBN 9781138218901 (hbk) | ISBN 9781315436739 (ebk)
Subjects: LCSH: Peace-building–Africa, Eastern–International cooperation. | Conflict management–Africa, Eastern–International cooperation. | Peace-building–Burundi. | Conflict management–Burundi. | Peace-building–Zimbabwe. | Conflict management–Zimbabwe.
Classification: LCC JZ5584.A354 W64 2017 | DDC 327.1/170967–dc23
LC record available at https://lccn.loc.gov/2016044282

ISBN: 978-1-138-21890-1 (hbk)
ISBN: 978-1-315-43673-9 (ebk)

Typeset in Times New Roman
by Wearset Ltd, Boldon, Tyne and Wear

Contents

	Acknowledgements	vi
	List of abbreviations	viii
1	Introduction	1
2	The field of intervention: crisis, hegemony, and subjectivity	12
3	Studying regional interventions	34
4	Regional forces in Burundi: 'we are able to act!'	50
5	Regional forces in Zimbabwe: 'will we become like them?'	105
6	Regional interventions in Africa and beyond	166
	Index	175

Acknowledgements

This book is the final product of a long academic process that started at the beginning of my PhD. Here I want to thank all those people and institutions, without whose support the book would not have been written or would have been written in quite a different way. This book would not have come together without the academic and financial support of GIGA, the German Institute of Global and Area Studies, which I joined in 2010 as a graduate student. The graduate programme on the study of regional powers directed my attention to regional interventions; the research process greatly benefitting from the rich expertise at GIGA on comparative area studies in general and politics on the African continent in particular. When I began my research on regional interventions in eastern and southern Africa, Dirk Nabers encouraged me to think about the practices of regional intervention beyond disciplinary limits and read the work of Ernesto Laclau and Chantal Mouffe. Subsequently, their thinking (or better said, my reading of their work) became the primary theoretical inspiration for this book. Thank you, Dirk, for your assistance.

I will depart from the custom of thanking one's partner at the end of the acknowledgements as André Bank was a principle source of academic and personal inspiration. The book greatly benefitted from his deep understanding of 'violence in the neighbourhood', his advice during the research process, as well as his commenting on countless versions of the manuscript. I also owe him credit for sharpening the research question that guides the analysis of this book. Thank you for supporting me throughout the process of researching and writing this book – and much beyond!

This book would be very different without the two research stays in Tanzania 2011 and South Africa 2012, which were generously funded by GIGA. I particularly want to thank the people that I conducted interviews with in Tanzania, South Africa, and Zimbabwe. The interviewees devoted their time for my questions without receiving much in return. A special thanks goes to Azaveli Lwaitama who was very supportive in addressing the diverse challenges I faced while conducting research in Tanzania. Kristina von Knobelsdorff and Emilie Lacroux gave me a warm welcome, rendering my stay a very pleasant experience. While I was a guest scholar at the University of Witwatersrand in Johannesburg, Gilbert Khadiagala was very helpful in providing me with additional contacts.

Thanks to Julia Scheller, Martina Schwikowski, Ash Jewnarain, and his friends for helping me to explore the non-scholarly side of this fascinating country.

Some people who have helped me along the way also deserve credit. I am very grateful to Ulf Engel who provided substantial comments on earlier versions of the manuscript. A special thanks goes to Johannes Plagemann, with whom I shared an office during my PhD at GIGA and who devoted much time and effort to comment on earlier versions. On a similar note, it has been really insightful and fun to discuss Burundi and Zimbabwe with Julia Grauvogel. I also wish to acknowledge the contributions of Lucie Chamlian, Charlotte Heyl, Kai Koddenbrock, Nicola Nymalm, Ina Peters, Ryoma Sakaeda, Maren Wagner, and Franzisca Zanker who in one way or another sharpened the argument. The book of course also immensely benefitted from the numerous encounters I had during conferences, such as the annual meetings of the International Studies Association, and workshops, as well as during the Essex summer school course on political discourse theory, organised by Jason Glynos and David Howarth.

Lastly I would like to thank my family. Theo, you brightened my days after plunging into the complexity of a research process. Thank you, Helga and Horst Timm. A special thanks goes to my parents Hilke and Jürgen Wodrig, who supported me throughout this research process and pretty much everything that lead to it. I am very grateful for your life-long backing!

Abbreviations

ANC	African National Congress
AU	African Union
BRICS	Brazil, Russia, India, China, and South Africa
CNDD-FDD	Conseil national pour la défense de la démocratie – Forces pour la défense de la démocratie
COMESA	Common Market for Eastern and Southern Africa
COSATU	Congress of South African Trade Unions
DA	Democratic Alliance
EAC	East African Community
EU	European Union
Frodebu	Front pour la démocratie au Burundi
ICG	International Crisis Group
IR	international relations
MDC	Movement of Democratic Change
OAU	Organisation of African Unity
Palipehutu-FNL	Parti pour la liberation du peuple hutu – Forces nationales de liberation
SACP	South African Communist Party
SADC	Southern African Development Community
SADC Organ	Organ on Politics, Defence and Security Cooperation
Uprona	Union pour le progrès national
ZANU-PF	Zimbabwe African National Union – Patriotic Front

1 Introduction

In 1995 eastern African elites became increasingly anxious that Burundi might become a 'second Rwanda', that is, a place of genocidal violence, which still reminds the world of having done nothing to stop it. Such analogical reasoning between the Rwandan past and the Burundian future prompted the former Tanzanian President to say: 'we must therefore act, and act quickly' (Mkapa 1996). A few years later, in southern Africa, what was going on in Zimbabwe attracted much attention from distant and not so distant places. On the top of the violence and uncertainty in 2008, the former South African President argued: 'the pain your country [Zimbabwe] bears, is a pain that is transferred to the masses of our people' (Mbeki 2008). The crises in Burundi and Zimbabwe, without denying the difference between the two trajectories of violence and crisis, both became fields of regional politics that not just transformed the societies under intervention but also the political landscape of those states and societies intervening. With articulating a *We need to act!* so typical for interveners (Bliesemann de Guevara and Kühn 2011), governments claimed agency that, at least in IR, have hardly ever been considered as possessing it (Harman and Brown 2013). This claim for agency prompts us – as researchers – to reconsider what we know about the subjectivity of Tanzania and other eastern and southern African states. It potentially unsettles our understanding of such commonly considered marginal places that themselves became interveners. The quote from the former South African President warns us against judging the search for African solutions to African problems by universal standards. Rather, spatial proximity between those intervening and those being under intervention might generate new constellations and new dynamics that considerably differ from what we know about international interventions. This book wants to contribute to our understanding of what can be called regional interventions.

Regional interventions on the African continent

Area studies have long pointed to transformations in practising interventions on the African continent. This change is best epitomised by the replacement of the Organisation of African Unity (OAU) with the African Union (AU) at the beginning of the new millennium. For intervention politics, this organisational make-up meant, speaking with metaphors here, a departure 'from non-intervention to non-indifference' (Williams 2006). Under the OAU – founded in 1963 by the newly independent states on the continent – intervention and sovereignty was entwined in a particular way (more generally, see Weber 1992). The newly independent member states authorised the OAU to defend their sovereignty vis-à-vis their former colonisers. But internal instabilities and Cold War politics undermined this quest for sovereign equality. Many OAU member states became again places of non-African intervention. As a means to discourage these non-African interventions, OAU member states refrained from criticising each other on their internal affairs (van Walraven 1999). The signifier 'non-intervention' thus wants to encapsulate these complex postcolonial dynamics that structured African politics from 1963 to 2001. The authors of the African Union, by contrast, promised to break with this practice of 'non-intervention'. In its charter, the AU is given the right to politically and militarily intervene in cases of war crimes, genocide, crimes against humanity, as well as serious threats to legitimate order. The constitutive act thus authorised the AU to intervene in a variety of internal crises. The signifier 'non-indifference' points to this legal authorisation.

This transformation 'from non-intervention to non-indifference' was neither abrupt nor complete (see Williams 2006, Witt 2013). Although the transformation is widely associated with the institutional reform culminating in the emergence of the AU, traces of it can already be reconstructed in the 1990s, most visibly at the regional scale. An early example of these changes is the intervention of the Regional Peace Initiative in Burundi (see Boulden 2003, Bellamy and Williams 2005). This Regional Initiative was not a formal regional organisation but an ad hoc coalition of Burundi's neighbours that performed intervention politics from 1995 to 2009. While intervening, the forces in the Regional Initiative identified a new subjectivity for themselves, paving the way for the institutional reforms as codified in the AU charter. But the transformation has not been a linear process, as the regional politics towards Zimbabwe illustrate. Beginning at the end of the twentieth century, the crisis in Zimbabwe activated a controversy among southern African societies about sovereignty and intervention, in the course of which the subjectivity normally attributed to interveners became questioned.

In this book, the transformation 'from non-intervention to non-indifference' becomes visible as a non-linear, complex process full of frictions. It is not as if the intervention politics scrutinised here only unfolded at the regional scale. In the case of Burundi and Zimbabwe the continental organisation contributed to the intervention politics as did forces from outside the continent. Institutionally the African peace and security architecture tries to integrate the multiscalarity of an intervention, with the AU being sought to coordinate the heterogeneity of forces involved in crafting peace (Engel and Gomes Porto 2010). But in practice such multiscalarity is not without frictions, as was already pointed out elsewhere: 'At the AU there is a feeling that the Regional Economic Communities [e.g. the Southern African Development Community] are not always fully committed to AU leadership. Conversely, in the regions the AU is sometimes felt to be overstepping itself' (Vines 2013, p. 101). In this book, these frictions and tensions will become visible as part of the emergence of new agents in the politics of intervention, enabled to articulate an elusive and fragile difference to hegemonic peacebuilding, as I will further explain in the next section.

The research gap of critical intervention studies

Interventions constitute a field in which multiple and heterogeneous interpretations about violence, crises, as well as political futures more generally 'meet'. The heterogeneity of the field created by interventions was, for a long time, most explicitly emphasised by mediation research. According to a popular definition, mediation (as a form of intervention) is commonly considered as a process 'where the disputants seek the assistance of, or accept an offer of help from, an individual, group, state or organization to settle their conflict or revolve their differences' (Bercovitch, Anagnoson, and Wille 1991, p. 8). Hence, mediation is imagined as a dialogical process, a representation that clearly crumbles when related to the intervention process more broadly, which tends to be associated with force rather than dialogue. The unevenness of the field constituted by an intervention will be scrutinised more closely in this section.

Prior to that, it should be clarified that intervention is here understood in the broad sense to include all external practices and articulations towards the place under intervention. IR has traditionally comprehended interventions as military force by states. Following Audra Mitchell:

> An uninvited military mission across state borders can certainly be an act of intervention, but so can the speech-acts of public figures attempting to influence warring actors, the efforts of 'grass-roots' peace-builders to restore social order in the wake of violence, and even the calculations of researchers attempting to predict and control the outbreak of conflict.
> (Mitchell 2014, p. 3)

Interventions are comprehended as a combination of already sedimented and novel discourses of former and current interveners as well as of people under intervention. Whereas those societies under intervention have little choice in joining the discourse, those outside the society under intervention do so by enunciating speech-acts and practising societal, political, military or economic interventions. In more conventional terms, all sorts of external undertakings aimed at ending violence and crisis are here understood as constituting the intervention (see also Autesserre 2014, p. 10). However, as will become explicit in the second chapter of this book, these discourses are not only shaped by discourse participant, but are also shaping them. The field of intervention is understood as an ever-changing virtual space, which constitutes subjects as interveners or recipients of intervention; as global, regional or local; as Western or non-Western (Björkdahl and Höglund 2013, Kappler 2014, 2015).

4 *Introduction*

Studies of peacebuilding had long privileged the analysis of the intervener's agency. The interveners were represented as being guided by liberal peacebuilding and statebuilding ideals, that is, an ideology that aims to comprehensively transform the society under intervention by importing liberal institutions (Paris 2002, Bliesemann de Guevara 2012). It was argued that this aspiration to comprehensively transform the crisis also shaped the self-understanding of the interveners, at least for a while (Sending 2011). Aiming to transform the society in crisis is not a dialogical approach, but implies the power of agency to shape politics according to one's own projections of good order (Mac Ginty and Richmond 2013, p. 177, Holmqvist, Bachmann, and Bell 2015, pp. 5–7). These exclusive projections of agency onto interveners have contributed to the image of the field of intervention as an uneven space. This understanding of interventions made plausible a particular imagination of the place under intervention as a terra incognita, that is, a political place without a history that could be remodelled from the outside (Lemay-Hébert 2011). Not surprisingly, the limits of such representation soon became visible: domestic forces wanted to shape their own futures. Both in academia as well as in practice, an intervention could no longer be thought without 'the local' (Mac Ginty and Richmond 2013).

Although the research field emerged with a focus on the interveners and immensely contributed to our understanding of this subject position, it has not yet specifically engaged in what might become a *regional turn*. The abovementioned transformations of the nexus of sovereignty and intervention on the African continent have been reflected upon by area studies and more sporadically in IR publications. But, largely, critical intervention scholarship has not yet specifically discussed the increasing number of interventions conducted by regional organisations, neighbouring governments, or other subjects that are relatively close to the violence and crisis. Recently, this research gap has also been noted by two leading scholars of the field: 'the regional aspect of liberal peace interventions has been under-researched' (Richmond and Mac Ginty 2015, p. 183). Hence, this book seeks to address this gap.

Political discourse theory and the subjectivity of the regional interveners

The book engages political discourse theory as articulated by Ernesto Laclau to analyse the regional interventions into Burundi and Zimbabwe. Peace and conflict studies in general and intervention studies in particular have a long history of aiming to improve the practices of peace and intervention. This had led to research which has often justified its relevance according to its ability to affect the practice of peacemaking. Engaging Laclau's complex theorising of the political does not seem to be the most practice-oriented path. Therefore, it was important when Lemay-Hébert, Onuf, and Rakic (2014, p. 2) argued for broadening the scope of the research by engaging political theory for studying interventions and statebuilding. I argue that studying regional interventions on the basis of political discourse theory facilitates thinking about, seeing, and expressing elements of regional interventions that otherwise might remain in the dark. This is obviously a strong claim. However, looking at these practices with political discourse theory makes the complex agency of the regional interveners visible. Regional interveners are not just intermediaries of liberal policy blueprints, nor are they entertaining a radically different peace. Political discourse theory allows for an understanding of regional intervention as a precarious counter-discourse, trying to emancipate itself from a hegemonic intervention discourse mostly preached in headquarters and government buildings located in the Global North. Yet, political discourse theory also knows that such emancipation is doomed to fail since counter-discourses produce new exclusions, reductions, and hence force. The analysis thus shows how African organisations, governments, and societal groups have tried to break out of their former subject position as passive bystanders by becoming interveners themselves. Being an intervener is associated with the ability to shape the future. In other words, political discourse theory helps to grapple with the transformations of subjectivity still ongoing in the field of intervention and beyond.

Political discourse theory is generally considered as contributing to poststructuralism, sharing with it a certain understanding of language and contingency. Like other poststructuralist approaches, in their opus magnum *Hegemony and socialist strategy* (2001 [1985]), Laclau and Mouffe critically engaged the structural linguistics once articulated by Ferdinand de Saussure, thoroughly studied the deconstruction of Jacques Derrida, and – with their help – offered a re-reading of Antonio Gramsci's take on hegemony. In the writing of Laclau and Mouffe, discursive hegemony became the modus of the political. Political discourse theory rests on the apprehension that language and discourse do not merely reflect reality but constitute it. The theory does not deny materiality exists, but it emphasises that we cannot directly access materiality: our understanding of materiality is always mediated by structures of signification (Laclau 1993, p. 541). In this sense, we cannot escape discourse. Accordingly, discourse has to be the primary level of analysis. Accentuating the discursive character of the political should not be misunderstood as a conceptualisation of the political as a fluid space in which anything goes. On the contrary, discourse in the Laclauian sense refers to a highly structured field. This structure is not independent from discourse, but it is produced by hegemonic, rather stabilised significations as well as by more floating elements that are controversial.

Regarding the subject of this book, political discourse theory facilitates thinking of interventions as hegemonic and counter-hegemonic discourses. Interventions can be understood as a hegemonic structure that rests on sedimented power-relations, knowledges, and practices (as discussed in the previous section). These traces of hegemony permeate the emergence of any particular intervention. But an intervention in the making also immediately becomes part of the discourse that had previously constituted it. This implies that any particular intervention can re-articulate and even potentially question the hegemonic structure, that is, the power-relations, knowledges, and practices, on which interventions rest. In this book, I will enquire how two particular interventions politicised and questioned existing significations but likewise perpetuated others.

Political discourse theory enables us to understand a particular intervention as a field in which this perpetuation, politicisation, and questioning of previous significations is performed. It is a discursive field, in which many heterogeneous forces are involved: government officials, staff from international and regional organisations as well as from non-governmental organisations, journalists, public intellectuals, and researchers are just a few job descriptions for the forces that engage into this discourse. Their involvement in this field likewise rests on sedimented discourses: significations that, for instance, solidified in international organisations like the UN, authorising the latter to manage matters of international peace and security. Theoretically, their involvement in this discourse can be understood as a subject position, that is, a discursive authorisation to do certain things. This discursive positioning produces but also constrains the agency of subjects in the field of intervention. Prior to the emergence of a particular field of intervention, discourses have already constituted subjects as authorised to shape the discourse, thereby however also excluding many others.

Political discourse theory goes beyond conceptualising subjects as a discursive product. Once the non-necessity of the discourse reveals itself, the agent that was previously discursively enacted can re-articulate and hence change the discourse. In these moments, subjects become subjects in the strong sense, being able to re-articulate their own subjectivity. This book wants to reconstruct the transformations of subjectivity in two particular fields of intervention, namely Burundi and Zimbabwe. It comes down to one guiding question which to my knowledge has not been asked yet: *How did the interventions shape the interveners?* In asking this question, the subjectivity of the regional interveners comes into focus, which seems especially relevant in the context of African intervention practices that have transformed so radically in the last two decades. In this time period, sedimented power-relations, knowledges, and practices broke open, changing the discursive order such that regional forces on the African continent became enacted as interveners. In this book, I analyse how, once enacted as a subject, the regional interveners re-articulated their subjectivity, finding their own voice with it.

Reconstructing the regional discourse on Burundi and Zimbabwe

Political discourse theory provides us with an ontology of the political. It is well equipped to chart the logics of regional interventions. However, Laclau was quite hesitant to translate the theoretically rich grammar into a method-driven research programme. With the translation from theory to praxis, terms such as 'antagonism', that constitute the political, often lose their theoretical complexity. As was argued with respect to the first generation of scholars analysing policies with political discourse theory, they 'deploy their ontological categories [e.g. 'antagonism'] in undertaking an ontic analysis of specific political discourses' (Townshend 2003, p. 132). Although Laclau warned that any antagonism escapes a fixation through language (Laclau and Mouffe 2001 [1985], p. 125), this first generation of policy-oriented political discourse theory scholars had exactly done this: theoretical notions like 'antagonism' were deductively imposed onto a reality, without making explicit the process of deduction (Keller 2011, p. 165). Such non-reflexivity on method, however, is not consistent with current standards in the social sciences. Since the first generation of political discourse theorists, much has changed. A new generation of policy-oriented political discourse theory scholars has made inroads in articulating different pathways of how to bridge theory and praxis. This book aims to follow these undertakings. Rather than subsuming text under the terms provided by political discourse theory, the subsequent analysis proceeds retroductively (Glynos and Howarth 2007), that is, constantly moving back and forth between political discourse theory, critical intervention studies as well as a large text corpus on regional articulations on Burundi and Zimbabwe. The retroductive proceeding is further explicated in Chapter 3.

Since the theoretical understanding of discourse is not limited to language but all kinds of representations, it would be theoretically sound to consider practices as well. That said, the corpora used here only include text data. For both Burundi and Zimbabwe, I compiled two distinct corpora that together comprise 300 individual documents. The corpora are constituted differently. The regional forces contributing to the discourse on Burundi were mostly elites, that is, heads of state, former government officials, staff of regional organisations, and other forces closely related to the respective incumbent governments. The text genres are therefore communiqués of the Regional Initiative, transcripts of speeches given by officials, interviews printed in newspapers, as well as Hansards if available. By contrast, the crisis in Zimbabwe was subject to a broad debate among the publics in southern Africa. Hence, the speakers included in the corpus are not just government elites, but national oppositional forces, NGO staff, journalists, as well as academics. The corpus is thus more diverse.

Additionally, between 2011 and 2012, I conducted thirty-two interviews with present and former policy-makers, former diplomats, journalists, and academics in Tanzania and South Africa – two countries that played an important role in shaping the discourses on Burundi and Zimbabwe. The interviews supplement the text data. Above all, the interviews sharpened my understanding of the two cases of regional intervention. On that note, the knowledge mediated by the interviews was of great help to read, code, and analyse the text corpora.

Structure of the book

The argument will be developed in five chapters. The next chapter, Chapter 2, proposes a Laclauian reading of the field of intervention. By making use of political discourse theory as a grammar for studying such a complex environment as an intervention, the focus is directed to the emerging subjectivities of the regional interveners as well as their struggle to fill the intervention with meaning. This provides a view on regional interventions that neither subjects the latter to universalist frameworks, which tend to pathologise African politics as deviant, nor over-enthusiastically embraces them as the solutions to all problems.

The chapter also discusses the state of the art of other literature strands and relates them to political discourse theory. Critical intervention scholarship is very helpful in sharpening our understanding of an intervention as a crowded and conflictual political space in which international and regional diplomats, militaries, staff of international organisations, journalists, and academics encounter domestic elites, current and former entrepreneurs of violence, activists, refugees, as well as 'ordinary' people. Additionally, post-Western IR has enabled us to think of non-Western orders as different, although this difference is neither essential, absolute, nor stable. Post-Western IR inspired the argument to the extent that regional peace efforts cannot be easily subsumed under allegedly universalist templates to craft peace. Instead, the researcher should display a sensitivity for difference that too often escapes our own realities.

Chapter 3 discusses the methodological approach used here to analyse the text data. As mentioned before, Laclau contributed to political theory rather than to empirical research. Therefore, political discourse theory has often been associated with a methodological deficit that, however, has been addressed by a more recent generation of researchers working with it. This chapter therefore complements these approaches that have mostly been developed to study discourses in the Global North. It is argued that the discourse analytical approach needs to account for certain practical constraints in doing research on intervention politics in eastern and southern Africa.

The two following chapters are the result of the coding of the two text corpora on Burundi and Zimbabwe. In Chapter 4, on the Burundian intervention scene, I analyse how the Regional Initiative as well as the subordinate mediation team – subsequently led by Julius Nyerere, Nelson Mandela, Jacob Zuma, and Charles Nqakula – struggled to fill the intervention with meaning. Not surprisingly, the Regional Initiative frequently made use of hegemonic signifiers generally structuring international interventions such as democracy and power-sharing. In the first part of this chapter, I show how these signifiers were emptied of any particular meaning allowing otherwise ideologically differing ruling elites like the Rwandan, Ugandan, and Tanzanian authorities to demand democratic change. In contradistinction to those authors, who subsume regional interventions under an allegedly universal logic of peace-making, I show in the second part of Chapter 4 how the Regional Initiative clearly differed from this universalist template. Unlike many other interveners in the Burundian intervention scene, the Regional Initiative also referred extensively to the regional scale for solutions. Temporarily, regional interveners identified the emerging East African Community and the successful South African transition from apartheid as common nodal points promising hope and emancipation – not just for Burundi but also for the wider region. By being responsible for the mediation as well as by imposing sanctions, the regional elite's agency in shaping politics became visible. In the third part of Chapter 4, I reconstruct how this new interpretative authority fosters new exclusions, delimitations, and depreciations. I show how the regional interpretative authority emerged only by antagonising both Burundian politics as well as Western approaches to peace-making. The construction of antagonisms towards other forces on the intervention scene enabled the regional forces to claim their authority over others.

Chapter 5 is on the Zimbabwean intervention scene. Unlike the Regional Initiative on Burundi, southern African forces including the Southern African Development Community, ruling parties such as the African National Congress, as well as national oppositions failed to identify common signifiers that were able to structure politics on Zimbabwe. In the first part of Chapter 5, I show how regional forces differed in their sense-making in Zimbabwe. Some regional forces, especially South African opposition and civil society, comprehended the crisis in Zimbabwe in terms of an increasingly authoritarian government. In reverse, this meant that the region should push for a democratic opening. The regional forces thus embraced an allegedly universal template of peace-making to make sense of the intervention. By contrast, the regional governments particularly were keen to argue that unequal land redistribution and sedimented racism were at the heart of the crisis. By putting emphasis on inequality and racism, they thus differed from the discourse usually constituting peace-making interventions. In the second part of this chapter, I show how the regional authorities failed to reinvent themselves as a progressive force that was able to represent itself as acting with regard to Zimbabwe. Instead, the crisis in Zimbabwe seemed to infect the neighbouring societies as well. In the third part of Chapter 5, it becomes clear that the intervention scene remained complex. It was criss-crossed by controversies about who has to be considered as the problem and about who should act.

The final chapter, Chapter 6, discusses how the interventions in Burundi and Zimbabwe have shaped the regional interveners. It discusses commonalities and differences between the regional interventions in Burundi and Zimbabwe. It therefore contributes to a better understanding of the forms of agency of regional interveners on the African continent in a particular historical time period, that is, from 1995 to 2013. Based on this answer to the guiding question, I will then discuss how this book contributes to our better understanding of regional interventions more generally.

References

Autesserre, S., 2014. *Peaceland: Conflict resolution and the everyday politics of international intervention*. New York: Cambridge University Press.
Bellamy, A.J., and Williams, P.D., 2005. Who's keeping the peace? Regionalization and contemporary peace operations. *International Security*, 29 (4), 157–195.
Bercovitch, J., Anagnoson, T.J., and Wille, D.L., 1991. Some conceptual issues and empirical trends in the study of successful mediation in international relations. *Journal of Peace Research*, 28 (1), 7–17.
Björkdahl, A., and Höglund, K., 2013. Precarious peacebuilding: Friction in global–local encounters. *Peacebuilding*, 1 (3), 289–299.
Bliesemann de Guevara, B., ed., 2012. *Statebuilding and state-formation: The political sociology of intervention*. London: Routledge.

Bliesemann de Guevara, B., and Kühn, F.P., 2011. 'The international community needs to act': Loose use and empty signalling of a hackneyed concept. *International Peacekeeping*, 18 (2), 135–151.

Boulden, J., 2003. *Dealing with conflict in Africa: The United Nations and regional organizations*. New York: Palgrave Macmillan.

Engel, U., and Gomes Porto, J., eds., 2010. *Africa's new peace and security architecture promoting norms, institutionalizing solutions*. Farnham: Ashgate.

Glynos, J., and Howarth, D., 2007. *Logics of critical explanation in social and political theory*. Abingdon: Routledge.

Harman, S., and Brown, W., 2013. In from the margins? The changing place of Africa in international relations. *International Affairs*, 89 (1), 69–87.

Holmqvist, C., Bachmann, J., and Bell, C., 2015. Assemblages of war: Police: An introduction. In: J. Bachmann, C. Bell, and C. Holmqvist, eds., *War, police and assemblages of intervention*. Abingdon: Routledge, 1–14.

Kappler, S., 2014. *Local agency and peacebuilding: EU and international engagement in Bosnia-Herzegovina, Cyprus and South Africa*. Basingstoke: Palgrave Macmillan.

Kappler, S., 2015. The dynamic local: Delocalisation and (re-)localisation in the search for peacebuilding identity. *Third World Quarterly*, 36 (5), 875–889.

Keller, R., 2011. *Wissenssoziologische Diskursanalyse: Grundlegung eines Forschungsprogramms*. 3rd edn., Wiesbaden: VS Verlag für Sozialwissenschaften.

Laclau, E., 1993. Discourse. In: R.E. Goodin and P. Pettit, eds., *The Blackwell companion to contemporary political philosophy*. Oxford: Blackwell, 541–547.

Laclau, E., and Mouffe, C., 2001 [1985]. *Hegemony and socialist strategy*. 2nd edn., London: Verso.

Lemay-Hébert, N., 2011. The 'empty-shell' approach: The setup process of international administrations in Timor-Leste and Kosovo, its consequences and lessons. *International Studies Perspectives*, 12 (2), 190–211.

Lemay-Hébert, N., Onuf, N., and Rakic, V., 2014. Introduction: Disputing Weberian semantics. In: N. Lemay-Hébert, N. Onuf, V. Rakic, and P. Bojanic, eds., *Semantics of statebuilding: Language, meanings and sovereignty*. Abingdon: Routledge, 1–18.

Mac Ginty, R., and Richmond, O.P., 2013. The local turn in peace building: A critical agenda for peace. *Third World Quarterly*, 34 (5), 763–783.

Marchart, O., 2010. *Die politische Differenz*. Berlin: Suhrkamp.

Mbeki, T., 2008. Letter to Morgan Tsvangirai of 22 November. Available from: https://www.flickr.com/photos/sokwanele/3065872812/in/photostream/ (accessed 20 November 2013).

Mitchell, A., 2014. *International intervention in a secular age: Re-enchanting humanity?* Abingdon: Routledge.

Mkapa, B.W., 1996. Speech of 8 July. Yaoundé, Cameroon: OAU summit.

Paris, R., 2002. International peacebuilding and the 'mission civilisatrice'. *Review of International Studies*, 28 (4), 637–656.

Richmond, O., and Mac Ginty, R., 2015. Where now for the critique of the liberal peace? *Cooperation and Conflict*, 50 (2), 171–189.

Sending, O.J., 2011. The effects of peacebuilding: Sovereignty, patronage and power. In: S. Campbell, D. Chandler, and M. Sabaratnam, eds., *A liberal peace? The problems and practices of peacebuilding*. London: Zed Books, 55–68.

Townshend, J., 2003. Discourse theory and political analysis: A new paradigm from the Essex School? *British Journal of Politics and International Relations*, 5 (1), 129–142.

Vines, A., 2013. A decade of African peace and security architecture. *International Affairs*, 89 (1), 89–109.

van Walraven, K., 1999. *Dreams of power. The role of the Organization of African Unity in the politics of Africa 1963–1993*. Aldershot: Ashgate.
Weber, C., 1992. Reconsidering statehood: Examining the sovereignty/intervention boundary. *Review of International Studies*, 18 (3), 199–216.
Williams, P.D., 2006. From non-intervention to non-indifference: The origins and development of the African Union's security culture. *African Affairs*, 106 (423), 253–279.
Witt, A., 2013. The African Union and contested political order(s). In: U. Engel and J. Gomes Porto, eds., *Towards an African peace and security regime*. Farnham: Ashgate, 11–30.

2 The field of intervention
Crisis, hegemony, and subjectivity

A peace intervention constitutes a field where different forces encounter each other whose ways otherwise do not intersect. Think of the crowd of internationals being dispatched by their governments or organisations to mediate, police, organise, or teach. Had there not been any intervention, most of these people would probably not have come to Burundi, the Democratic Republic of Congo, or South Sudan – to name just a few of the African places under intervention. In recent years, numerous studies have specifically focused on the people of 'peaceland', as Séverine Autesserre (2014a, p. 6) called a 'metaphorical world, inhibited by the transnational community of interveners'.[1] The horror enacted by widespread violence certainly attracts many governments, organisations, and individuals from distant and not so distant places. But not everybody in this field, which is constituted by performances of intervention, needs to actually *be* in the place under intervention. The field I speak of is scattered around many locations (cf. Kappler 2014, pp. 16–49). An intervention is not only performed in the place under intervention, but heads of state or civil society meet and discuss what is going on in the said place in near or far-away places. What keeps this field together is not a shared place but discourse, as I will argue in this chapter.

The following conceptualisation of the field of intervention is heavily in debt to political discourse theory as articulated by Ernesto Laclau, partly together with his co-author Chantal Mouffe. This chapter theorises the field of intervention based on the re-reading of the critical intervention literature with political discourse theory. As explicated in the introduction to this book, this theory can enhance our understanding of interventions – and particularly of regional interventions – as it conceptualises the transforming subjectivities of those forces engaged in this discursive field. As will become more apparent throughout this chapter, critical intervention literature has neither explicitly payed attention to regional interventions nor to the transformation of subjectivity during the practice of intervention. Re-reading the existing literature with political discourse theory thus closes these gaps, allowing for an empirical analysis of how the two cases of regional intervention shaped the respective interveners.

The structure of this chapter follows the logic of political discourse theory. Initially I will introduce discourse as an ontological concept, discuss previous work on discourses and interventions, as well as explicate this book's take on interventions as discourses. Normalised and stabilised significations – that is, for instance, sedimented power-relations, knowledges, and practices – destabilise according to political discourse theory when they are dislocated. In the second section, the concept of dislocation is introduced, relating it to research on violence and emergency. I will argue that interventions are often imagined as an external attempt to reinsert closure into a dislocated space. In the third section I will conceptualise this external closure as hegemony, introducing the concept and relating it to research on the liberal peace and the local turn. This leads me to discuss how to situate regional interventions into the logic of hegemony and, as I need to add, counter-hegemony, before introducing the concept of antagonism in the fifth section. Lastly this re-reading of the literature with political discourse theory will culminate in the conceptualisation of subjectivity in the field of intervention.

Interventions as discourses

Understanding interventions as discourses in the Laclauian sense implies a particular ontology (Howarth 2009, p. 313), which I will introduce in this section. Political discourse theory departs from the everyday use of the term, where discourse is often used as a synonym for speech, rhetoric, debate, justification, and so on. Not surprisingly, this conceptualisation of discourse is also different from other discourse analytical and theoretical approaches that, for example, differentiate between discursive and non-discursive elements (cf. Fairclough 1993, 2003).[2] Political discourse theory does not differentiate between speech and practice, between discursive and non-discursive elements. It rather stretches the concept of discourse such that, ultimately, practices, institutions, and (our signification of) materiality are forced into this logic of signification. That does not imply that political discourse theory denies the existence of materiality. But, as Laclau and Mouffe (2001 [1985], p. 108) emphasised, processes of signification mediate our apprehension of this materiality as well as the world at large. This also applies to practices and institutions, which are considered stabilised and normalised discourses. We thus cannot escape discourse.

Discourse in the Laclauian sense functions as a synonym for structure, implying that structure cannot be independent from discourse. As we cannot escape from signification, the structure has to be discursive and relational, chaining infinite institutions, practices, and speeches together or setting them apart. The discursivity of the structure furthermore implies that the structure is open to re-significations and contingent change. There is nothing necessary about the structure. This does not imply that meaning is constantly in flux. The flow of signification and re-signification can be temporarily stabilised (Laclau 1990, pp. 34–35). A relative fixity of a discursive formation is important for 'reality' to emerge. 'We act as if the "reality" around us has a stable and unambiguous structure' (Jørgensen and Phillips 2010, p. 33). According to political discourse theory, 'reality' can thus be understood as a relatively stabilised discursive formation, in which we are thrown and which we share with others. If such a 'reality' did not emerge, we would live in a psychotic universe. Political discourse theory can thus apprehend what we sense as 'reality' as a normalisation of signification. Such a normalisation allows those situated within a discursive formation to act without getting lost in a struggle of signification.

That discourses constitute the world in which we live is nothing new for critical intervention scholarship. After all the latter has emerged as a critique of the dominant and, one might add, structured discourse of intervention at that time, the so-called liberal peace. In a widely cited article, Roland Paris (2002) argued that post-1989 interventions would globalise a particular liberal model of governance. Paris thereby did not only reconstruct an existing discourse among the so-called international community,[3] but he also enacted 'liberal peace' as a metaphor for the diverse power-relations, institutions, and knowledges of international interventions. The signifier 'liberal peace' subsequently came to represent an otherwise complex assemblage of practices and speeches. The metaphor 'liberal peace' tried to make sense of complexity and tried to describe the discursive structure of said broader terrain. The scholarship on liberal peace-building can be read as an attempt to register the normalised significations behind any particular intervention. However, any registering of a discourse is also incomplete and likewise subjected to the logic of signification. For a short time, the signifier 'liberal peace' seemed adequate to represent the complex assemblage of interventions. But soon it was argued that Paris had suggested homogeneity where there was none. A debate emerged regarding how far all practices of intervention could be subsumed under such an allegedly universal leitmotiv. Oliver Richmond (2004, p. 132) argued that the international community had only simulated such a liberal 'peacebuilding consensus'. All sorts of interveners had frequently used liberal peace as a reference point. But in practice such an agreement was missing. Instead, international forces held different conceptions of what peace meant (see also Heathershaw 2008). Shortly after the publishing of Paris' ground-breaking article, liberal peace as a homogeneous category for all institutions, practices, and knowledges concerning interventions was destabilised, paving the way for a more sophisticated understanding of the discursive structuring in which interventions are embedded. But despite these differences in approaches, in a certain time period it was difficult to escape the representational regime of liberal peace that functioned as the then *normal* horizon of change. The critical intervention literature has thus conceptualised interventions as discourses from the very outset.

Political discourse theory theorises the processes of discursive structuring. Basically a discourse is structured relationally.[4] The discursive structure can be visualised as a network of signifiers. Each signifier becomes meaningful through its relations with other signifiers. This relational ontology thus departs from the notion that words refer to a definite signified. This relational ontology can be illustrated with the help of a quote. Richmond (2006, p. 309) wrote of interventions, that they target 'the hard shell of the state' instead of the society at large. He continued: 'This results in a virtual peace ... especially from the perspective of those who are experiencing it.' In this quote 'peace' cannot refer to a definite signified, that is, a 'reality' that is unambiguously peaceful. Peace only becomes meaningful by relating it to other signifiers. In this example, the international community related peace to the transformation of the state. In times of statebuilding (Bliesemann de Guevara 2008) the external re-building of the state alongside an idealised template filled the signifier 'peace' with meaning. At the beginning of the 2000s 'peace' seemed to be metonymic with statebuilding – at least internationally. Richmond alerted his readers to the fact that on the ground 'peace' was related to different signifiers. These more complex relations locally were excluded from the rather reductive signification internationally (Koddenbrock 2016, pp. 56–83). A signifier like 'peace' thus does not refer to one definite signified but is related to many signifiers like 'state' or 'non-violence', 'welfare', and so on that try to fix its meaning. According to political discourse theory, 'any discourse is constituted as an attempt to dominate the field of discursivity, to arrest the flow of differences, to construct a centre' (Laclau and Mouffe 2001 [1985], p. 112). As has already been suggested with the latter example, the determination of the meaning of a particular signifier can imply an infinite play of references: each of the signifiers that are invoked to specify 'peace' likewise need to be specified by new signifiers. This is what Laclau and Mouffe refer to as the flow of differences. But instead of being caught in this infinite flow, a (structured) discourse tries to arrest it. It tries to determine a signifier like 'peace' to mean, for example, a particular set of state institutions.

In this section, I have specified the relational ontology of political discourse theory on which the argument of this book rests. The concept of discourse as employed here should not confused with our everyday use of the term. It is a structural concept that is stretched so as to not only encompass speech. In the next section I will discuss how violence – as a physical real – becomes integrated into signification and discourse.

Violence, crisis, and dislocation

When terms like 'large-scale violence', 'catastrophe', or 'mass migration' become associated with a place, the outside world tends to comprehend the place in terms of crisis. According to Didier Fassin and Mariella Pandolfi (2010, p. 10), 'disasters and conflicts are now embedded in the same global logic of intervention' that rests, among others, on 'the temporality of emergency, which is used to justify a state of exception'. The problematisation of large-scale violence as an emergency that needs to be acted upon is not a necessary representation but has a tradition. In one yet influential current in Western thought, large-scale violence has been considered as 'the ultimate Other of the Civilising Process' that has tamed 'us' to such a degree that we can finally let go the pleasures of exercising violence (Barkawi 2011, p. 706, Malešević and Ryan 2012, p. 178). According to this current of thought, contemporary large-scale violence is considered as 'a residue of the past' (Malešević and Ryan 2012, p. 169). Some research suggests that this current of thought has been partly reproduced in our knowledge and interpretation of distant violence, at least until recently. 'Discussions of humanitarian atrocities from Rwanda to Srebrenica focused on evil "others", particularly evil individuals and elites, held to bear direct individual moral responsibility for war crimes' (Chandler 2014, p. 442). When the outside world looks at such a place, it often sees an uncivilised, disordered, and abnormal Other, thereby, however, forgetting to mention that in all states and societies, including the 'civilised' and 'ordered' ones, particular forms of violence are deemed legitimate (Jabri 1996, pp. 98–115, Schlichte 2009, p. 65, Barkawi 2011, p. 703, Jackson and Dexter 2014, p. 6). The problematisation of large-scale violence as crisis nevertheless reveals a certain structuring of the field of intervention. A place with large-scale violence is generally comprehended as a place in disorder that is in need of external intervention. Kai Koddenbrock (2016, p. 1) noted that 'in places like the Democratic Republic of the Congo', where violence is widespread and many people are displaced, 'intervention actors assume they hardly have to justify and substantiate their case for intervention'. In other words, large-scale violence and related processes are often considered synonymous with crisis. But what does this conceptualisation of violence as crisis imply? How does violence become integrated into discourse?

Research on violence argues that those perpetrating and suffering from the violence are trapped in the particularity of the event. By contrast, those talking about violence render it politically and socially meaningful. The talk about violence integrates it into discourse; it attaches names to it; it categorises it. Yet, instead of being representable, the horror of violence seems to elude any simple labelling but also language as such. The *real*[5] of the violence cannot find its equivalent in a particular name given to it, in a particular signifier (Kapust 2014, p. 53). The talk about violence will never be able to enclose the horror of the moment as well as its implications. It will always be reductive. Tarak Barkawi has pointedly described this failure to integrate large-scale violence into (a particular kind of academic) discourse:

> The Second World War, which still appears every day on our television screens, its victorious order of battle still sitting on the UN Security Council, its discourses and contested memories still informing identity politics in and beyond the West, is safely contained by CoW [Correlates of War] between the dates of 1939 and 1945.
>
> (Barkawi 2011, p. 710)

It is important to emphasise that the Correlates of War project is not unique in its reductions. It seems to be the ontology of violence as something real that resists being integrated into our symbolic order. However, despite this incomprehensibility of violence – and this is an important point – 'its incomprehension is an invitation for (re)interpretation' (Ayyash 2010, p. 104). Violence thus opens the discourse instead of closing it. It allows for divergent interpretations to flourish. This stimulation of controversy can be considered as the nucleus of crisis.

On the basis of political discourse theory, violence *can* be comprehended as an empirical expression of a dislocation. In this theory a dislocation unsettles a discursive order, that is, the stabilised discursive formation through which the material world is mediated. As Dirk Nabers put it:

> In linguistic terms, a discourse is dislocated when it cannot integrate or explain certain 'events.' Those 'events' remain incomprehensible; they are characterized by uncertainty over what they signify and imply. They cannot be incorporated within existing frameworks of intelligibility.
> (Nabers 2015, p. 120)

A dislocation is thus an ontological category that upsets the discursive structure of the moment. It cannot be unambiguously assigned to a physical real like violence, even though violence might be really dislocating for those suffering the violence (considering that they can still suffer). But for those talking about it, the violence does not manifest itself as a physical real. It had already become a signifier in the infinite field of the discursive. In this sense, it is subjected to the same relational ontology of discourse as introduced in the previous section. The signifier 'violence' can be discursively constituted as normal or as a small disturbance (Hansen and Sørensen 2005, p. 97) or a crisis: that is, a moment 'when the symbolic system needs to be radically recast' (Smith 1998a, p. 167, see also Laclau and Mouffe 2001 [1985], p. 136, Laclau 2005, p. 132). The constitution of violence as a dislocation is thus already based on an act of signification. The physical real that violence reveals is immediately covered by discourse. That said, the signification of violence as an indicator of a crisis is deeply ingrained into our discursive orders, implying that we often perpetuate this signification when faced with large-scale violence.

In the discourse theoretical ontology, dislocations enable alternative discourses to arise. As a dislocation reveals the contingency of normalised discursive formation, by implication it 'opens possibilities of multiple and indeterminate re-articulations for those freed from its coercive force' (Laclau 1990, p. 42). A dislocation brings home to us that our 'reality' is contingent upon a certain discursive order that thereby loses its appearance of normality. By accounting for the contingent foundations of the discursive structure, so political discourse theory, alternatives become thinkable again. By constituting violence as a dislocation of the normalised order, it almost automatically gives rise to the question *what next?* Constituting violence as a dislocation almost by definition gives rise to conflicting, antagonistic propositions about the future to come. In this sense, violence as dislocation opens the discourse instead of closing it. However, a caveat is necessary here. By constituting violence as dislocatory, not all elements of a discursive formation will be called into question. Many layers of signification will always outlast dislocatory moments (Smith 1998a, p. 168, Hansen and Sørensen 2005, p. 97). That said, the place that becomes constituted as an object of intervention is commonly a place where multiple and antagonistic interpretations of the inflicted violence circulate. It is a place, where the contingency of the political is exposed. It is a place of uncertainty.

This place is also a place that is widely considered as having lost its ability to reintroduce discursive closure. The 'post-conflict spaces, almost by definition, are characterized far more by diversity and division than by unity' (Donais 2009, p. 11). Discursive closure refers to a drive to cover the dislocation and to arrest the divisions it revealed by constructing a new discursive fundament. The failure of domestic forces to re-articulate such a shared discursive fundament, so the hegemonic argument, creates the need for an external intervention in the first place (Donais 2009, p. 12). Against this backdrop, external forces become interveners by convincing themselves (and others) that they can bring back discursive closure. 'What liberal peacebuilding represents is a closure and diminishing of debate over the nature and path toward peace' (Peterson 2013, p. 323, see also Duffield 2007, p. 29). As Mitchell wrote,

> human beings [and in this case specifically interveners] are framed as the ultimate arbiters of meaning, solely responsible for ensuring the value of human life and the order of the universe. They attempt to do so by projecting meaning onto other beings, and by restoring it when it is lost.
> (Mitchell 2014, p. 2)

In the wake of the void of stabilised meaning in the place inflicted with violence, interveners are widely considered as functioning as ultimate arbiters of meaning. In the remainder of this chapter, I will discuss how to analyse the intervener's drive for closure.

Hegemony in the field of intervention

With political discourse theory the interveners' drive to bring back closure can be conceptualised in the 'turbulent modus of hegemony' (Nonhoff 2007, p. 7). Here the political is a discursive field that lacks any ultimate foundation. Instead a normalised, hegemonic discourse mediating our understanding of the world temporarily acts as this foundation. By conceptualising the political as being subjected to the logic of hegemony, nothing can be taken for granted. It rather allows for theorising the discursive emergence of a hegemony as well as its disintegration. Liberal peace has functioned as this normalised discourse constituting interventions and their subjects. It has imagined interveners as closing the void by exporting a set of institutions and practices deemed as liberal. Based on the discourse theoretical terminology, it can be said that the signifier 'liberal peace' has acted as an empty signifier: that is, a temporarily stabilised centre in a relational discursive formation that gripped peaceland (cf. Richmond 2006, p. 295). The empty signifier lost its origin or source. It does not signify a particular policy, but it 'serves as the container for shifting significations' (Žižek 2000, p. 224). The signifier is empty because it represents the discursive formation as a whole. It is 'only if the signifiers empty themselves of their attachment to particular signifieds and assume the role

The field of intervention 19

of representing the pure being of the system ... that such a signification is possible' (Laclau 2007 [1996], p. 39). For example, the signifier 'peace' is empty, not signalling a particular policy but order after chaos. 'Liberal peace', by contrast, is comparably less empty, signalling a set of 'liberal' institutions and practices as a response. Empirically it is thus difficult to reconstruct a pure empty signifier, just representing the being of the system. Most of the signifiers that represent a discursive formation still expose traces of signification, thus being rather tendentially empty (Laclau 2000, p. 304).

The relative emptiness renders an empty signifier hard to challenge. Due to the vagueness of its signification, alternative discourses can be either integrated or rejected as not to the point. The empty signifier therefore stabilises a discourse. This persistence of the empty signifier 'liberal peace' was also noted by critical intervention scholarship. Some scholars challenged this 'only game in town' (Mac Ginty 2010, p. 403) by directing the attention to the local scale. It has been critiqued on the grounds that – in the framework of liberal peacebuilding – interveners have been exporting liberal institutions *irrespective* of the domestic politics in the state under intervention that have often been deemed as irrelevant, illiberal, or illegal (Zürcher 2011, Chandler 2013, pp. 17–18, Koddenbrock 2016, pp. 28–55). Interveners have often understood the state under intervention as an empty shell, which could be shaped and re-built by external forces from scratch (Lemay-Hébert 2011b). By directing attention to domestic discourses and signification processes,[6]

> the local turn is something of a terra nullius for the liberal peace epistemology. It represents a dangerous and wild place where Western rationality, with its diktats of universality and modernisation, is challenged in different ways.
> (Mac Ginty and Richmond 2013, p. 763)

The liberal peace discourse was considered not capable of integrating local rationalities into its discursive formation, therewith questioning 'the "natural" right of the North to intervene in the political formations of the South' (Mac Ginty and Richmond 2013, p. 764). However, Roger Mac Ginty also recognised the limitations of challenging liberal peacebuilding.

> Given the pervasive nature of liberal peacemaking and the internationalized nature of civil war, it is difficult to conceive of actors completely outside of the liberal peace ambit. To some extent, virtually all actors involved in peacemaking and peacebuilding have to take cognizance of structures, principles and laws shaped by the liberal peace.
> (Mac Ginty 2010, p. 396)

This statement illustrates the hegemony ascribed to liberal peacebuilding. It is difficult to avoid being gripped by this hegemonic discursive formation. Research is thus illuminating the extent, to which the tendentially empty signifier 'liberal peace' can be disputed. Therefore, scholars have focused on micro-alternatives.[7] But these alternative signifiers do not travel well beyond a particular context. They do not empty themselves to such an extent as to function as common reference point for other violent places as well.

Given the alleged stability of the empty signifier 'liberal peace' that seems to structure our understanding of interventions, it is questionable to what extent it is plausible to analyse a particular regional practice of intervention in the turbulent modus of hegemony. Before coming back to this question, I discuss the Laclauian understanding of hegemony and counter-hegemony. Laclau (2005, pp. 139–141) argued that every hegemonic discourse conceals heterogeneity. The signifier 'liberal peace', for instance, obscures the heterogeneity of the concepts of peace that are subsumed under this signifier. These otherwise *different* policies subsumed under the empty signifier together constitute a *chain of equivalence*. They are only equal in their depreciation and exclusion of local politics as an Other. In political discourse theory, each hegemonic discourse ultimately rests on exclusions, that is antagonisms (Thomassen 2005, p. 14). Later I will discuss antagonisms in more detail. For now, it suffices to argue that the antagonistic excluded Other more likely registers the contingency of the hegemonic discourse. By taking into account the contingency of a discursive order, alternatives become possible again. For example, as the liberal peace discourse had long attached little value to domestic politics, it was very plausible to expect the local to be the place for a counter-hegemony to the liberal peace to emerge. It was expected that local forces would begin to disarticulate elements from the hegemonic discourse, rearticulating them into an emerging counter-discourse (Mouffe 1979, p. 197). Political discourse theory reminds us that the counter-hegemonic discourse which allows a different understanding of politics is likewise not atemporal. Rather, the alternative discursive formation is constantly in danger of being integrated into the hegemonic discourse (Smith 1998b, pp. 234–235). Laclau and Mouffe (2001 [1985], p. 178) therefore argued that counter-hegemonies should be understood as *processes* of transformation that – like any discourse – will not be able to fully embody the 'right' and 'emancipated' political order (Smith 1998a, p. 167). Rather, the counter-hegemonic discourse rests on homogenisations, reductions and exclusions. As I will argue in this book, this counter-hegemonic logic is highly relevant for understanding regional practices of intervention.

Situating regional interveners into the logic of hegemony and counter-hegemony

Critical intervention scholarship has mostly ignored regional interventions. Recently, Richmond and Mac Ginty (2015, p. 183) noted that 'the regional aspect of liberal peace interventions has been under-researched and [this] is especially pertinent given the ascent of the BRICS [Brazil, Russia, India, China and South Africa] and others'. There seems to be an understanding that 'no clear alternative model, ideology, model of state, or model of peace is on offer by the

BRICS or other emerging powers' (Richmond and Tellidis 2014, p. 578). Regional organisations in general and the African Union in particular do not counter liberal peace but embrace it to a certain extent (Mac Ginty 2008, p. 143). David Chandler (2009, p. 22) even argued that the spread of regional organisations is primarily a sign of the West's 'desire to divest policy responsibility'. Accordingly, phrases like 'African solutions to African problems' were highly misleading since member states of the regional organisation would lack any capacity to articulate an autonomous intervention policy (Chandler 2006, p. 192). By contrast, Richmond and Ioannis Tellidis acknowledged that BRICS have created some space for alternative discourses on interventions. 'The positionality of [the BRICS states] is complex. They resist aspects of the liberal peacebuilding and neoliberal statebuilding process while embracing others' (Richmond and Tellidis 2014, p. 576). Hence, if regional interveners articulate counter-hegemonic elements, this counter-discourse has not yet been stabilised to such a degree as to escape the danger of being integrated into the hegemonic discourse. This book contributes to the reconstruction of regional intervention practices as temporal and unstable counter-hegemonic discourses that are always on the verge of becoming integrated into 'normal' international intervention politics.

If regional practices of intervention can neither be easily subsumed under an allegedly universal template of doing interventions nor be considered as a fully articulated alternative model of peacemaking, it is imperative to reflect upon the possible constitution of difference. I argue that post-Western approaches to IR enable us to conceptualise this difference. According to a now familiar critique, the field of IR is Eurocentric, with most research institutions being located in North America and Europe (e.g. Hoffmann 1977, Wæver 1998a). These centres, so the argument goes, are more or less deaf to the experiences of the world of the beyond. The numbness is sustained by theories as well as publication policies. This structuration of knowledge production has shaped our understanding of non-Western politics as dissenting and rebellious (Acharya 2011, p. 629), thereby stabilising the distinction between core and periphery, in which the core is able to function as a model for the rest. The filling of theoretical signifiers such as 'sovereignty' with Western significations render historical differences in the emergence of sovereignty and especially the legacies of colonialism invisible (Grovogui 2001). This is not to say that there is 'such a thing as pure, untainted African knowledge' (Smith 2012). We should give up expecting to find a radically alternative way of non-Western thinking (Bilgin 2008, p. 10). Yet, as Pinar Bilgin rightly pointed out:

> Such seeming absence of 'difference' cannot be explained away through invoking assumptions of 'teleological Westernization' ('they all seek to become like us!') but requires becoming curious about the effects of the historical relationship between the 'West' and 'non-West' in the emergence of ways of thinking and doing the same but not quite – to use Bhabha's turn of phrase.
>
> (Bilgin 2008, p. 6)

22 The field of intervention

Accordingly, difference can be understood in terms of *doing the same but not quite*. Post-Western IR facilitates the thinking of non-Western politics as different (Tickner and Blaney 2012, p. 6), although this difference is neither essential, absolute, nor stable. Referring to post-conflict, developmental interventions in Mozambique, Meera Sabaratnam argued that Mozambicans did not resist the politics of intervention because they identified with a radically different peace. Critique of Western intervention should not be considered as 'assertions of a fundamental alterity' to liberal peace. Mozambicans rather questioned the unfairness, inequality, and hypocrisy of the intervention (Sabaratnam 2011, pp. 254–255). This critique was not technical but inherently political as these resistances 'reveal much about the nature of the experiences of intervention' (Sabaratnam 2011, p. 261). Thus, post-Western IR inspired the argument to the extent that regional interventions do not simply perpetuate allegedly universalist templates to craft peace. Instead, the researcher should display sensitivity for difference; that is, he or she should be alert to articulations and practices that escape such allegedly universal categorisations like liberal peace.

According to political discourse theory, this constitution of difference is a complex process involving the articulation of antagonisms and the claiming of floating signifiers. In the section on hegemony, I argued that counter-hegemonic discourses disarticulate elements from the hegemonic discourse and rearticulate them into their own discourse. Political discourse theory calls them floating signifiers: that is, the meaning of the signifier is becoming indeterminate because it is claimed by different discourses (Laclau 2005, p. 131).

> Only the presence of a vast area of floating elements and the possibility of their articulation to opposite camps – which implies a constant redefinition of the latter – is what constitutes the field permitting us to define a practice as hegemonic.
>
> (Laclau and Mouffe 2001 [1985], p. 136)

It has to be expected that a regional intervention employs signifiers already articulated in the broader discourse on interventions. But these signifiers are integrated into the regional discourse, thereby becoming filled with different meaning. For example, when regional interveners embrace democracy as the aspired post-conflict order, they do not necessarily perpetuate the liberal peace discourse. By integrating it into a different system of signification, the signifier might be filled differently. Floating signifiers thus only reveal difference on the second view. They are not different signifiers, heralding difference through its orthography. The difference only reveals itself after a layer of sameness.

Theoretically, floating and empty signifiers differ in their hegemonic accomplishment. A floating signifier indicates the fluidity of a discursive formation. Empirically, however, the distance is not as great: 'A situation where only the category of empty signifier was relevant, with total exclusion of the floating moment, would be one in which we would have an entirely immobile frontier – something that is hardly imaginable' (Laclau 2005, p. 133). Difference is not

The field of intervention 23

only constituted by claiming certain signifiers. It is also constituted by differentiating the own discourse from hegemonic knowledge and practices. In order to stabilise these floating moments, the counter-discourse needs to be delimited against a preceding discourse. 'There is no emancipation without oppression, and there is no oppression without the presence of something which is impeded in its free development by oppressive forces' (Laclau 2007 [1996], p. 1). In other words, in order to emancipate themselves from the preceding liberal peace discourse that privileged 'liberal'/Western interveners, regional forces have to consider the preceding discourses as oppressive.

> If we are speaking about *real* emancipation, the 'other' opposing the emancipated identity cannot be a purely positive or neutral other but, instead, an 'other' which prevents the full constitution of the identity.
>
> (Laclau 2007 [1996], p. 2)

Against this theoretical backdrop, it has to be expected that regional forces also constitute difference by demarcating themselves from previous practices.

It is now possible to conceptualise the field of interventions as an inherently conflictual one where different forces, among them the regional, struggle to stabilise discursive elements. A counter-hegemonic discourse claims discursive elements already articulated in other discourses and delimits itself from an already existing discursive order. In such a field, regional interventions can be conceptualised as a precarious counter-hegemonic discourse that is always on the verge of becoming integrated into 'normal' peacebuilding.

Antagonism in the field of intervention

Critical intervention scholarship has increasingly emphasised disagreement and conflict among *all* forces constituting the field of intervention. As argued earlier, the liberal peace discourse has comprehended the intervener as someone who brings back discursive closure into a polity that has lost its ability to do so (Peterson 2013). In view of the violent antagonism in the place under intervention, the external response is represented as *ideally* being homogeneous and unanimous. The visible heterogeneity and diversity among interveners is, by contrast, considered as a problem. 'A common critique of postwar statebuilding operations is that they suffer from a lack of coordination among the myriad international actors involved in these missions' (Paris 2009, p. 53). Instead of perpetuating the myth that the crafting of consensus in the field of intervention is possible, the theoretical reflection about interventions has begun to emphasise the normality of conflicts and *frictions* involved in the process of crafting peace.

> A range of actors, ideas and practices rub against each other at sites of peacebuilding, and these encounters create new power relations, agencies, ideas and practices that may or may not resemble their originals.
>
> (Björkdahl and Höglund 2013, p. 292)

24 *The field of intervention*

Frictions do not arise only among domestic forces but among all forces participating in the discourse of intervention. They are not per se be considered as destructive. They may also serve as a 'catalyst for change' through which (violent, authoritarian, or neo-imperialistic) social and political practices can be challenged (Björkdahl and Höglund 2013, p. 290). Rather than conceiving of interventions as something planned and controllable, the conceptual metaphor of friction 'stresses the emergent and unexpected nature of unintended and unplanned consequences' (Millar, van der Lijn, and Verkoren 2013, p. 139).

For political discourse theory, conflicts – or more precisely antagonisms – are constitutive of the political. They create the possibilities for politics in the first place. An antagonistic frontier marks the presence of exclusions from hegemony that, at one point, potentially challenge the stabilised discourse (Laclau 1990, p. 35, Mouffe 2005, p. 13). Antagonisms are thus ontologically necessary. Politics is not able to eliminate antagonisms and to replace them with consensus and harmony, but it can transform the antagonistic discursive markers in such a way as to make them compatible to non-violent politics (Mouffe 2005, p. 22). Like the literature on friction, political discourse theory emphasises how ontological antagonisms are both destructive and productive. Antagonisms have a paradoxical double function. On the one hand, antagonisms threaten the truth, normality, and rationality of a discourse. Their mere presence calls into question the discursive hegemony. They block the full constitution of the discourse as representing reality. Regarding the field of intervention, the local scale is considered to embody the antagonism, putting into question the rationality of the liberal peace discourse. On the other hand, the antagonising force also constitutes the discourse. It reveals what the discourse is radically not (Laclau 1990, p. 21, for IR see Campbell 1998), as the local scale represents what the interveners are radically not.

An intervention tends to respond to an antagonism that became massively violent. Against this backdrop, it is astonishing to speak of a productive function of antagonisms. It is pertinent to understand that political discourse theory does not comprehend antagonism as an empirical, discursive form but rather an ontological logic that structures an empirical discourse. Ontologically, an antagonism – as the radical limit of our own discourse – escapes the apprehension through language and meaning.

> Insofar as there is antagonism, I cannot be a full presence for myself. But nor is the force that antagonizes me such a presence: its objective being is a symbol of my non-being and, in this way, it is overflowed by a plurality of meanings which prevent its being fixed as full positivity.
> (Laclau and Mouffe 2001 [1985], p. 125)

That said, in empirical discourses particular collectivities often embody and symbolise an antagonism. 'What forms this exclusion takes, how it is performed, and how strongly it is insisted upon are questions for empirical inquiry' (Neumann 1998, p. 399). The empirical filling of an antagonism with a particular meaning is a discursive process. Mouffe (2005, pp. 98–107) argued that politics is about articulating antagonisms such that they question the hegemonic discourse without denying the existence of the people representing the discursive formation. In this empirical filling of antagonism, the antagonising force is no longer conceptualised as an enemy but an adversary, 'that is, somebody whose ideas we combat but whose right to defend those ideas we do not put into question' (Mouffe 2005, p. 102). Recently some work on interventions incorporated this agonistic pluralism, arguing that interventions should 'assist in creating platforms on which agonistic contestation can take place' (Aggestam, Cristiano, and Strömbom 2015, p. 1741).

> Differences cannot simply be removed; they remain, and more importantly, because they are given no 'outlet' in formal modes of liberal governance and institutions, they manifest themselves in dangerous and often violent ways.
> (Peterson 2013, p. 322)

The increasing body of work on local conceptions of peace, frictions, and agonistic pluralism suggests that intervention scholarship has already begun to conceptualise the field of interventions as criss-crossed by antagonisms. 'Evidence suggests that movements toward an as of yet undefined post-liberal order in which the non-liberal alternatives and liberal hegemonic order collide is already occurring' (Peterson 2013, p. 325). Making these empirical articulations of antagonism in the practices of regional intervention visible thus further contributes to understanding the function of conflict and friction in the field of intervention. As I will argue in the next section, antagonisms are formative for new subjectivities to arise.

Regional subjectivity in the field of intervention

Critical intervention scholarship has begun conceptualising subjectivity in the field of intervention. The literature on friction argued that these encounters transform the subjectivity of those involved (Björkdahl and Gusic 2013, p. 333). Stefanie Kappler (2013, pp. 349–350) specified that 'the boundaries between different categories of actors (local, civil society, national, international) are subject to constant re-negotiation in the formation of frictions'. In other words, by engaging in frictional encounters, the boundaries separating 'us' from 'them' are either reinforced or shifted. Instead of being unambiguously represented as either international or local, such categorisations are, to a certain degree, fluid and emerging through a particular kind of boundary work. Kappler argued that the forces located in the place under intervention often de-emphasise or re-emphasise their local subjectivity, thereby positioning themselves in a particular configuration of peacebuilding.

26 *The field of intervention*

> The positionality as 'international', on the one hand, seems to go hand in hand with a notion of authority and competence. Local identity, which is, on the other hand, performed in parallel, suggests local ownership and legitimacy of projects and facilitates access to funding.
>
> (Kappler 2015, pp. 883–884)

These discursive categories thus position a force, equipping it with a particular agency. Being identified as 'international' positions someone as a representative of universal, morally desirable values (Bliesemann de Guevara and Kühn 2011). According to this claim, a representative of the international community is viewed as authoritative and competent, whereas – under the framework of local ownership – being positioned as local imparts legitimacy on his or her statements. Critical intervention scholarship thus began to theorise the positionalities in the field of intervention.

Discourse theory helps to further conceptualise the emergence, perpetuation, and transformation of subjectivity in the field of intervention in general and in regional interventions in particular. It departs from the understanding that subjects are not pre-social, but that they are always discursively constituted (Epstein 2011, p. 330). The forces in a particular field of intervention are positioned through a previously existing discursive formation (Laclau and Mouffe 2001 [1985], pp. 114–122). In this sense, the basic conceptualisation is similar to already existing approaches to subjectivity in the field of interventions, as discussed in the previous paragraph. External forces are only taking part in this field of intervention because a discourse had previously enacted them as interveners, authorising the respective forces to manage matters of international peace and security. In the terminology of political discourse theory, this is a subject position; that is, a discourse contouring the sedimented agency and its limits.

> Bound to seek recognition of its own existence in categories, terms, and names that are not of its own making, the subject seeks the sign of its own existence outside itself, in a discourse that is at once dominant and indifferent.
>
> (Butler 1997, p. 20)

Once enacted as an intervener, the latter cannot escape thinking of its existence in these categories, terms, and names. Even though such a force might not previously have felt like an authoritative representative of a universal peace project, once positioned as intervener such agency suggest itself. Being positioned as a representative of the international community provides subjects with a strong 'can do' attitude, suggesting that they are able to transform whole societies (Bliesemann de Guevara 2010, p. 1). The international community and, closely related, interveners are generally represented as being powerful and as being able to act (Sending 2011). Mitchell wrote that 'intervention is a way of imagining action, predicated on a simple belief: that humans can change the course of events by interposing themselves in it' (Mitchell 2014, p. 3). An intervener can thus be comprehended as a subject position that is generally attributed with a particular form of agency. Regarding the subject of this book, how this positioning transforms regional forces needs to be specifically analysed. How does this subject position implicate forces that formerly have lacked agency in international relations?

Political discourse theory goes beyond conceptualising subjects as discursive products. It is therefore able to process this question analytically, thereby moving beyond existing research. As discussed in previous sections of this chapter, a discourse is never stable but performative: its elements can be re-articulated. Once the contingency of the discursive order reveals itself, forces that were previously discursively enacted as agents can re-articulate – and hence change – the discourse. In these moments of dislocation, subjects become subjects in the strong sense, re-articulating their own subjectivity (Laclau 1990, p. 44). They can step outside the representational regime that attributed them in a particular way, searching for new categories, terms, and names which seem to be more fitting. In this sense, subjectivity is also subjected under the logic of hegemony and counter-hegemony. Once the contingency of the subjectivity reveals itself, a hegemonic discourse can be questioned from within, articulating new antagonisms and claiming floating signifiers.

The transformation of subjectivity thus evolves as a discursive process in the unstable interspace between counter-hegemonic distinction and hegemonic re-integration. When scholars argued that frictional encounters transform agency, they were referring to this process of marking a frontier. As argued earlier, an antagonism frustrates but also constitutes our being. The antagonism thus symbolises what we are radically not. Against this backdrop, IR scholars have drawn attention to radical others that are constitutive for the subjectivities of states or continents (e.g. Campbell 1998, Neumann 1998, Wæver 1998b). A repositioning of subjectivity thus involves re-articulating the antagonistic frontier, rendering the self radically different from the other. Slavoj Žižek however warned that our subjectivity cannot be ultimately attributed to a radical other: 'the external enemy is simply the small piece, the rest of reality upon which we "project" or "externalize" this intrinsic, immanent impossibility' (Žižek 1990, p. 252). That the antagonising force is blocking our full constitution is thus only a projection that conceals 'an inherent "maladaptation" of a self that can never be fully socialized' (Epstein 2011, p. 335). In this sense, the subject is ultimately a subject of lack.

> There is nothing in me which was oppressed by the [discursive] structure or is freed by its dislocation.... The freedom thus won in relation to the structure is therefore a traumatic fact initially: I am condemned to be free ... because I have a *failed* structural identity. This means that the subject is partially self-determined. However, as this self-determination is not the expression of what the subject *already* is but the result of its lack of being instead, self-determination can only proceed through processes of *identification.*
> (Laclau 1990, p. 44, emphasis in original)

28 *The field of intervention*

In other words, a dislocation ultimately exposes our essential lack. We are nothing without discursive structures positioning us. A dislocation thus partially exposes the contingency of our identity. Instead of being liberating, a dislocation provokes anxiety about lacking any virtues of our own, driving us to re-identify with an altered discourse that subjects us anew to a discursive structure.

This conceptualisation of subjectivity goes beyond existing approaches regarding interventions. Kappler argued that the 'two centres of gravity between which identity formation meanders' are the poles 'local' and 'international' (Kappler 2015, p. 876). They could thus decide between these two subject positions. With political discourse theory it is possible to move beyond this binary. By becoming enacted as agents able to shape the discourse, the regional forces are able to re-articulate it, crafting potentially counter-hegemonic moments, before being re-integrated into discursive structure. As will be argued in the remainder of the book, while intervening, the regional forces have constantly referred to the regional scale for creating these moments of counter-hegemony and thus re-articulating the discourse, in which they were thrown (Wodrig 2014, Wodrig and Grauvogel 2016).

Conclusion

In this chapter, I proposed a Laclauian reading of the field of intervention that helps thinking about, seeing, and expressing elements of regional interventions that otherwise might remain in the dark. Such theory-driven analysis seems especially relevant given the absence of critical engagement with regional interventions in general and the transformation of subjectivity this entails in particular. On the basis of political discourse theory, regional interventions can be analysed as potentially counter-hegemonic discourses, through which regional forces transcend their discursive positioning by re-articulating new antagonistic frontiers and claiming floating signifiers. The transformation of subjectivity thus evolves as a discursive process, in the unstable interspace between counter-hegemonic distinction and hegemonic re-integration. Even if a counter-hegemonic discourse becomes temporarily effective, it is always in danger of becoming integrated into the discursive hegemony, which also constantly evolves. According to Mac Ginty, in this field of interventions, 'all actors are compelled to operate in an environment shaped in some way by others' (Mac Ginty 2010, p. 392). It is difficult to sustain a discourse of counter-hegemony, as constant dislocations – events – in the field of intervention disturb its stabilisation.

This analysis of the regional interventions into Burundi and Zimbabwe cannot reveal timeless 'truths' about regional interventions, but it accounts for the transformation of interveners in a set historical context. The theorisation of the field of intervention is however more general, applicable to other cases as well. It is a formal theorisation of this field, open for the contingency of specific politics of intervention.

Notes

1 For other studies on this metaphorical world inhibited by interveners, see Lemay-Hébert 2011a, Goetze and Bliesemann de Guevara 2014, Koddenbrock 2016.
2 In a review of discourse analytical approaches in the field of IR, Milliken (1999, p. 226) argued that the problem was not that there was little discourse analytical research. But no common understanding had emerged among scholars about the concept of discourse. Still, many different understandings of discourse theory and discourse analysis circulate.
3 For a critical engagement with the signifier, see Bliesemann de Guevara and Kühn 2011.
4 Other scholars in this field have argued for a comparable relational ontology as a theoretical lens guiding the analysis of interventions (see Holmqvist, Bachmann, and Bell 2015, pp. 3–5, Koddenbrock 2016, pp. 2–4).
5 Beyond the social reality that is always mediated via discourse and thus has to be understood as immanently symbolic, some authors who explicitly allude to the thinking of the psychoanalyst Jacques Lacan argue that the real is something unrepresentable, something that escapes the realm of discourse (e.g. Solomon 2012, pp. 914–917). The real makes itself felt by thinking that 'things are not quite right' (Glynos and Howarth 2007, p. 143), that the symbolic fails to capture something. Against this backdrop, the horror of violence cannot be adequately mediated by the symbolic.
6 For a review, see Autesserre 2014b.
7 For indigenous peacemaking, see Mac Ginty 2008.

References

Acharya, A., 2011. Dialogue and discovery: In search of International Relations theory beyond the West. *Millennium: Journal of International Studies*, 39 (3), 619–637.
Aggestam, K., Cristiano, F., and Strömbom, L., 2015. Towards agonistic peacebuilding? Exploring the antagonism–agonism nexus in the Middle East peace process. *Third World Quarterly*, 36 (9), 1736–1753.
Autesserre, S., 2014a. *Peaceland: Conflict resolution and the everyday politics of international intervention.* New York: Cambridge University Press.
Autesserre, S., 2014b. Going micro: Emerging and future peacekeeping research. *International Peacekeeping*, 21 (4), 492–500.
Ayyash, M.M., 2010. Hamas and the Israeli state: A 'violent dialogue'. *European Journal of International Relations*, 16 (1), 103–123.
Barkawi, T., 2011. From war to security: Security studies, the wider agenda and the fate of the study of war. *Millennium: Journal of International Studies*, 39 (3), 701–716.
Bilgin, P., 2008. Thinking past 'Western' IR? *Third World Quarterly*, 29 (1), 5–23.
Björkdahl, A., and Gusic, I., 2013. The divided city: A space for frictional peacebuilding. *Peacebuilding*, 1 (3), 317–333.
Björkdahl, A., and Höglund, K., 2013. Precarious peacebuilding: Friction in global–local encounters. *Peacebuilding*, 1 (3), 289–299.
Bliesemann de Guevara, B., 2008. The state in times of statebuilding. *Civil Wars*, 10 (4), 348–368.
Bliesemann de Guevara, B., 2010. Introduction: The limits of statebuilding and the analysis of state-formation. *Journal of Intervention and Statebuilding*, 4 (2), 111–128.
Bliesemann de Guevara, B., and Kühn, F.P., 2011. 'The international community needs to act': Loose use and empty signalling of a hackneyed concept. *International Peacekeeping*, 18 (2), 135–151.
Butler, J., 1997. *The psychic life of power: Theories in subjection.* Stanford: Stanford University Press.

30 The field of intervention

Campbell, D., 1998. *Writing security: United States foreign policy and the politics of identity*. Manchester: Manchester University Press.

Chandler, D., 2006. *Empire in denial: The politics of state-building*. London: Pluto Press.

Chandler, D., 2009. *Hollow hegemony. Rethinking global politics, power and resistance*. London: Pluto Press.

Chandler, D., 2013. Peacebuilding and the politics of nonlinearity: Rethinking 'hidden' agency and 'resistance'. *Peacebuilding*, 1 (1), 17–32.

Chandler, D., 2014. Beyond good and evil: Ethics in a world of complexity. *International Politics*, 51 (4), 441–457.

Donais, T., 2009. Empowerment or imposition? Dilemmas of local ownership in post-conflict peacebuilding processes. *Peace and Change*, 34 (1), 3–26.

Duffield, M., 2007. *Development, security and unending war: Governing the world of peoples*. Cambridge: Polity Press.

Epstein, C., 2011. Who speaks? Discourse, the subject and the study of identity in international politics. *European Journal of International Relations*, 17 (2), 327–350.

Fairclough, N., 1993. *Discourse and social change*. Cambridge: Polity Press.

Fairclough, N., 2003. *Analysing discourse. Textual analysis for social research*. London: Routledge.

Fassin, D., and Pandolfi, M., 2010. Introduction: Military and humanitarian government in the age of intervention. In: D. Fassin and M. Pandolfi, eds., *Contemporary states of emergency*. New York: Zone Books, 9–25.

Glynos, J., and Howarth, D., 2007. *Logics of critical explanation in social and political theory*. Abingdon: Routledge.

Goetze, C., and Bliesemann de Guevara, B., 2014. Cosmopolitanism and the culture of peacebuilding. *Review of International Studies*, 40 (4), 771–802.

Grovogui, S., 2001. Sovereignty in Africa: Quasi-statehood and other myths in international theory. In: K.C. Dunn and T.M. Shaw, eds., *Africa's challenge to international relations theory*. Basingstoke: Palgrave Macmillan, 29–45.

Hansen, A.D. and Sørensen, E., 2005. Polity as politics: Studying the shaping and effects of discursive polities. In: D. Howarth and J. Torfing, eds., *Discourse theory in European politics*. Basingstoke: Palgrave Macmillan, 93–116.

Heathershaw, J., 2008. Unpacking the liberal peace: The dividing and merging of peacebuilding discourses. *Millennium: Journal of International Studies*, 36 (3), 597–621.

Hoffmann, S., 1977. An American social science: International relations. *Daedalus*, 106 (3), 41–60.

Holmqvist, C., Bachmann, J., and Bell, C., 2015. Assemblages of war:police. An introduction. In: J. Bachmann, C. Bell, and C. Holmqvist, eds. *War, police and assemblages of intervention*. Abingdon: Routledge, 1–14.

Howarth, D., 2009. Power, discourse, and policy: Articulating a hegemony approach to critical policy studies. *Critical Policy Studies*, 3 (3–4), 309–335.

Jabri, V., 1996. *Discourses on violence: Conflict analysis reconsidered*. Manchester: Manchester University Press.

Jackson, R., and Dexter, H., 2014. The social construction of organised political violence: An analytical framework. *Civil Wars*, 16 (1), 1–23.

Jørgensen, M., and Phillips, L., 2010. *Discourse analysis as theory and method*. Los Angeles: Sage.

Kappler, S., 2013. Peacebuilding and lines of friction between imagined communities in Bosnia-Herzegovina and South Africa. *Peacebuilding*, 1 (3), 349–364.

Kappler, S., 2014. *Local agency and peacebuilding. EU and international engagement in Bosnia-Herzegovina, Cyprus and South Africa*. Basingstoke: Palgrave Macmillan.

Kappler, S., 2015. The dynamic local: Delocalisation and (re-)localisation in the search for peacebuilding identity. *Third World Quarterly*, 36 (5), 875–889.

Kapust, A., 2014. Die Bedeutung von Gewalt und die Gewalt von Bedeutung. In: M. Staudigl, ed., *Gesichter der Gewalt. Beiträge aus phänomenologischer Sicht*. Paderborn: Wilhelm Fink, 51–73.

Koddenbrock, K., 2016. *The practice of humanitarian intervention: Aid workers, agencies and institutions in the Democratic Republic of the Congo*. Abingdon: Routledge.

Laclau, E., 1990. *New reflections on the revolution of our time*. London: Verso.

Laclau, E., 2000. Constructing universality. In: J. Butler, E. Laclau, and S. Žižek, eds., *Contingency, hegemony, universality: Contemporary dialogues on the left*. London: Verso, 281–307.

Laclau, E., 2005. *On populist reason*. London: Verso.

Laclau, E., 2007 [1996]. *Emancipation(s)*. London, New York: Verso.

Laclau, E. and Mouffe, C., 2001 [1985]. *Hegemony and socialist strategy*. 2nd edn. London: Verso.

Lemay-Hébert, N., 2011a. The bifurcation of the two worlds: Assessing the gap between internationals and locals in state-building processes. *Third World Quarterly*, 32 (10), 1823–1841.

Lemay-Hébert, N., 2011b. The 'empty-shell' approach: The setup process of international administrations in Timor-Leste and Kosovo, its consequences and lessons. *International Studies Perspectives*, 12 (2), 190–211.

Mac Ginty, R., 2008. Indigenous peace-making versus the liberal peace. *Cooperation and Conflict*, 43 (2), 139–163.

Mac Ginty, R., 2010. Hybrid peace: The interaction between top-down and bottom-up peace. *Security Dialogue*, 41 (4), 391–412.

Mac Ginty, R., and Richmond, O.P., 2013. The local turn in peace building: A critical agenda for peace. *Third World Quarterly*, 34 (5), 763–783.

Malešević, S., and Ryan, K., 2012. The disfigured ontology of figurational sociology: Norbert Elias and the question of violence. *Critical Sociology*, 39 (2), 165–181.

Millar, G., van der Lijn, J., and Verkoren, W., 2013. Peacebuilding plans and local reconfigurations: Frictions between imported processes and indigenous practices. *International Peacekeeping*, 20 (2), 137–143.

Milliken, J., 1999. The study of discourse in international relations: A critique of research and methods. *European Journal of International Relations*, 5 (2), 225–254.

Mitchell, A., 2014. *International intervention in a secular age: Re-enchanting humanity?* Abingdon: Routledge.

Mouffe, C., 1979. Hegemony and ideology in Gramsci. In: C. Mouffe, ed., *Gramsci and Marxist theory*. London: Routledge & Kegan Paul, 168–204.

Mouffe, C., 2005. *The democratic paradox*. London: Verso.

Nabers, D., 2015. *A poststructuralist discourse theory of global politics*. New York: Palgrave Macmillan.

Neumann, I.B., 1998. European identity, EU expansion, and the integration/exclusion nexus. *Alternatives*, 23 (3), 397–416.

Nonhoff, M., 2007. Politische Diskursanalyse als Hegemonieanalyse. In: *Diskurs, radikale Demokratie, Hegemonie. Zum Politischen Denken von Ernesto Laclau und Chantal Mouffe*. Bielefeld: Transcript Verlag.

32 The field of intervention

Paris, R., 2002. International peacebuilding and the 'mission civilisatrice'. *Review of International Studies*, 28 (4), 637–656.

Paris, R., 2009. Understanding the 'coordination problem' in postwar statebuilding. In: R. Paris and T.D. Sisk, eds., *The dilemma of statebuilding: Confronting the contradictions of postwar peace operations*. Abingdon: Routledge, 53–78.

Peterson, J.H., 2013. Creating space for emancipatory human security: Liberal obstructions and the potential of agonism. *International Studies Quarterly*, 57 (2), 318–328.

Richmond, O., 2004. The globalization of responses to conflict and the peacebuilding consensus. *Cooperation and Conflict*, 39 (2), 129–150.

Richmond, O., 2006. The problem of peace: Understanding the 'liberal peace'. *Conflict, Security and Development*, 6 (3), 291–314.

Richmond, O., and Mac Ginty, R., 2015. Where now for the critique of the liberal peace? *Cooperation and Conflict*, 50 (2), 171–189.

Richmond, O., and Tellidis, I., 2014. Emerging actors in international peacebuilding and statebuilding: Status quo or critical states? *Global Governance*, 20, 563–584.

Sabaratnam, M., 2011. Situated critiques of intervention: Mozambique and the diverse politics of response. In: S. Campbell, D. Chandler, and M. Sabaratnam, eds., *A liberal peace? The problems and practices of peacebuilding*. London: Zed Books, 245–264.

Schlichte, K., 2009. *In the shadow of violence*. Frankfurt am Main: Campus Verlag.

Sending, O.J., 2011. The effects of peacebuilding: Sovereignty, patronage and power. In: S. Campbell, D. Chandler, and M. Sabaratnam, eds., *A liberal peace? The problems and practices of peacebuilding*. London: Zed Books, 55–68.

Smith, A.M., 1998a. *Laclau and Mouffe: The radical democracy imaginary*. London: Routledge.

Smith, A.M., 1998b. Das Unbehagen der Hegemonie. Die Politischen Theorien von Judith Butler, Ernesto Laclau und Chantal Mouffe. In: O. Marchart, ed., *Das Undarstellbare der Politik: zur Hegemonietheorie Ernesto Laclaus*. Vienna: Turia und Kant, 225–237.

Smith, K., 2012. Africa as an agent of international relations knowledge. In: S. Cornelissen, F. Cheru, and T.M. Shaw, eds., *Africa and international relations in the 21st Century*. London: Palgrave Macmillan, 21–35.

Solomon, T., 2012. 'I wasn't angry, because I couldn't believe it was happening': Affect and discourse in response to 9/11. *Review of International Studies*, 38 (4), 907–928.

Thomassen, L., 2005. From antagonism to heterogeneity: Discourse analytical strategies. *Essex Papers in politics and government: Sub-series in ideology and discourse analysis*, 21, 1–37.

Tickner, A.B., and Blaney, D.L., 2012. Introduction: Thinking difference. In: A.B. Tickner and D.L. Blaney, eds., *Thinking international relations differently*. London, New York: Routledge, 1–24.

Wæver, O., 1998a. The sociology of a not so international discipline: American and European developments in IR. *International Organization*, 52 (4), 687–727.

Wæver, O., 1998b. Insecurity, security, and asecurity in the West European non-war community. In: E. Adler and M. Barnett, eds., *Security communities*. Cambridge: Cambridge University Press, 69–118.

Wodrig, S., 2014. Crafting a region while intervening? Regional discourses on Burundi. *Journal of Intervention and Statebuilding*, 8 (2–3), 214–239.

Wodrig, S., and Grauvogel, J., 2016. Talking past each other: Regional and domestic resistance in the Burundian intervention scene. *Cooperation and Conflict*, 51 (3), 272–290.

Žižek, S., 1990. Beyond discourse-analysis. In: E. Laclau, ed., *New reflections on the revolution of our time*. London: Verso, 249–260.
Žižek, S., 2000. Da capo senza fine. In: J. Butler, E. Laclau, and S. Žižek, eds., *Contingency, hegemony, universality: Contemporary dialogues on the left*. London: Verso, 213–262.
Zürcher, C., 2011. The liberal peace: A tough sell? In: S. Campbell, D. Chandler, and M. Sabaratnam, eds., *A liberal peace? The problems and practices of peacebuilding*. London: Zed Books, 69–88.

3 Studying regional interventions

In order to analyse the guiding question of how these regional interventions shaped the respective interveners, the theoretical conceptualisation as developed in the last chapter has to be 'operationalised'. The reconstruction of the transformation of subjectivities in the intersection between the articulation of counter-hegemonic moments and hegemonic reintegration has to be explicated. Reflecting on the 'operationalisation' of political discourse theory is a relevant endeavour, as Laclau aimed at articulating an ontology of the political. He objected to the discipline of the critical impetus of this ontology with methodology and, even worse, methods. Is this so? Are methodology and method always constraining? In the course of this chapter, I will argue that, on the contrary, methodology and method can be creative and critical. It can help us to see and, one might add, enact elements that otherwise would have remained unnoticed and *unreal*. This promise of creativity is especially relevant given that regional interventions have not received much attention from critical intervention scholarship. In this sense, no previous research had illuminated the twilight zone between the perpetuation of a dominant peace and the articulation of difference for regional interventions more generally and for Burundi and Zimbabwe in particular. Methodology and method can thus help us not to simply impose theoretical concepts onto an allegedly transparent empirical reality. Instead methodology and method help to thoroughly re-read empirical complexity with the help of the theoretical terminology outlined in the last chapter.

The most familiar objection against the constricting discipline of methods for our scientific inquiry was articulated by Paul Feyerabend (1986). In recent years, IR scholars have reclaimed the critical potential of methodologies and methods as performative, political, and creative (Friedrichs and Kratochwil 2009, Aradau and Huysmans 2014). For enabling political discourse theory to speak *to* and *with* regional practices of intervention in eastern and southern Africa, it seems necessary to scrutinise the function of methodology and method. As Claudia Aradau and Jef Huysman (2014, p. 598) argued, methods are 'performative practices experimentally connecting and assembling fragments of ontology, epistemology, theories, techniques and data through which substantive effects are obtained'. This chapter is structured as follows: First I will discuss the methodological deficit of political discourse theory, introducing 'retroduction' as a possible way out. In the second section I will introduce coding as the technique for analysing a huge amount of text data on regional interventions. The third section discusses the difficult assembling of text data on regional interventions into Burundi and Zimbabwe. Lastly I will present the coding scheme as employed with respect to the analysis of these two instances of regional intervention.

The methodological deficit of political discourse theory – and a possible way out

Scholars working empirically with political discourse theory almost by necessity have to think about the translation of this terminology into empirical research (Howarth 2000, 2009, Herschinger and Renner 2014, Nabers 2015, pp. 129–148). Most of these scholars have attested that political discourse theory has a *methodological deficit*. The difficulty of articulating a methodology for political discourse theory can be illustrated with respect to the ontology of antagonism, which strongly differs from the everyday meaning attached to it. In political discourse theory, antagonism is a constitutive element of any structure. Any political formation lacks an ultimate foundation that would stabilise its being. Therefore, it constantly needs to perform its stability as a whole, by projecting the responsibility for its lack to the outside (Laclau 1990, Laclau and Mouffe 2001 [1985]). Political discourse theory thus understands an antagonism as a projection rather than a stable frontier that separates us from them. The antagonism is constitutive, but also elusive at the same time. How to get hold of an empirical but elusive manifestation of antagonism, without essentialising it?

Laclau contributed to the theory of the political as such rather than focusing on more definite policy fields like interventions (Townshend 2003, p. 132). From the point of view of political discourse theory, a policy field has to be comprehended as a 'fixed variety of the political' (Dyrberg 1998, p. 27). By scrutinising regional intervention politics, this book tries to reconstruct a fixed variety of the political: that is, a policy field, in which the ontological impossibility of ultimate foundations is concealed through temporarily stabilised, empirical substitutes. It is important to understand the difference between the political and a fixed variety of the political (see also Marchart 2010). The ontological depth of concepts like 'antagonism' gets partially lost with its fixation. It is very difficult to reconstruct empirically the process of projection. Therefore, it has been argued that an ontological antagonism resists being verified empirically (Dyrberg 1998, p. 27, Marchart 2010, p. 27).

The first generation of political discourse theorists tried to transcend this gap between ontology and empirical discourse by 'deploying their ontological categories in undertaking an ontic analysis of specific political discourses' (Townshend 2003, p. 132). In other words, ontological concepts like antagonism were deductively imposed onto a fixed variety of the political, without making explicit the process of deduction and subsumption (Keller 2011, p. 165). What is so bad with subsumption? As it is usually understood, subsumption separates abstract concepts from empirical complexity. It postulates a hierarchy in favour of the abstract that remains sacrosanct (Herborth 2011, p. 138), thereby encircling an already enacted reality and forestalling creative thinking. Indeed, it has been argued elsewhere that the most influential contributions to IR have not followed such a logic of subsumption (Friedrichs and Kratochwil 2009, Herborth 2011). Such a deductive procedure is especially irritating when embracing political discourse theory, as the latter denies the possibility of any ultimate foundations.

How can this theory then function as an ultimate foundation for a research design? Like all articulations, political discourse theory was articulated in a particular historical context, a context which the theory, however, later partially left behind. In *Hegemony and socialist strategy*, Laclau and Mouffe positioned the book as an intervention into left-wing politics. It was a time when 'evident truths' of the left were seriously questioned by failures 'from Budapest to Prague' as well as by the rise of new social movements. These developments seemed to be not explainable by classical Marxism that elevated the economic antagonism as the ultimate driver of resistance and change. Against this dislocation of classical Marxist thinking, their intervention aimed at filling the theoretical speechlessness of left-wing politics (Laclau and Mouffe 2001 [1985], pp. 1–2). Although the current reception of Laclauian thinking has stepped out of this particular historical context and hence, to a certain degree, became universalised, it would contradict the theoretical ontology to argue that political discourse theory is atemporal. Deductive or subsumptive reasoning would thus contradict political discourse theory, as they would further stabilise the theory by subordinating everything under this logic. Jacob Torfing (1999, p. 292) therefore warned against filling the methodological deficit with a 'totalising master methodology'.

In the last few years, another research logic has gained momentum: abduction, or retroduction. Those who embrace retroduction, trace it back to Charles Sanders Peirce (1839–1914), even though there are some doubts about the congruence of contemporary and historical understandings of retroduction. Twenty years ago, retroduction was something like an 'insiders' tip' among social scientists (Reichertz 2012, p. 276, 2013, p. 11), but recently it has received some notable endorsement (Glynos and Howarth 2007, pp. 18–48, Friedrichs and Kratochwil 2009, pp. 709–711). Contrary to deduction, with retroduction, the abstract does not remain sacrosanct, but – through endless cycles between theory and praxis – the empirical complexity alters our abstract grammar as well. Various scholars of political discourse theory have identified retroduction as a possible way out of the methodological deficit (Glynos and Howarth 2007, Nonhoff 2010, Herschinger 2012). In accordance with discourse theory terminology, the research process can be comprehended as an act of articulation, constructing new relations between previously dispersed elements (cf. Laclau and Mouffe 2001 [1985], p. 113). The research process is thus not detached from the constitution of the world. Rather, it is itself part of constituting that world. Hence, 'any full-fledged explanation of a social phenomenon will invariably involve a plurality of heterogeneous theoretical and empirical elements that need to be assembled together into a complex, though singular, explanation' (Glynos and Howarth 2007, p. 178). This book is thus the endpoint of a constant back and forth movement between theory, method, and praxis, through which I was able to re-assemble the heterogeneous theoretical and empirical elements into a more or less coherent argument. Hence, the argument I articulate in this book is not an objective depiction of an external world, but enacts a representation of regional interventions that might not have been enacted before.

A retroductive and articulatory methodology should not be misunderstood as 'anything goes' (see also Friedrichs and Kratochwil 2009, p. 707), a claim that will become more plain in the course of this chapter. The book apprehends social sciences as pluralistic. Therefore, the scientificity of an argument can only be evaluated by its systematicity, intelligibility, and plausibility (Jackson 2011, p. 189, Nonhoff 2011, p. 100). What renders social science different from everyday thinking is the systematic questioning of all elements of the argument, but also the systematic presentation of the argument in the course of this book.

A retroductive and articulatory methodology has implications for the whole research process on regional interventions. The initial problematisation has already transformed the object of research (Glynos and Howarth 2007, p. 34, Friedrichs and Kratochwil 2009, p. 712). First, by understanding the interventions in Burundi and Zimbabwe as examples of regional interventions, I homogenised and synthesised the otherwise heterogeneous practices. Heterogeneous interventions became chained together as manifestations of 'regional interventions'. Second, methods likewise transform the object of research. Contrary to the common understanding of methods as techniques of representing an externally given world, they are enacting worlds 'in the sense that it is an active force that is part of a process of continuous production and reproduction of relations, an endless process of bring worlds into being' (Aradau and Huysmans 2014, p. 603). The method used here – coding – helped to articulate the world of regional interventions. On the basis of systematic reading and coding of two text corpora (see below), the difference between international and regional interventions is not simply represented as it was. Instead it is a narration about an elusive relation of difference that contributes to the constituting of regional interventions as different. Without articulations like these, this difference might have remained unreal (cf. Latour 2015, chs 4, 5).

The process of constitution as delineated with respect to regional interventions is not unidirectional – as deduction claims it is. By understanding a research process as cyclical – that is, as a constant back and forth movement – the explanatory concepts 'cannot remain fully intact in the process of explaining' (Glynos and Howarth 2007, p. 186). Therefore, third, it also has to be asked how the method and the empirical elements have transformed political discourse theory? At this point, it can be responded that the empirical analysis de- and re-contextualised the theory. Here, it is no longer a theory aimed at filling a theoretical void of left-wing politics, but a theory that enables to render visible international agency, and diversity beyond the usual suspects.[1] In the following, I will introduce coding as a method that allowed for proceeding retroductively while developing the argument on regional interventions.

Situating coding in retroductive methodology

Coding as a method comes from a different research tradition, namely grounded theory. The latter was originally conceived as an inductive methodology, enabling researchers to articulate abstract theories from empirical complexity. In *The discovery of grounded theory* (1967), Barney Glaser and Anselm Strauss aimed at countering the dominance of deductive reasoning in social sciences. Therefore, they presented grounded theory as a purely inductive methodology. The possibility of generating abstract conclusions by systematically studying empirical complexity was, however, soon called into question. From there on, abduction was identified as a more adequate methodological proceeding. Both grounded theory methodologists and political discourse theorists thus demand an abductive or retroductive procedure, even though strong differences remain. This shared endorsement of the research methodology is the strongest argument for combining political discourse theory with coding.

Coding can be understood as a technique of re-assembling heterogeneous textual and theoretical elements. It requires an assemblage of text material. Grounded theory methodologists have developed a three-step procedure: open, axial, and selective coding. During open coding the researcher tags relevant text passages, still being strongly guided by the wording of the text. Only in the next phase the researcher condenses the code system. In this axial phase codes should function as categories with a 'more complex "inner life"' (Berg and Milmeister 2007, p. 187), being products of creative moments, in which 'bounds of sense are redrawn' (Friedrichs and Kratochwil 2009, p. 712). This phase thus corresponds to retroductive reasoning, articulating new relations between previously dispersed elements. In the last phase, the researcher scrutinises the creative re-assemblage of elements for plausibility. This phase is rather technical. Selective re-coding aims to find empirical support for the argument. If the argument cannot be supported by textual material, the research returns to the second phase.

There are some reservations about combining coding with political discourse theory (Glasze, Husseini, and Mose 2009, Diaz-Bone and Schneider 2010). Coding from a grounded theory perspective aims at constructing categories. This contradicts non-essentialism as embraced by political discourse theory (Diaz-Bone and Schneider 2010, p. 500). Categories suggest the possibility of stabilised, atemporal, and uncontested knowledge, whereas political discourse theory aims to question such fixed representations of reality, by making visible instabilities, ruptures, and ambiguities. Therefore, it was proposed that the codes be reinterpreted as 'temporary marks': that is, 'hypotheses about elements and reciprocal references in a discursive order' (Diaz-Bone and Schneider 2010, p. 501). In the initial phase, relevant discursive elements are coded. These codes function as a 'search grid', from which the researcher, in a second step, can reconstruct the relational entanglements of the discursive structure (Glasze Husseini, and Mose 2009, pp. 295–296). In other words, in the open coding phase, the researcher tags all those empirical elements that have a *potential* structural function. I call them potential key elements. During the axial coding phase, the researcher articulates relations between previously dispersed empirical and theoretical elements: for example, that the signifier 'democracy' temporarily functioned as an empty signifier in the field of intervention.

This research practice of re-articulating theoretical and empirical elements can be comprehended as acts of judgement (Glynos and Howarth 2007, pp. 183–186). Judgement is often associated with arbitrariness – as the opposite of scientific rigour, thereby however disregarding how researchers develop a 'situated ability' to judge by participating in their academic field (Glynos and Howarth 2007, pp. 184–185). This familiarity with the respective academic field(s) allows the creative re-articulation of elements, thereby enacting new analytical perspectives on the subject matter.

It should have become clear that coding is not a 'neutral' method. It is another device contributing to the final argument. The researcher cannot hide behind a method that supposedly extracts information from an external world, but – by re-assembling the elements – the researcher is part of the constitution of this world. Other scholars working in political discourse theory argued for different methodical approaches – such as corpus linguistics, quantifying the frequency of discursive elements in a given corpus (Glasze 2007, Nabers 2009, 2015). Coding as described above runs into the danger of only analysing those elements which the dominant narratives consider relevant. By contrast, a frequency analysis renders the identification of potential key signifiers more intelligible, directing the focus to the most frequent occurrences. But corpus linguistics also requires a closed text corpus. That is a corpus that is sampled according to a well-defined principle, incorporating all texts that are subsumed under this principle. With respect to the regional interventions in Burundi and Zimbabwe, such a closed corpus could not be assembled. This book is interested in the regional polyphony on Burundi and Zimbabwe. It was impossible to define one or more definite principles for sampling the text corpus that could satisfy this polyphony, as I will discuss in more detail in the next section.

Regional polyphony: the difficulties of assembling text material

A variety of socio-political forces were involved in shaping the discourses on Burundi and Zimbabwe. The regional polyphony created certain challenges for assembling the text material, which I will discuss in this section. Such discussion is crucial as it facilitates intelligibility – one criterion, which ensures scientific reasoning among a pluralistic social science community. The composition of the text corpus was also decisive for the analysis itself. It predetermined whose significations became visible and whose disappeared. Certain questions thus arose with the collection of text material: which texts are relevant and which are not? Who contributed to the regional discourse on Burundi and Zimbabwe? Who not enough? These questions point to the difficult relations between text and theory.

The way text material should be assembled is controversial. The concept of text corpora was developed in linguistics. These corpora allowed for study of real rather than ideal language data. Basically, a text corpus signifies a principled text collection (Teubert 2005, p. 4) rather than a specific method or way of analysis. It was proposed to start the sampling process by defining a virtual corpus: that is, all those documents which ideally should be included in the analysis (Teubert 2010, pp. 393–394). The virtual corpus on Burundi and Zimbabwe would include all those texts regarding how regional forces positioned themselves on the crises in the two countries. The realisation of this virtual corpus however failed due to practical constraints. The real corpus only includes those texts which I could access (cf. Teubert 2010, pp. 393–394). For example, the real text corpus on Burundi includes most but not all communiqués of the Regional Peace Initiative on Burundi, as access was limited.

Ultimately the differentiation between virtual and real text corpus does not help to define the text corpus as it does not specify the principle for its compilation: that is, all those texts regarding how regional forces positioned themselves on the crisis in the two countries. I compiled the corpora by including texts from commonly accepted regional 'actors' on these cases (see also Hajer 1993, p. 46). This principle of compilation is partly at odds with political discourse theory. The latter emphasises the inseparability of discourse and subjectivity, as detailed in the last chapter. By assembling corpora on the basis of sedimented 'actors', subjects become essentialised. This is a critical incompatibility between theory and methodology, which is however difficult to transcend. In empirical research, the limits of a text corpus will always remain controversial and theoretically vulnerable. Martin Nonhoff (2010, pp. 310–311) proposed understanding these sedimented 'actors' as provisory subject positions that will however change while reconstructing the discourse. This is an important argument, especially considering that this book analyses the transformation of regional subjectivity. I followed this pragmatic approach, compiling the text corpus according to commonly accepted 'actors' in these two cases of intervention.[2]

The text corpus on Burundi includes 180 different texts: communiqués and statements produced by the Regional Peace Initiative on Burundi and the subsequent facilitation teams; speeches and interviews given by regional heads of state and other government officials; communiqués, reports, and resolutions by the Organisation of African Unity (and, later, by the African Union); as well as Hansards of parliamentary debates in Uganda and South Africa. This text corpus most notably echoes voices from regional government elites: the former Tanzanian Presidents Julius Nyerere, Benjamin Mkapa, and Jakaya Kikwete; the Ugandan President Yoweri Museveni; the Rwandan President Paul Kagame; as well as the former (and current) South African Presidents Nelson Mandela, Thabo Mbeki, and Jacob Zuma. It was difficult to include voices other than the government officials or the facilitation team, reflecting the discrepancy between virtual and real corpora.

The regional intervention in Burundi was an elite undertaking. This does not however imply that non-governmental elites and ordinary citizens had nothing to say on the crisis in their neighbourhood. In light of the broad definition of intervention, the inclusion of their voices would also have suggested itself. Local residents in north-western Tanzania witnessed the arrival of many people fleeing from Burundi and other violent crises in the neighbourhood. From 1993 to 2000, Tanzania hosted almost 1,500,000 refugees. The majority of local residents are said to have responded with fear, a sentiment that in the context of the first multiparty elections in Tanzania's history was also mediated politically (Rutinwa 1996, p. 229).[3] The government did its best to avert a broader politicisation of Burundi. In 1997, the Tanzanian Ministry of Home Affairs warned NGOs not to engage in 'hostile exchanges of words with the government' (Landau 2008, p. 69, see also Tripp 2000, Mercer 2003, Hoffman and Robinson 2009). Thus, at that time, neither non-governmental organisations nor the opposition (which was still in its infancy) were able to freely articulate positions on Burundi. Even though the Tanzanian discourse on Burundi was broad-based, it was difficult to reanimate these rather semi-public or private voices almost two decades later. This was thus one constrain in compiling the corpus on Burundi.

Another important force on Burundi was the Ugandan Government. In contrast to Tanzania, the Burundian crisis did not widely resonate among Ugandan society. In this sense, the Ugandan debate about Burundi was mostly shaped in the capital Kampala. At the time foreign policy decisions were generally taken by the president, bypassing the cabinet, civilian advisors, the bureaucratic apparatus, parliament, or other relevant domestic groups. However, the Burundian crisis fell at a time when Ugandan parliamentarians were able to publicly criticise government policy. In the sixth legislative period from 1996 to 2001, open debate temporarily became possible (Mair 2001, p. 45). During this period, the Ugandan Parliament and especially the committee on foreign affairs actively contributed to the government's foreign and security policy,[4] including regarding Burundi. Yet, this relative open atmosphere in parliament did not last. In 2004, a constitutional amendment limited the parliament's competences (Mwenda 2007, p. 24), also diminishing the societal contribution to the discourse on Burundi.

The communiqués issued by the Regional Peace Initiative on Burundi were one of the most important text sources on regional intervention politics. But the Regional Initiative was an ad hoc coalition with diverging memberships, having no permanent secretariat, which meant I could not access communiqués through a single institutional webpage. Instead these communiqués and similar statements are dispersed across the internet.[5] Even in case of fully institutionalised 'actors' like the Rwandan, Tanzanian, or Ugandan presidency statements, speeches, and interviews had to be collected from diverse sites and sources.[6] Access to text material from the South African Government, by contrast, was much easier. Yet, compared to the amount of text on Zimbabwe, the South African Government only rarely spoke about Burundi. In the aftermath of the intervention, the facilitation team and specifically the Mwalimu Nyerere Foundation published an edited volume on their practices, which likewise served as text material. Under Nyerere, however, public relations remained in his hands, whereas, later, under shifting South African facilitators, the foreign ministry regularly briefed the media on Burundi. Both South African and Ugandan parliaments discussed Burundi. Hansards could be downloaded from the respective institutional websites.

The text corpus on Zimbabwe includes 185 single documents: texts produced by the Southern African Development Community (SADC); statements, speeches, and interviews given by regional heads of state and other government officials; and, infrequently, texts issued by the African Union. Contrary to Burundi, this corpus is more heterogeneous, not only echoing government elites, but also including voices from wider society – especially from South African society (see below). The South African President Thabo Mbeki initially intervened bilaterally into the Zimbabwean crisis, but from 2007 to 2013 he and later Jacob Zuma were officially appointed as facilitators by SADC. The South African Government was thus one of the most vocal speakers on Zimbabwe. But they also avoided publicly commenting on details of their intervention politics (Sachikonye 2005, p. 581, Gumede 2007, p. 220).[7] The presidency and the foreign ministry nevertheless had to regularly issue press releases, as the South African constitution codifies the right to access to government documentation. It was therefore relatively easy to gather a vast amount of government documentation on Zimbabwe.[8] The president also had to respond to parliamentary questions,[9] providing insights into otherwise 'quiet diplomacy' (see Hamill and Hoffman 2009, Moore 2010). President Mbeki also regularly published comments on Zimbabwe in the party outlet *ANC Today*. In the aftermath of his presidency, internal communications about regional intervention politics was leaked to the public (e.g. Mbeki 2008).

SADC was another vocal regional voice on Zimbabwe. In contradistinction to the Regional Peace Initiative on Burundi, SADC is a well-established regional organisation with its own institutional website. This facilitated easy access to summit communiqués and other documents. Moreover, other SADC heads of state also commented on the crisis in their neighbourhood.[10] The access to their statements and speeches on Zimbabwe was however more difficult. None of these governments have had a comparable documentation policy to South Africa. The process of identifying relevant statements was thus cumbersome, relying on secondary references to specific speeches or statements. As a result, their voices are rather underrepresented in the corpus.

In contrast to their eastern African counterparts, the southern African elites were not able to monopolise the articulations on Zimbabwe. The following statement partially elucidates the polyphony on Zimbabwe: 'Except for the Zimbabwe situation, foreign policy issues generate precious little public debate in South Africa and hardly feature in election campaigns' (Geldenhuys 2010, p. 154). The Zimbabwean crisis, by implication, was met with a heated debate among South African society at large (Sachikonye 2005, p. 581). Domestic criticism was voiced by oppositional parties, civil society organisations, foreign policy thinktanks, the media, but also by coalition partners from the government. Since the end of apartheid, the African National Congress has formed a coalition with the Congress of South African Trade Unions as well as the South African Communist Party (see Botiveau 2013). Regarding Zimbabwe, these coalition partners soon became the 'top internal opposition' (Booysen 2011, p. 3), voicing their critique in statements and interviews but also by co-organising a boycott against the Zimbabwean Government (see Larmer 2008), which can likewise be comprehended as a distinct contribution to the discourse.[11] Within the ANC rank and file, Zimbabwe likewise emerged as a subject of debate. Especially vocal was the ANC Youth League and its former secretary general, Julius Malema. In parliament, the major opposition party the Democratic Alliance kept Zimbabwe on the national agenda. However, due to the ANC dominance in parliament, the Zimbabwean crisis was only a few times subject to parliamentary debate. More often, the opposition posed formal questions to the president, to which he had to respond.

Besides these state elites, numerous civil society organisations like Crisis in Zimbabwe Coalition, Solidarity Peace Trust, and the South African Liaison Office articulated critiques of Zimbabwe and the regional intervention policy. According to an interviewee, the Zuma administration was indeed more willing to consider the views of the civil society organisations on Zimbabwe:

> We had meetings with the facilitation team around President Zuma. We had the opportunity to present to them and to the presidency our views in terms of how we see things, what we want. Not only that. We also had the privilege to see our submissions reflected in policy in terms of the SADC resolutions on Zimbabwe. So for us, it has been a significant success in terms of acceptance of our analysis, and proposals, and recommendations, and seeing them reflected in actual practice.[12]
>
> (Interview with activist, 15 August 2012)

Yet, others were less optimistic:

> When [Lindiwe Zulu, facilitation team member] came in, you knew she would say: 'Yes, we want to listen to civil society in Zimbabwe, in South Africa. This is not just about state to state.' And then she said all these nice liberal things.... She made all these promises and nothing would ever happen.
>
> (Interview with scholar, 21 August 2012)

Although the civil society organisations were well connected and shaped the domestic debate about Zimbabwe, I was not able to systematically include all statements into the corpus, since this would have overextended the scope of the project. Therefore, the voice of civil society organisations is only included sporadically – at moments where their statements resonated with other regional intervention forces.

The two corpora are thus rather different. Whereas the regional discourse on Burundi was mostly shaped by government elites, Zimbabwe became a subject of broader, societal debate. The corpus on Zimbabwe is thus more heterogeneous, integrating diverse regional forces. In the course of the analysis, the stable frontiers separating one 'actor' from another collapse. Defining the corpus along these lines was a pragmatic choice, rendering the sampling more intelligible.

A coding scheme for analysing regional interventions

These two corpora functioned as the underlying text data for the coding process. In total, the text data consist of 365 individual documents. Given the sheer amount of text data, using a qualitative data analysis software like Atlas.ti almost seemed a natural choice.[13] During the first phase of coding, I tagged all those elements which I considered as potentially structuring the discourse. The first phase of coding was not inductive as grounded theory methodologists had originally anticipated. My decision to tag a particular element was already pre-structured by previous discourse on the respective cases as well as on interventions more broadly. These discourses already informed my comprehension of the regional interventions. In the methodical reflections about coding, this pre-structuring is reflected as sensitising concepts. According to Juliet Corbin and Strauss (2008, p. 37), 'familiarity with relevant literature can enhance sensitivity to subtle nuances in data'. In this understanding, sensitising concepts are less rigid than pre-conceived, theoretically deduced categories and therefore allow for an openness towards unexpected significations. 'A researcher should remain open to new ideas and concepts and be willing to let go if he or she discovers that certain "imported" concepts do not fit the data' (Corbin and Strauss 2008, p. 40).

Before starting the open coding process, I therefore explicitly reflected upon those sensitising concepts that would necessarily pre-structure the coding of the text data. Apart from secondary literature, two research trips to Tanzania and South Africa, during which I conducted numerous semi-structured interviews with policy-makers, activists, journalists, and scholars,[14] were crucial for my comprehension of the discourses. The people I interviewed deepened my knowledge of the respective interventions, but they also attached particular significations to them, ultimately directing my attention to specific elements within the large amount of text data. In the following, I will reflect on which elements I considered as relevant prior to the coding process.

Most importantly my approach to the data was pre-structured by the problematisation of Burundi and Zimbabwe as regional interventions, which I expected to be *potentially* different to international interventions. Although I did not assume that these regional interventions were radically different from the liberal peace framework, I was interested in discursive elements generally associated with 'liberal peace' or 'democracy' as well as in elements associated with 'the West' or the 'international community', as these latter signifiers commonly refer to traditional interveners. At the same time, I was curious about elements potentially marking difference, like – for instance – the signifier 'region'. In the course of this first coding phase, it turned out that 'region' was not the only marker of difference, an argument which I will develop in the next two chapters. I also identified certain potential key elements on the basis of interviews and secondary literature. On Burundi, it seemed impossible to circumvent signifiers like 'ethnicity' and 'power-sharing', as well as 'sanctions'. During the coding process, I sensed that 'Burundi' functioned as an important signifier in the transformation of regional subjectivity, as did 'South Africa'. On Zimbabwe, the omnipresence of the signifier 'land' was almost impossible to ignore – as was 'democracy', 'human rights', and 'opposition'. Throughout the research process, I frequently encountered references to 'race' – a signifier I also had in mind while coding the text data. Furthermore, the figure of Mugabe is ubiquitous as well. These signifiers thus structured the initial, open-coding phase. This is not to say that, while coding, new signifiers or associated signifiers did not became important.

These codes functioned as a search grid, from which I proceeded with axial coding. Theoretical codes do not tag single elements but relations between elements. As an example, I was interested in reconstructing empirical manifestations of antagonisms. An empirical antagonism cannot be reduced to one articulation only. In order to function as an antagonism, this relation has to be perpetuated. The reconstruction of an antagonism therefore involves a rather holistic consideration of all those codes that could discursively represent this antagonism: for example, the signifiers 'the West' and 'international community'. In the axial-coding phase, I derived a list of all of those codes, reading them in sequence. Yet, not surprisingly, these signifiers were signified quite differently in different statements, rendering a homogenising reading very reductive and distorting. It is therefore also important to keep in mind that empirical manifestations of antagonisms are always elusive: a frontier separating 'us' from 'them' is a fundamentally instable projection that is subject to much resistance and questioning. In the next two chapters, I will thus also try to disclose the constant failure of such projections. In a third phase (selective coding), I re-considered whether this structuring was plausible, complex, and to the point. With it, slowly, the final narrative, which I present in the next two chapters, assumed shape.

Notes

1 The 'usual suspects' are all those states, organisations, and forces more generally which are considered powerful in international relations: US, EU, China, Russia. The expression is deliberately indeterminate: who is powerful is obviously up for debate, but it is not purpose of this book to determine who is or is not powerful.
2 I identified these sedimented 'actors' with the help of secondary literature as well as interviews. I started with the assumption that a wide array of regional/transnational, national, and local 'actors' as well as representatives of civil society, business men and women, corporations, and social movements shaped the discourse on Burundi and Zimbabwe (cf. Hagmann and Péclard 2010, pp. 546–547).
3 For a more complex analysis of the local dynamics, see Landau 2008. For the changing Tanzanian refugee policies, see Chaulia 2003.
4 In the late 1990s, the Ugandan Parliament was among others investigating military corruption (Tangri and Mwenda 2003, p. 539). This was very remarkable considering that, during the same legislative period, forty seats were compulsorily allocated to representatives of the Ugandan armed forces (Tripp 2010, p. 142)

46 *Studying regional interventions*

5 Communiqués were published among others by the UN, ReliefWeb, and the South African Department of International Relations and Cooperation.
6 One fruitful source was the African Presidential Archives and Research Centre at Boston University but also newspaper archives from *Le Monde* or *Christian Science Monitor*. Another source was the documentation system of the UN. I also searched for specific speeches or interviews mentioned elsewhere – however, with different degrees of success.
7 According to members of the facilitation team, the negotiations relied on secrecy, therefore limiting the public's right to know (Mufamadi 2008, Zulu 2010).
8 The information portal of the South African Government as well as the homepage of the foreign ministry were important sources in this regard.
9 After the 1994 elections, the opposition used the right to ask questions of the president extensively. Yet, in 2000, the then ANC chief whip used the ANC majority to change the rules. Whereas the previous rules allowed opposition parties to raise as many questions as they saw necessary, the modified regulations restricted this possibility (Jeffery 2010, pp. 16–17).
10 The SADC heads of state publicly contributing to the regional discourse on Zimbabwe were the former and current Botswanan Presidents Festus Mogae and Ian Khama, former Zambian Presidents Levy Mwanawasa and Michael Sata, and former Tanzanian President Kikwete.
11 As argued in the last chapter, political discourse theory does not differentiate between linguistic and non-linguistic articulations. Practices like this boycott are thus also acts of signification. According to Laclau and Mouffe (2001 [1985], p. 108), 'what constitutes a differential position and therefore a relational identity with certain linguistic elements, is not the idea of [a boycott], but the [boycott] as such'. Although the practice of boycotting is theorised as an act of signification, the corpus only incorporates linguistic data. The method is thus biased towards linguistic acts of signification, not so political discourse theory.
12 The view that campaigning by civil society organisations to a certain extent was able to shape the regional discourse on Zimbabwe was also shared by a scholar interviewed on 5 September 2012.
13 For the compatibility of qualitative data analysis software and political discourse theory, see Diaz-Bone and Schneider 2010.
14 In late 2011, I stayed in Tanzania for three months and was able to interview fifteen policy-makers, facilitators, members of civil society, as well as journalists. The interviews were conducted either in Dar es Salaam or Arusha. Less than a year later, I went to South Africa, where I was able to speak to eighteen people, most of them located in Johannesburg, Pretoria, and Cape Town.

References

Aradau, C., and Huysmans, J., 2014. Critical methods in international relations: The politics of techniques, devices and acts. *European Journal of International Relations*, 20 (3), 596–619.
Berg, C., and Milmeister, M., 2007. Im Dialog mit den Daten das eigene Erzählen der Geschichte finden: Über die Kodierverfahren der Grounded Theory Methdologie. *Historical Social Research, Supplement: Grounded Theory Reader*, 182–210.
Booysen, S., 2011. *The African National Congress and the regeneration of political power*. Johannesburg: Wits University Press.
Botiveau, R., 2013. Longevity of the tripartite alliance: The post-Mangaung sequence. *Review of African Political Economy*, 40 (138), 620–627.

Chaulia, S.S., 2003. The politics of refugee hosting in Tanzania: From open door to unsustainability, insecurity and receding receptivity. *Journal of Refugee Studies*, 16 (2), 147–166.

Corbin, J., and Strauss, A., 2008. *Basics of qualitative research: Techniques and procedures for developing grounded theory*. Los Angeles: Sage.

Diaz-Bone, R., and Schneider, W., 2010. Qualitative Datenanalysesoftware in der sozialwissenschaftlichen Diskursanalyse. Zwei Praxisbeispiele. In: R. Keller, A. Hirseland, W. Schneider, and W. Viehöver, eds., *Handbuch sozialwissenschaftliche Diskursanalyse*. Vol. 2: *Forschungspraxis*. Wiesbaden: VS Verlag für Sozialwissenschaften, 491–529.

Dyrberg, T.B., 1998. Diskursanalyse als postmoderne politische Theorie. In: O. Marchart, ed., *Das Undarstellbare der Politik: Zur Hegemonietheorie Ernesto Laclaus*. Vienna: Turia und Kant, 23–51.

Feyerabend, P., 1986. *Wider dem Methodenzwang: Skizzen einer anarchistischen Erkenntnistheorie*. Frankfurt am Main: Suhrkamp.

Friedrichs, J., and Kratochwil, F., 2009. On acting and knowing: How pragmatism can advance international relations research and methodology. *International Organization*, 63 (4), 701–731.

Geldenhuys, D., 2010. South Africa: The idea-driven foreign policy of a regional power. In: D. Flemes, ed., *Regional leadership in the global system: Ideas, interests and strategies of regional powers*. Farnham: Ashgate, 151–168.

Glasze, G., 2007. Vorschläge zur Operationalisierung der Diskurstheorie von Laclau und Mouffe in einer Triangulation von lexikometrischen und interpretativen Methoden. *Forum: Qualitative Sozialforschung/Forum: Qualitative Social Research*, 8 (2): art 14.

Glasze, G., Husseini, S., and Mose, J., 2009. Kodierende Verfahren in der Diskursforschung. In: G. Glasze and A. Mattissek, eds., *Handbuch Diskurs und Raum: Theorien und Methoden für die Humangeographie sowie die sozial- und kulturwissenschaftliche Raumforschung*. Bielefeld: Transcript, 293–314.

Glynos, J., and Howarth, D., 2007. *Logics of critical explanation in social and political theory*. Abingdon: Routledge.

Gumede, W., 2007. *Thabo Mbeki and the battle for the soul of the ANC*. London: Zed Books.

Hagmann, T., and Péclard, D., 2010. Negotiating statehood: Dynamics of power and domination in Africa. *Development and Change*, 41 (4), 539–562.

Hajer, M.A., 1993. Discourse coalitions and the institutionalization of practice: The case of acid rain in Britain. In: F. Fischer and J. Forester, eds., *The argumentative turn in policy analysis and planning*. Durham, NC: Duke University Press, 43–76.

Hamill, J., and Hoffman, J., 2009. 'Quiet diplomacy' or appeasement? South African policy towards Zimbabwe. *Round Table*, 98 (402), 373–384.

Herborth, B., 2011. Methodenstreit – Methodenzwang – Methodenfetisch. *Zeitschrift für Internationale Beziehungen*, 18 (2), 137–151.

Herschinger, E., 2012. 'Hell is the other': Conceptualising hegemony and identity through discourse theory. *Millennium: Journal of International Studies*, 41 (1), 65–90.

Herschinger, E., and Renner, J., 2014. *Diskursforschung in den Internationalen Beziehungen*. Baden-Baden: Nomos.

Hoffman, B., and Robinson, L., 2009. Tanzania's missing opposition. *Journal of Democracy*, 20 (4), 123–136.

Howarth, D., 2000. *Concepts in social sciences: Discourse*. Buckingham: Open University Press.

48 Studying regional interventions

Howarth, D., 2009. Power, discourse, and policy: Articulating a hegemony approach to critical policy studies. *Critical Policy Studies*, 3 (3–4), 309–335.

Jackson, P.T., 2011. *The conduct of inquiry in international relations: Philosophy of science and its implications for the study of world politics*. London: Routledge.

Jeffery, A., 2010. *Chasing the rainbow: South Africa's move from Mandela to Zuma*. Johannesburg: South African Institute for Race Relations.

Keller, R., 2011. *Wissenssoziologische Diskursanalyse: Grundlegung eines Forschungsprogramms*. 3rd edn., Wiesbaden: VS Verlag für Sozialwissenschaften.

Laclau, E., 1990. *New reflections on the revolution of our time*. London: Verso.

Laclau, E., and Mouffe, C., 2001 [1985]. *Hegemony and socialist strategy*. 2nd edn. London: Verso.

Landau, L.B., 2008. *The humanitarian hangover: Displacement, aid and transformation in western Tanzania*. Johannesburg: Wits University Press.

Larmer, M., 2008. The Zimbabwe arms shipment campaign. *Review of African Political Economy*, 35 (117), 486–493.

Latour, B., 2015. *Die Hoffnung der Pandora: Untersuchungen zur Wirklichkeit der Wissenschaft*. Frankfurt am Main: Suhrkamp.

Mair, S., 2001. *East African co-operation: Regionale Integration und Kooperation südlich der Sahara*, Part 1. Berlin: SWP-Studie.

Marchart, O., 2010. *Die politische Differenz*. Berlin: Suhrkamp.

Mbeki, T., 2008. Letter to Morgan Tsvangirai of 22 November. Available from: www.flickr.com/photos/sokwanele/3065872812/in/photostream/ (accessed 20 November 2013).

Mercer, C., 2003. Performing partnership: Civil society and the illusions of good governance in Tanzania. *Political Geography*, 22 (7), 741–763.

Moore, D., 2010. A decade of disquieting diplomacy: South Africa, Zimbabwe and the ideology of the National Democratic Revolution, 1999–2009. *History Compass*, 8 (8), 752–767.

Mufamadi, S., 2008. Media briefing of 15 April. Pretoria: South African Department of International Relations and Cooperation. Available from: www.politicsweb.co.za/iservice/transcript-of-mufamadis-briefing-on-zimbabwe (accessed 27 February 2013).

Mwenda, A.M., 2007. Personalizing power in Uganda. *Journal of Democracy*, 18 (3), 23–37.

Nabers, D., 2009. Filling the void of meaning: Identity construction in U.S. foreign policy after September 11, 2001. *Foreign Policy Analysis*, 5 (2), 191–214.

Nabers, D., 2015. *A poststructuralist discourse theory of global politics*. New York: Palgrave Macmillan.

Nonhoff, M., 2010. Hegemonieanalyse: Theorie, Methode und Forschungspraxis. In: R. Keller, A. Hirseland, W. Schneider, and W. Viehöver, eds., *Handbuch sozialwissenschaftliche Diskursanalyse*. Vol. 2: *Forschungspraxis*. Wiesbaden: VS Verlag für Sozialwissenschaften, 299–331.

Nonhoff, M., 2011. Konstruktivistisch-pragmatische Methodik. Ein Plädoyer für die Diskursanalyse. *Zeitschrift für Internationale Beziehungen*, 18 (2), 91–107.

Reichertz, J., 2012. Abduktion, Deduktion und Induktion in der qualitativen Forschung. In: U. Flick, E. von Kardorff, and I. Steinke, eds., *Qualitative Forschung: Ein Handbuch*. Reinbeck: Rowolt, 276–286.

Reichertz, J., 2013. *Die Abduktion in der qualitativen Sozialforschung. Über die Entdeckung des Neuen*. 2nd edn., Wiesbaden: VS Verlag für Sozialwissenschaften.

Rutinwa, B., 1996. Beyond durable solutions: An appraisal of the new proposals for prevention and solution of the refugee crisis in the Great Lakes region. *Journal of Refugee Studies*, 9 (3), 312–325.

Sachikonye, L.M., 2005. South Africa's quiet diplomacy: The case of Zimbabwe. In: J. Daniel, R. Southall, and J. Lutchman, eds., *State of the nation: South Africa 2004–2005*. Cape Town: Human Sciences Research Council Press, 569–585.

Tangri, R., and Mwenda, A.M., 2003. Military corruption and Ugandan politics since the late 1990s. *Review of African Political Economy*, 30 (98), 539–552.

Teubert, W., 2005. My version of corpus linguistics. *International Journal of Corpus Linguistics*, 10 (1), 1–13.

Teubert, W., 2010. Provinz eines föderalen Superstaates – regiert von einer nicht gewählten Bürokratie? Schlüsselbegriffe des europakritischen Diskurses in Großbritannien. In: R. Keller, A. Hirseland, W. Schneider, and W. Viehöver, eds., *Handbuch sozialwissenschaftliche Diskursanalyse*. Vol. 2: *Forschungspraxis*. Wiesbaden: VS Verlag für Sozialwissenschaften, 387–422.

Torfing, J., 1999. *New theories of discourse: Laclau, Mouffe and Žižek*. Oxford: Blackwell.

Townshend, J., 2003. Discourse theory and political analysis: A new paradigm form the Essex School? *British Journal of Politics and International Relations*, 5 (1), 129–142.

Tripp, A.M., 2000. Political reform in Tanzania: The struggle for associational autonomy. *Comparative Politics*, 32 (2), 191–214.

Tripp, A.M., 2010. *Museveni's Uganda: Paradoxes of power in a hybrid regime*. Boulder: Lynne Rienner.

Zulu, L., 2010. Interview. *SW Radio*, 17 June. Available from: http://nehandaradio.com/2010/06/22/sa-mediator-lindiwe-zulu-speaks-to-bth/ (accessed 27 February 2013).

4 Regional forces in Burundi
'We are able to act!'

At the end of 1995, the former US President Jimmy Carter facilitated a meeting between the heads of state of Burundi, Rwanda, Tanzania, Uganda, and Zaire to discuss the multiple crises and mass violence unsettling not just one state but the whole region. This November meeting, convened in distant Cairo, marks the beginning of the Regional Peace Initiative on Burundi. The year 1995 was of little significance in itself, yet it was enclosed by two years of mass violence and war: the 1994 genocide in Rwanda and the beginning of the Congo wars in 1996 during which many neighbouring governments and their armed forces waged war against each other. Against the backdrop of mass violence and the diverse antagonisms the violence exposed, the emergence and persistence of a regional peace initiative is remarkable, to say the least. This does not mean that the antagonisms criss-crossing the political and societal landscape in the Great Lakes and beyond did not become manifest in one form or another in the speeches, interviews, and communiqués issued by representatives of the regional intervention. This chapter reconstructs how the Regional Initiative, its representatives and associated forces such as the mediation team – subsequently led by Julius Nyerere, Nelson Mandela, Jacob Zuma, and later Charles Nqakula – enacted and performed a regional intervention despite these antagonisms and despite knowing little about undertaking an intervention.[1]

The Regional Peace Initiative on Burundi – a coalition dominated by the regional heads of state – appointed Julius Nyerere, former Tanzanian President, as chief facilitator. Nyerere defined his mandate as a 'freelance facilitator', who was not directly accountable to the Regional Initiative (Butiku 2004, p. 82). However, as the 'father of the nation', Nyerere is said to have remained decisive for Tanzanian politics until his death in 1999: 'the really important issues of Tanzanian diplomacy had always remained his prerogative' (Prunier 2009, p. 67). Initially, the facilitation team under Nyerere – recruited from the networks of the eponymous Mwalimu Nyerere Foundation – faced some difficulties in bringing the diverse Burundian forces to the negotiating table. A first round of negotiations was held in the northern Tanzanian town of Mwanza in April and June 1996 that, however, led nowhere. Disappointed by the negotiations, and understanding Burundi as potentially 'another Rwanda', the Regional Initiative began planning for a regional security assistance force. These plans were, however, interrupted by the *coup d'état* of July 1996. As a bold, and for many, surprising response, the regional intervention enacted sanctions against landlocked Burundi, demanding that the new government under Pierre Buyoya accepted the regionally led facilitation. Only in 1998 did regionally sponsored peace negotiations commence in Arusha, a city in northern Tanzania and host of the East African Community. The negotiations culminated in the Arusha Peace and Reconciliation Agreement (Arusha Agreement), signed by fourteen parties in August 2000. Yet, the agreement did not mark the end of the regional intervention.

Nyerere died in 1999. As his replacement, the Regional Initiative appointed Nelson Mandela who had just retired from the South African presidency.[2] Geographically speaking, the 'regional' intervention thus broadened. The signifier 'regional' also came to imply South Africa. Burundi's immediate neighbourhood was worried about their position in the Burundian field of intervention. Therefore, Mandela initially hung on to the previous facilitation team and brought in just a few new faces (Bomani 2004, p. vii, Rautenbach and Vrey 2010, p. 15). This compromise is said to have 'ensured a modicum of regional control' (Khadiagala 2003, p. 236). Yet, shortly after the Arusha Agreement, the facilitation team members associated with the Mwalimu Nyerere Foundation were disempowered. From then on South African Government staff performed the everyday tasks of regional intervention. At that time the heterogeneity of the regional interveners became more visible. The facilitation performed the intervention mostly from South Africa, whereas the Regional Initiative was still in the hands of the Tanzanian and Ugandan Governments.

After the Arusha Agreement, South African Deputy President Zuma dominated the politics of facilitation. Two major armed movements had not yet signed the peace agreement, which rendered their inclusion a continuous objective of the intervention. In 2003, the Pretoria Protocols integrated one of the two armed movements into the government. The other armed movement did not sign a ceasefire agreement until 2008. In the meantime, the facilitation was handed over to a South African minister, Charles Nqakula, who remained in this position from 2006 to 2009.

This brief outline suggests a linearity and unity of regional intervention that becomes blurred on closer inspection. In the subsequent chapter, this linearity and unity is undermined, disclosing a more complex representation of these practices. In the first section, I show how the Regional Initiative frequently made use of hegemonic signifiers generally structuring international interventions such as 'democracy' and 'power-sharing'. These signifiers were emptied of any particular meaning, allowing ideological differences and antagonisms to be transcended. In contradistinction to those authors, who subsume regional interventions under an allegedly universal logic of peacemaking, I show in the second section how the Regional Initiative clearly differed from this universalist template. Unlike many other forces in the Burundian intervention scene, the regional interveners identified the emerging East African Community and the successful South African transition from apartheid as common nodal points promising hope and emancipation – not just for Burundi but also for the wider region. By being responsible for the mediation as well as by imposing sanctions, the regional elite's agency in shaping politics became visible. In the third section, I reconstruct how this new interpretative authority fostered new exclusions, delimitations, and depreciations. I show how the regional interpretative authority emerged only by antagonising both Burundian politics as well as Western approaches to peacemaking. The construction of antagonisms towards other forces in the intervention scene enabled the regional forces to claim authority over others.

'Democracy and security for all': the rise and fall of an empty signifier

At the time the Regional Initiative emerged, democracy functioned as one of many horizons of change among the members of the Regional Initiative. The identification with liberal peacebuilding was thus not an obvious choice. In Tanzania, the 'father of the nation' Nyerere began to identify democracy as a political objective by the mid-1980s and thereby created space for public debate. As an intellectual, he embraced the signifier 'democracy' at a moment when its future was still hampered internationally by the iron curtain and domestically by the lack of an articulate opposition (Hoffman and Robinson 2009, p. 124).[3] In 1995, the first multiparty elections represented another nodal point in the national discourse on democracy, thereby, however, bringing new legitimacy to the rule of Chama Cha Mapunduzi, the party of the presidents from independence until today. In Uganda, by contrast, change and progress were not primarily associated with democracy. In 1986, Yoweri Museveni and the National Resistance Movement came to power at the barrel of a gun, thereby ousting the hated regime of Milton Obote (Makara, Rakner, and Svåsand 2009, p. 187). In his inauguration speech, Museveni promised: 'No one should think that what is happening today is a mere change of guard: it is a fundamental change in the politics of our country.'[4] The new government wanted fundamental change to be understood as the transcendence of the societal divisions that bedevilled Ugandan politics from independence onwards. Change thus referred to a future national unity.[5] Whereas at the beginning, the Ugandan non-party system was said to be relatively open to diverging positions, the space for contestation shrank by the mid-1990s (see Furley and Katalikawe 1997, Mwenda 2007, Makara Rakner, and Svåsand 2009, pp. 190–191, Muhumuza 2009). Thus, for two of the leading members of the Regional Initiative, liberal democracy was still one among many horizons of change.

It was Burundi that provided the heads of state in the Regional Initiative with the most far-reaching example of democratic transition. From 1966 to 1993, this small, landlocked country was governed by three successive military governments who barred the majority of the people from political participation and economic well-being. In this period, Burundi witnessed recurrent cycles of violence (Lemarchand and Martin 1974, Lemarchand 1994, Daley 2006). In most accounts, including the regional ones, the excluded people are comprehended as Hutu (discussed in the next section). In 1988, a renewed cycle of mass violence marked the emergence of new practices. Dismayed by the renewed violence, donors put pressure on the government to initiate institutional reforms (Reyntjens 1993, p. 564). The constitutional reforms enabled the inclusion of some of those formerly excluded in leading state positions and initiated a policy of reconciliation 'but without democratisation', as Stef Vandeginste (2009, p. 66) clarified. These reforms thus did not fundamentally alter the state institutions. When regional forces referred to Burundi as the most far-reaching example of democracy in the region (e.g. Ugandan Parliament 1995, p. 17), none of them had these reforms in mind but were thinking of the first multiparty election in 1993 which was described as a 'virtual political earthquake' (Reyntjens 1993, p. 573). After having ruled Burundi since 1965, the Union pour le progrès national (Uprona) lost the elections – to everybody's surprise, one may add. With the former opposition party, the Front pour la Démocratie au Burundi (Frodebu), appointing the government, a large portion of the political and bureaucratic elite (minus the armed forces) was replaced, thereby enabling the democratically legitimised emergence of a Hutu elite (Reyntjens 1993, p. 579, Uvin 2009, pp. 12–13). By mid-1993, this fundamental and, for a short moment, peaceful change of ruling practices enabled Burundi to emerge as a model for the rest of Africa (Vandeginste 2009, p. 64). Yet, the short glory of Burundi soon faded in a *coup d'état* in October 1993, in the course of which members of the armed forces executed the then recently elected President Melchior Ndadaye. This (eventually failed) *coup d'état* marked the beginning of a renewed cycle of violence and civil war.

The violence following the *coup d'état* of 1993 shook the regional understanding of Burundi as a model for the rest of Africa. Burundi could no longer be represented in these terms. According to political discourse theory, violence, and especially mass violence, has the potential to dislocate normalised reality. A dislocation discloses the non-necessity of things and questions our representations and practices. In this sense, the coup of 1993 disclosed the non-necessity of a democratic transition. The moment revealed the fragility of change. However, the dislocation was immediately integrated into speech and interpretation. This discursive reintegration of the dislocatory moment is analysed in the next section. As I will show in the section after that, this signification of the violence also suggested a politics of intervention. In Chapter 2, I argued that interventions can be understood as an external closure to a dislocated space. By constituting the Burundian violence as the expression of an antagonistic divide, the leitmotiv 'democracy and security for all' – a paraphrase for power-sharing – soon asserted itself as the empty signifier, even though – at the dawn of the regional intervention – democracy did not function as the undisputed horizon of change in Tanzania or Uganda.

The signification of mass violence in Burundi: the persistence of ethnicity

It has to be remembered that, from a theoretical point of view, the horror of violence is such a dislocatory moment, at least for those experiencing it, that some part of it will always remain incomprehensible. However, those witnessing the violence – like the regional interveners but also, more broadly, the international community – usually do not hesitate to categorise violence, to make sense of it, and therewith to reintegrate it into discourse. This regional sense-making of violence will be reconstructed in this section. Against this background, it can be asked: How did the Regional Initiative signify the *coup d'état* of October 1993, the subsequent institutional imbroglio, as well as the fear of another genocide? In this section, I argue that regional forces – like most of the interveners including academics and international journalists – discursively reintegrated the violence as being ascribable to an *ethnic* or otherwise demographically defined antagonism. They were not able to transcend this sedimented representation of violence in Burundi that had a long tradition (Lemarchand 1994). According to this line of reasoning, the violence can be attributed to the political, economic, and social exclusion of the Hutu majority and the respective dominance of the Tutsi, a demographic minority. By 1993, this representation had become hegemonic within Burundi as well, while other possible representations were suppressed: for instance, that the socio-political hierarchies were much more complex than the differentiation between Hutu and Tutsi suggested, emerging from clan and family ties as well as from patron-client networks (Lemarchand 1994, p. 14, Ould-Abdallah 2000, pp. 43–44).[6] The increasingly stabilised antagonism differentiating between Hutu and Tutsi structured subsequent politics. After the June 1993 elections, the new Hutu President Ndadaye became the liberating hope of those identifying with the oppressed Hutu. By contrast, the army, which, at that time, was still dominated by the old Tutsi elite, likewise reproduced this antagonism by interpreting these changes as a threat to the Tutsis in general.

In the initial years of the regional intervention, the representatives of the Regional Initiative aimed at transcending the representation of the violence as being ethnic. In their official communiqués, the Regional Initiative hardly addressed ethnicity directly. An exception is the Cairo Declaration of November 1995. Here the heads of state of Burundi, Rwanda, Tanzania, Uganda, and Zaire condemned 'the ethnic and political genocide ideology used in competition for conquest and monopoly of power' (Regional Initiative 1995). Similar statements were repeated by the Ugandan and Tanzanian Presidents in 1998 and 1999 (Museveni 1998a, 1998b, Mkapa 1999a). Comprehending ethnicity as ideology highlights the non-necessity of the ethnic structuring of the political landscape. From this point of view it was an antagonism that could in principle be transcended. Against this backdrop, the regional interveners tried to articulate positions that would overcome this antagonism. The first chief facilitator Nyerere rejected the understanding of the Burundian crisis in ethnic terms. He argued that other elements like low economic development had been more decisive for the outbreak of violence (Nyerere 1996a). Museveni, the chair of the Regional Initiative, proposed stopping thinking in terms of ethnicity. Instead, Hutu and Tutsi should be understood as 'occupational guilds based on job specialization', such as agriculturalists, cattle-keepers, rulers, and hunter-gatherers (Museveni 1998b). The second chief facilitator Mandela suggested that the antagonistic differentiation between Hutu and Tutsi could be comprehended as 'perceptions' about historical legacies (Mandela 2000a). The representatives of the Regional Initiative also continuously emphasised that their mediation aspired to include 'all' forces in the peacemaking (Regional Initiative 1995, 1996a, 1996b, 1997b, 1998, Mkapa 1996c, 1997, 1998a), thereby articulating a counter-position to the antagonistic differentiation.

Yet, the regional interveners were not able to move beyond the sedimented antagonism. Although Nyerere claimed to refuse to understand the violence as ethnic, the facilitator soon relapsed into the same categorisations: 'Since their [Burundi's and Rwanda's] independence in 1962, both have been torn by fighting between factions from the majority Hutu tribe and the minority Tutsis' (Nyerere 1996a). In line with the hegemonic representation, he conceived of the political as being divided by a more or less clear frontier separating Hutus from Tutsis. Others faced similar problems with transcending the hegemonic representation. Then Tanzanian President Mkapa (1996c, 1997) argued that the regional intervention could guarantee 'the security and well-being of all groups, but especially the minority'. For Mandela, the facilitation had to balance between a responsive form of democracy and ensuring 'security for those who for reasons of demography feel vulnerable within such a system' (Mandela 2000a). By replacing ethnicity with demography, the regional interveners did not transcend the representation of the Burundian political space as divided by a clearly definable frontier.

The persistence of these representations in the regional discourse can also be attributed to the personal histories of the regional heads of state, among them Nyerere, Tanzanian President from 1960 to 1985. In 1972, the Burundian military government crushed anti-regime protests with what a UN Commission of Inquiry (1996, para. 85) later called genocidal repression against the educated Hutu elite. This event was interpreted as the watershed in Burundian politics, marking the climax of Tutsi hegemony in Burundi. Yet, the exclusion of the Hutu was a breeding ground for a counter-hegemony. Many of the oppressed and haunted fled to neighbouring Tanzania. In the refugee camps, a revanchist interpretation of Burundian politics, directed against Tutsi hegemony, flourished (Lemarchand 1994, pp. 76–105). These were the beginnings of a counter-ideology that later nourished the armed Hutu movements in the Burundian civil war. The violent episode of 1972 had altered the way Nyerere comprehended Burundi, namely as a state divided by societal antagonism. On the eve of Burundian independence in 1962 Nyerere still constituted Burundi – a pre-colonial kingdom – as a unified state. Nyerere is quoted as having said to the Burundian independence leader: 'You [Louis Rwagasore] are lucky, you have a nation ... but I am trying to build one' (cited in Ameir 2008, p. 66). Yet, the genocidal violence of 1972 dislocated this view of Burundi, revealing the relations of domination and oppression. In that year, the Burundian army raided Tanzanian territory to break the Hutu protesters, who fled to the borderlands. In response, Tanzanian dockworkers, with the active encouragement of the government, including Nyerere, boycotted the transfer of goods towards land-locked Burundi (White House 1973, Lemarchand and Martin 1974, p. 32). It is plausible that these personal entanglements brought about a new understanding of Burundi, as the former US special envoy to the Great Lakes noticed. Despite his awareness of Tutsis fearing genocide themselves, 'it was clear that Nyerere emotionally identified with the struggle of the majority Hutu to overcome their history of subordination and discrimination' (Wolpe 2011, p. 15). Personally Nyerere had thus stabilised the signification of violence in Burundi long before the violence once again escalated in 1993.

The Ugandan President likewise drew on past categorisations and understandings to make sense of the mass violence unfolding from 1993 onwards. Museveni relied on an analogy between Burundi, Uganda, and other African countries:

> We must reject the sectarian ideology of reactionaries that ... is based on false history.... We should only work with people who believe in Burundi, in Rwanda, in Uganda and in Africa and not with those who believe in sectarianism.... Sectarianism is nothing but criminal opportunism, seeking cheap popularity.
>
> (Museveni 1998b)

When the Ugandan National Resistance Movement under Museveni ousted the Obote regime, the new government reinvented itself as a force against division and sectarianism. It claimed to bring a unitary future. In this statement, Museveni constituted a chain of equivalence between Uganda and Burundi as places bedevilled by sectarianism. Based on this analogy he was able to signify the violence in Burundi as an expression of sectarianism. Thus, at the end of the day, thinking with and against ethnicity was deeply embedded in the personal, societal, and political histories of the regional space.

With the beginning of the official peace negotiations in mid-1998, thinking in ethnic categories openly imposed itself onto the regional intervention. Jean-Pierre Chrétien (2000, p. 142) provokingly argued that 'the negotiations themselves have contributed to re-enact the "interethnic" dual' (translation mine). In May 1999, the facilitation led by Nyerere divided the Burundians into Hutu and Tutsi parties, thereby – visibly for everybody – reproducing and further stabilising this antagonistic differentiation. Scholars differ in how far this ethnicisation of the intervention was promoted by the interveners. Kristina Bentley and Roger Southall (2005, p. 68) argued that the Hutu-dominated parties decided to unite as a bloc. Their decision, by implication, prompted the formation of a Tutsi bloc. In this reading, the regional interveners could do nothing against it. According to Gregory Mthembu-Salter (2002, p. 33), however, Nyerere actively endorsed the formation of these ethnic blocs. A member of the facilitation team reasoned that the ethnic profile of the Burundian parties suggested such bloc-building (Mpangala 2004, pp. 122–134). This shift towards accepting ethnicity as a structure of Burundian politics also became manifest at other scales. At the UN, Mandela (2000a) argued that the differences between Hutus and Tusis must be 'properly adjusted'. It has been argued elsewhere that 'Mandela [was] more prepared than Nyerere [had been] to analyse Burundi's problems in explicitly ethnic terms' (Mthembu-Salter 2002, p. 33). The stabilised and sedimented antagonism thus came to structure the regional intervention. This shift rendered plausible certain interventions and, as I will argue in more detail below, enabled the production of power-sharing as an empty signifier.

All in all, the regional signification of the violence remained within the hegemonic discourse. It was not possible to think beyond the stabilised antagonism, from which the mass violence seemed to originate. The Regional Initiative was not able to permanently destabilise the ethnically defined antagonism that was made responsible for the violence. This inability points to the sedimentation of such antagonistic structuring. Rather than being a terra incognita waiting to be shaped by the interveners (Lemay-Hébert 2011), the regional forces – in the course of their intervention – had to acknowledge that the field of intervention was not without a history.

The production of 'power-sharing' as an empty signifier

Around 1995, that is, the year the regional intervention into Burundi began, the hegemony of the liberal peace seemed to be in full swing. As Paris (1997, p. 56) wrote, 'a single paradigm – liberal internationalism – appears to guide the work of most international agencies engaged in peacebuilding'. Within the realms of this 'enormous experiment in social engineering', the interveners aimed to enact a liberal democratic polity in the respective society under intervention (Paris 1997, p. 56). In the terminology of political discourse theory, 'liberal peace' had functioned as an empty signifier that structured the contemporary understanding of interventions. It has to be expected that, at the beginning of the regional intervention into Burundi, it was difficult to think beyond the hegemonic liberal peace. Therefore, it is especially interesting to ask how the Regional Initiative, the facilitation team as well as other representatives of the regional intervention has made use of the liberal peace. In this section, I argue that – instead of 'democracy' – 'power-sharing' functioned as an empty signifier, enacting unity among otherwise heterogeneous forces.

At the Regional Initiative's constitutional meeting in November 1995, neither 'democracy' nor 'power-sharing' made it into the final declaration. The communiqué said that the initiative was formed to commonly advance 'peace, justice, reconciliation, stability and development in the region' (Regional Initiative 1995). As stated before, Tanzania was in transition, holding its first multiparty elections. The Ugandan Government had already scheduled the presidential elections for May 1996, after years without any. But, at its first regular summit in June 1996, the fate of the signifier 'democracy' shifted. The Tanzanian President argued that regionally led negotiations were 'the best way to create a political and constitutional dispensation that will guarantee democratic rights to all groups, while safeguarding [their] security' (Mkapa 1996a, see also 1996b). A similar wording can be found in the communiqué, stating that the Regional Initiative (1996a) aimed at facilitating 'a durable settlement based on democracy and security for all'. These first two statements on democracy suggest that the signifier is signified in a particular way, namely 'democracy' stands for a consociational model (instead of a majoritarian democracy) that accommodates rather than transcends the stabilised antagonism.

This particular filling of the signifier 'democracy' at this early state of the intervention might seem odd, given that neither Tanzania nor Uganda had any experiences with consociational democracy and given that both governments still aimed at transcending the ethnically stabilised antagonism. The early identification of consociational democracy by the Regional Initiative might testify to the difficulties interveners have in shaping the polities they intervene in. In articulating 'democracy and security for all', the regional interveners engaged with Burundian history instead of referring to universalised, abstract conceptualisations of order.

During the constitutional reform process initiated by the first Buyoya government in 1988 consociational democracy emerged as a horizon for change within Burundi. The ruling (minority) elite feared majoritarian democracy. As Filip Reyntjens (1993, pp. 565–566) wrote of the 1992 constitution, 'certainly no other country's constitutional engineering has resulted in such an insistence on the need for "a spirit of national unity"'. The constitution envisioned that state institutions would integrate the diverse elements of the Burundian population, a circumscription for those ethnic groups widely considered as being the building blocks of Burundian society. Yet, those writing the constitution failed to stipulate power-sharing quotas for the armed forces, thereby indirectly enabling the *coup d'état* of October 1993 that heralded the civil war (Vandeginste 2009, p. 68). After the coup, the UN facilitator Ahmedou Ould-Abdallah sponsored the 1994 Convention of Government, an agreement that allowed the co-opting of the moderate opposition into government, as the UN facilitator explicated (Ould-Abdallah 2000, p. 74). Vandeginste (2009, p. 69) claimed that 'the legitimacy of the ballot box was henceforth formally replaced by the legitimacy of the power-sharing consensus'. Thus, prior to the identification of power-sharing as a solution by the Regional Initiative, Burundians had already experienced two episodes of power-sharing, each filling the signifier differently: whereas the 1992 constitution aimed at reforming the political system as a whole, the Convention of Government balanced positions.

In the first months of the regional intervention, 'power-sharing' became a relevant signifier without however completely dominating the regional discourse on Burundi. In the first round of regionally sponsored peace negotiations in July 1996, the regional mediation traced at least two different and potentially incommensurable fillings of the signifier 'democracy' that were discussed within the conference centres: one filling referred to the constitution of 1992 and the other one to the convention of 1994. And that is not counting the third filling of 'democracy' articulated by the major armed movement Conseil National Pour la Défense de la Démocratie – Forces pour la Défense de la Démocratie (CNDD-FDD). They were however excluded from the peace talks. The armed movement CNDD-FDD – formed after the coup of October 1993 – demanded the institutionalisation of majoritarian democracy and lent weight to this demand through violence (Nindorera 2008, p. 103). In the peace negotiations of June 1996, the old elite refused to negotiate with the armed movement, arguing that the demand for majoritarian democracy had to be considered as extremist. Hence, the old ruling elite tried to keep the third filling of the signifier 'democracy' from the negotiation table. They were successful. The regional intervention did not counter this exclusion.

In July 1996, the Burundian armed forces staged another *coup d'état*, the fourth successful one in Burundi's post-independence history,[7] reinstating Pierre Buyoya as president and expelling Frodebu from government. Immediately, Buyoya announced the suspension of the constitution and of the political parties (ICG 1998a, p. 4). As a response to the coup, the Regional Initiative imposed sanctions and demanded the return to 'constitutional order', meaning:

(a) Immediate restoration of the National Assembly, which is a democratic institution of legality that has derived its mandate from the people of Burundi;
(b) Immediate unbanning of political parties in the country.
(Regional Initiative 1996b)

Additionally, the Buyoya government was urged to commit to unconditional and inclusive negotiations under the auspices of the Regional Initiative. Although the National Assembly and the political parties were recognised as democratic institutions, the regional interveners argued that *only* regionally sponsored negotiations would bring democracy and security for all (Regional Initiative 1996b). By arguing that only the Regional Intervention could bring democracy and security for all, the Regional Initiative linked their fortune to Burundian power-sharing.

This moment signalled a discursive shift. Previously, the demand for power-sharing was one among others. A month before the coup, other signifiers like 'security' were still much more prominent in the regional communiqué (Regional Initiative 1996a). Although the communiqué already mentioned 'democracy and security for all', the signifier did not function as a nodal point in the regional discourse. Only after the coup, democracy became a justification for the regional sanctions. In the immediate post-coup communication, the regional interveners – rather than losing time on explicating their position on future democracy – highlighted the non-acceptability of a coup. Tanzanian President Mkapa (1996c) argued that the regional response to the coup was 'a declaration of principle – that the era of *coups d'état* was over' (see also Nyerere 1996a). In an interview, Nyerere (1996c) argued that 'Africans do not accept military regimes anymore' (translation mine). The regional demands and sanctions would serve as a precedent for other cases: 'hence also the stern warning which the countries of the region gave to the army and the King in Lesotho, when it looked as if those authorities were about to reject a democratically elected government there' (Nyerere 1998, p. 150).[8] The Tanzanian authorities constituted the regional sanctions as a pro-democratic policy: 'for once *we* took a bold step in support of democracy in our region' (Mkapa 1996c, emphasis mine, see also 1996d, Nyerere 1996c). This statement thus equates regional intervention with a democratic future: the 'we' of the quote refers to those governments having attended the Regional Initiative's summit on 31 July 1996, at which the heads of state decided upon the imposition of sanctions and the articulation of demands. These were the Ethiopian, Kenyan, Rwandan, Tanzanian, and Ugandan heads of state plus the Zairean Prime Minister. On closer inspection, this 'we' was not as united as the quote suggests but precarious and heterogeneous. How could power-sharing emerge as a nodal point among these heterogeneous regional forces?

After the coup, expectations were high that the Rwandan Government would join forces with the new Buyoya government instead of rallying behind the regional sanctions and the demand for power-sharing (Mthembu-Salter 1999, pp. 12–13). This expectation stemmed from constituting regional politics as being solely governed by an ethnic antagonism, chaining together the 'Tutsi' governments of Rwanda and Burundi. However, as Mthembu-Salter (1999, pp. 12–13) argued, the Rwandan Government was eager to re-position itself as a technocratic, competent government. Their identification with the regional position can thus be interpreted as a way to reinvent their subjectivity as progressive rather than sectarian. This analysis does not allow the inferance that the Rwandan Government fully subjected itself to the logic of democracy and power-sharing. Nor can it be inferred that the government identified with the principled condemnation of *coups d'état* and military regimes out of conviction. On the contrary, as has been argued by the International Crisis Group, if Burundi had transformed into a democracy, it would have been an unpleasant precedent for authoritarian Rwanda as well (ICG 1998a, pp. 12–13). According to political discourse theory, the Rwandan Government can be conceptualised as a split subject (Laclau 2007 [1996], pp. 14–15). On the one hand, they remained *different* from the regional position, meaning that their subjectivity was not completely absorbed by the regional intervention. This is the logic of difference. However, by (explicitly or implicitly) agreeing to the publication of the regional communiqué, the Rwandan Government partly suspended this difference. Together with other regional governments, they were *equal* in their endorsement of the regional position. This is what has been called a chain of equivalence. Understanding the Rwandan Government as a split subject helps grasp the precariousness of the regional position: the remaining difference led to the falling apart of the regional intervention.

A similar argument could be made with respect to the Ugandan Government, which can likewise be understood as a split subject. The Ugandan Government's understanding of the coup also differed from the official regional position.

Museveni reportedly understood the coup as another sign that Burundi lacked 'leaders motivated by the country's national interest rather than personal interests or those of a narrowly defined group' (Wolpe 2011, p. 14). In private, he demanded that the head of the Burundian armed forces relinquish power immediately, in order to side-line reactionaries and sectarians (Wolpe 2011, p. 14). In contrast to the Tanzanian authorities and the official regional communiqué, he did not perpetuate the signification of the regional sanctions as a bold step in support of democracy. However, the Ugandan Government nevertheless was a link in a chain constituting the regional position. The dislocatory coup of July 1996, including the increasing fear of large-scale violence and even genocide, prompted heterogeneous forces to rally behind the signifier 'democracy and security for all', thereby masking their heterogeneity for a while. Yet, this paraphrase for power-sharing was only partially emptied of any meaning and was therefore not beyond being questioned – as will be argued in the following.

It has to be recalled that an empty signifier is not attached to a particular meaning but 'serves as the container for shifting significations' (Žižek 2000, p. 224). Because of its emptiness, the signifier is hard to challenge. Potential counter-meanings can be either integrated or rejected as beside the point. The empty signifier therefore stabilises a particular discursive structure. I already pointed out that, in the Burundian intervention scene, different fillings of the signifier 'democracy' circulated: majoritarian democracy, consociationalism/power-sharing, and co-optation. The regional intervention mostly referred to the signifier 'power-sharing' but without specifying its meaning. They were not alone in this: As Patricia Daley (2006, p. 675) pointed out with respect to the Burundian parties, 'very few had a conceptualization of democracy that extended beyond the demand for equity'. Comprehending 'democracy' as at least a partially empty signifier that does not refer to a particular signified seems also in line with the self-understanding of the regional intervention. Directed towards the Burundian parties, Tanzanian President Mkapa (1996a) argued: 'we assure you that we in Tanzania do not have any ulterior motives – except the restoration of peace, security, stability, democracy, human rights, and dignity for each and every person in our region'. Mandela likewise assured the Burundian parties that he did not have any preconceived positions on power-sharing in post-conflict Burundi (paraphrased by Butiku 2004, p. 106). In a nutshell, the longer the regional intervention lasted, the more difficult it became to reconstruct the fillings of the signifier 'power-sharing', as well as its origin.

By mid-1998, the Buyoya government finally agreed to regionally sponsored peace negotiations. The negotiations culminated in the Arusha Peace and Reconciliation Agreement in August 2000 that states as a principle the reorganisation of state institutions 'to make them capable of integrating and reassuring all the ethnic components of Burundian society' (Arusha Agreement 2000, Protocol I, art. 5.2). As the new chief facilitator emphasised before the UN Security Council, the agreement institutionalised 'democracy and security for all'. In the words of Mandela (2000b), the agreement would ensure 'that the democratic rights of the majority are respected, while the fears and concerns of the minorities are simultaneously addressed'. The Arusha Agreement thus stabilised 'power-sharing' as a key signifier in the Burundian field of intervention, thereby fixing a common horizon of change. Post-Arusha, the signification of power-sharing as the best solution was widely shared among the regional interveners. Among the South African facilitation, the power-sharing agreement in Burundi became a symbol for their policy of external democratisation. A member of the South African Parliament (2001a, p. 10) argued that the Arusha Agreement was an 'important step ... to expand the frontiers of liberty and peace'. For South African President Mbeki, the Arusha Agreement was

> a practical manifestation of our government's and country's commitment to three matters central to the objective of a better life for the peoples of our continent, including ourselves – peace, democracy and development.
> (Mbeki 2001)

By contrast, for a member of the Ugandan Parliament (2001, p. 29), power-sharing as institutionalised in the Arusha Agreement testified to the Regional Initiative's achievement in preventing another genocide. Thus, the signifier 'power-sharing' was able to accommodate very different significations. For South Africans, 'power-sharing' in Burundi mostly functioned as a symbol for the diffusion of democracy on the continent, whereas for the Ugandan member of parliament it was a means to prevent mass violence. In this sense, it was partially empty, allowing heterogeneous subjects to embrace it.

With the passage of time, the hegemony of power-sharing became dislocated by political practices within Burundi. The signifier 'power-sharing' had only partially emptied itself, heralding instead some sort of democratic change. Initially democracy became a mythical order projected into the future. In 2003, AU representative Mamadou Bah (2003) explained that the Arusha Agreement '*will* help to democratise Burundi' (emphasis mine). In 2004, South African Deputy President Zuma (2004) argued that the regional intervention had contributed 'to build, defend and consolidate the democracy that *will* emerge in Burundi after elections' (emphasis mine). In 2007, the late South African chief facilitator Charles Nqakula (2007a) stated that 'it is important for Burundi as a country, for the development of that country, for the people of Burundi, at least to begin to have a sense that their country is democratizing' (see also Zuma 2011). Thus, the regionally sponsored signifier 'power-sharing' lost its ability to accommodate certain fillings, among them the internationally hegemonic signifier 'liberal peace'. The regional intervention was no longer able to represent itself as a force that could bring democracy to Burundi. This breaking apart of a partially empty signifier coincided with a less homogeneous performance of the regional intervention, as will become more explicit in the next section.

In short, the signifier 'power-sharing' was able to temporarily function as the contingent foundation of the regional intervention, thereby pretending to suture the violent dislocations in Burundi that became manifest after the assassination of Ndadaye in 1993. The regional interveners constituted their authority in the field of intervention by arguing that only a regionally led negotiation process could facilitate 'democracy and security for all' (cf. Wodrig and Grauvogel 2016). The signifier 'power-sharing' emerged as a nodal point, to which heterogeneous forces were able to refer. Even after Nyerere's death and the appointment of Mandela as chief facilitator, the signifier continued to function as a shared horizon of change. Different forces could fill the signifier with different meaning, which indicates its partial emptiness. Those studying interventions are probably not really surprised that 'power-sharing' asserted itself as a (partially) empty signifier of the regional intervention. Elsewhere, power-sharing has been described as the current panacea for interveners (Binningsbø 2013, p. 89). In this sense, embracing power-sharing as a shared horizon of change reflected a hegemonic zeitgeist. This section thus confirms the diagnosis that regional interventions have not yet offered an alternative peace (Richmond and Tellidis 2014, p. 578). This reading will, however, be supplemented and, one could even say, dislocated in the remainder of this chapter.

'We are able to act': a new subjectivity for regional interveners

The surprising element of intervention politics in Burundi was not the facilitation of a power-sharing agreement, but the emergence and persistence of regional forces claiming authority in the field of intervention. It is worth quoting the then Tanzanian President on how he justified the regional intervention before the Organisation of African Unity (OAU):

> Today the level of violence, murder, and militarisation of all the groups and parties has reached very dangerous proportions, and the international community is justified to fear a replay of the 1994 Rwandan tragedy in Burundi. The question we have to ask ourselves is whether we can afford another tragedy like that in our region. Clearly we cannot, and *we must therefore act and act quickly.*
>
> (Mkapa 1996b, emphasis mine)

The statement constitutes the violence in Burundi as an urgent object of intervention that necessarily demands external agency. A similar argument was also made by an Ugandan participant at the peace negotiations:

> After the genocide in Rwanda and after other forces like the UN and OAU failed to intervene, it was felt that the potential for violence and genocide in Burundi was so high.... Therefore, *we felt that the region should make an effort to prevent this kind of situation ever occurring.*
>
> (Ugandan Parliament 2001, emphasis mine)

The surprising element of the regional intervention into Burundi was not its identification of an alternative peace, but their agency.

The reluctance of the usual suspects: the emergence of a new subjectivity

In this section I will address how the Regional Initiative, albeit being an ad hoc coalition of governments without any previous experience in intervening, became the nodal point of the intervention. I will reconstruct the discursive shifts that positioned the Regional Initiative with its changing memberships and with no secretariat as interveners. These discursive shifts took place pre-eminently at the United Nations and the Organisation of African Unity.

Shortly after the abortive *coup d'état* of October 1993 and the assassination of Burundian President Ndadaye, the UN appointed the Mauritanian diplomat Ould-Abdallah as their special representative (see Ould-Abdallah 2000, pp. 37–40). His mandate was to restore democratic institutions and to facilitate dialogue. His intervention culminated in the Convention of Government of September 1994 that tried to settle the crisis by distributing positions (see above). But the agreement reportedly produced 'only a lull in the crisis' (Khadiagala 2003, p. 220). In September 1995, Ould-Abdallah submitted his resignation. His departure left a void, which was subsequently filled by the regional intervention. Like the UN, the OAU had been engaged in the Burundian crisis from 1993 onwards. For the OAU, dispatching the small Mission for Protection and Restoration of Trust in Burundi was 'a litmus test to the just established mechanism for conflict prevention, management and resolution' (Maundi 2004, p. 307, see also Tieku 2013, p. 518), which is generally considered as the first of a number of signs signifying the transformation of the African peace and security architecture. A Tanzanian diplomat argued that a few month earlier 'the organization would not even have dared to deal with such a conflict due to lack of appropriate and effective instruments' (Maundi 2004, p. 307). Although the OAU intervention was limited (Khadiagala 2003, p. 222), the presence of the OAU in Burundi arguably altered how the field of intervention was imagined.

When, at the beginning of 1996, the UN Security Council asked the Secretary-General to plan for a 'rapid humanitarian response in the event of widespread violence or a serious deterioration in the humanitarian situation in Burundi' (UN 1996c, see also 1996a), and most of the usual suspects were rather reluctant to commit to contingency planning, it was already possible to think of the OAU as a potential partner in forging such contingency planning. The UN Secretary-General reported:

> Following the adoption of resolution 1040 (1996), I wrote to the Secretary-General of OAU, Mr. Salim Ahmed Salim, on 25 January, setting out the options that I had identified for major preventive action.... In an oral response to my letter, Mr. Salim recalled that the OAU Summit of June 1995 had seriously considered the option of military intervention if there should be a dramatic deterioration in the security situation in Burundi.
>
> (UN 1996b)

Salim Ahmed Salim, who acted as the OAU Secretary-General from 1989 to 2001, was an important figure, re-articulating the continental discourse on interventions. Salim was a Tanzanian politician and diplomat, and Nyerere's preferred presidential candidate for the first multiparty elections in 1995 (Nyang'oro 2011, p. 92). He was a committed Pan-Africanist and, as the then acting OAU Secretary-General, he had initiated the reforms that a decade later culminated in the creation of the African Union. In the Burundian field of intervention, he initially functioned as a nodal point linking various scales and discourses. The quote suggests that it was primarily he who identified contingency planning as a potential field of engagement for the OAU. Yet, the OAU was not able to further engage in the Burundian field of intervention, lacking capacity, intelligence, and resources (Muyangwa and Vogt 2000, p. 15, Tieku 2013, p. 521). At that time the continental organisation lacked the means to reinvent itself as the authority in a field of intervention like Burundi and to plan for a contingency, as the UN Security Council demanded. The signifier 'contingency planning' was thus not stabilised at the OAU but instead travelled further down the scale.

However, by 1995, the OAU could neither simply delegate intervention politics to a 'local' sub-regional organisation as the latter was still practically non-existent. By mid-1990, Burundi's neighbourhood, often referred to as the Great Lakes Region, eastern or central Africa, had not yet coalesced into a definite region with its territoriality stabilised by a regional organisation. Throughout the 1980s, the Zairean government under Mobutu Sese Seko tried to establish the Economic Community of the Great Lakes Region as *the* sub-regional organisation. Yet, by the mid-1990s, the Economic Community of the Great Lakes Region already lost its position of strength and was widely considered as dysfunctional. The East African Community, meanwhile, was only on its way to being revived by the founding states Kenya, Tanzania, and Uganda. The first East African Community of the three states was founded in 1967 but collapsed a decade later in 1977. Its decline is generally ascribed to irreconcilable, ideological antagonisms between the three governments (Nye 1965, Mair 2001, pp. 7–8, Mngomezulu 2006). At the beginning of the 1990s, the ideological antagonisms destabilised and a common approach to international relations became conceivable again. In 1993, a Permanent Tripartite Commission for East African Cooperation was created, coordinating the negotiations that in 1999 culminated in the signing of the founding treaty for the current EAC. The treaty entered into force in 2001. In 2007, Burundi and Rwanda joined the EAC. Some analysts argued that chief facilitator Nyerere and Ugandan President Museveni aimed at 'making Burundi a test of political co-operation for the East African Community' (ICG 2000a, p. 18, see also Wolpe 2011, pp. 22–23). However, by mid-1995, neither the EAC nor any other 'local' sub-regional organisation was institutionalised enough to be charged with an intervention (see Wodrig 2014, pp. 219–221).

These discursive shifts thus created a void that was filled by the Regional Initiative. It was the OAU Secretary-General who paved the way for the emergence of the Regional Initiative as the nodal point in the Burundian field of intervention. The professional lives of Salim and Nyerere were closely linked and, hence, Nyerere was the obvious chief facilitator from the point of view of Salim – and for the UN Secretary-General as well. The latter said in a report dated February 1996:

> It is unrealistic to expect a handful of small-scale measures to have any real impact on the fundamental problems of Burundi. That was why I continued to believe that the international community needed to launch a major initiative to prevent another humanitarian tragedy in the subregion, as well as to promote dialogue embracing all the elements of the Burundian political spectrum.
>
> (UN 1996b, p. 3)

The UN Secretary-General Boutros Boutros-Ghali thus demanded 'a major initiative' to fill the void and excluded 'a handful of small-scale measures'. In this statement the UN Secretary-General implicitly rejected the numerous mediators, envoys, and non-government organisations that had reportedly 'taken over the official mediation process in Burundi' after the UN special representative Ould-Abdullah had departed (Hara 1999, p. 146, see also Ould-Abdallah 2000, p. 97). The UN Secretary-General thus positioned himself within a hegemonic struggle among a heterogeneous crowd of interveners that were trying to occupy the void in the field of intervention. Boutros-Ghali put his weight behind 'a major initiative' that would both intervene militarily and promote dialogue – and the Regional Peace Initiative on Burundi including Nyerere began to perform this major initiative.

The Regional Initiative, and especially the Tanzanian authorities, were quick to begin contingency planning. In June 1996, Nyerere (1996b) argued that 'you'll not solve the problem by military intervention, but you must not rule out military intervention'. At the first regular summit, the Regional Initiative (1996a) authorised a regional security assistance force that, however, never materialised. The contingency planning was interrupted by a *coup d'état* which rendered these plans implausible.[9] Thus, whereas the UN and the OAU were reluctant to prepare for such an eventuality, the Regional Initiative did. It filled the void in the Burundian field of intervention and marginalised alternative forces (Tieku 2013, p. 522).

By accepting the policy proposed by the UN Secretary-General, the Regional Initiative under Nyerere emerged as the nodal point in the field of intervention. Initially the authority of the regional forces as interveners was defined by traditional agents in the politics of intervention. The OAU (1996b, 1996d), for example, frequently expressed its full support for the Regional Initiative. The Regional Initiative's enactment as regional interveners were thus the result of broader discursive shifts that created a void in the Burundian field of intervention. As I argued in Chapter 2, discourses position subjects, endowing them with a form of agency or with the lack of it (Laclau and Mouffe 2001 [1985], pp. 114–122). Interveners are widely considered as being almost omnipotent subjects, able to transform whole societies. However, the discourse fragments analysed here only envisioned the regional forces as realising policies constructed elsewhere. The Regional Initiative had to plan for an emergency in case of mass violence or even genocide. They had also to enable negotiations and perform a major initiative. Yet, the traditional agents in the politics of intervention did not authorise the regional forces to craft their own policies. Those delineating the subject position of the regional interveners were taken by surprise by the discursive shifts that were yet to come.

A united regional response: sanctions as a sign of counter-hegemony

To everybody's surprise the Regional Initiative declared sanctions against Burundi shortly after becoming positioned as interveners. In this section I will reconstruct how the regional imposition of sanctions became overdetermined, signalling the regional distancing from those forces that brought them into this position. Even though the policy seemed to reveal the agency of an otherwise marginalised place, other forces were first to entertain sanctions. The spectre of sanctions started to enter the discursive field in January 1996 when the UN Security Council considered an arms embargo and travel restrictions against those Burundians who encouraged violence (UN 1996a). Thereafter, however, the signifier 'sanctions' disappeared from the discursive surface, only to reappear shortly before the *coup d'état* of 25 July 1996 that rehabilitated Buyoya as president. The UN Special Rapporteur on Burundi reviewed the possibility to enact sanctions:

> Should the Burundi authorities refuse to respect the commitments undertaken at Arusha, the international community should consider applying sanctions against Burundi.
>
> (UN 1996d)

On the day of the coup, the OAU (1996d) also demanded the complete isolation of 'any such regime that could take over leadership in Burundi through the use of force or on any other pretext', requesting the imposition of sanctions. The more traditional interveners had thus already considered sanctions as a potential policy prior to the Regional Initiative embracing them. The regional interveners were still not re-articulating their subject position. The signifier 'sanctions' was not yet signifying regional agency.

Despite the consideration of sanctions at the UN and the OAU, the actual regional declaration of sanctions was met with surprise. On 31 July 1996, the Regional Initiative announced:

> The Regional Summit decided to exert maximum pressure on the regime in Bujumbura, including the imposition of economic sanctions in order to bring about conditions which are conductive to a return to normalcy in Burundi. In this regard, the Summit strongly appeals to the international community to support the efforts and measures taken by the countries of the region.
>
> (Regional Initiative 1996b)

68 *Regional forces in Burundi*

The declaration of sanctions was not previously coordinated with the international community (Hoskins and Nutt 1997, p. 8, Wohlgemuth 2005, p. 130). Subsequently neither the UN nor the OAU explicitly endorsed the regional imposition of comprehensive economic sanctions. The OAU (1996e) formally appealed to the international community 'to lend its strong support for the speedy implementation of those decisions'. Here, 'decisions' partially functions as a synonym for 'sanctions', leaving room, however, for interpretation. The avoidance of the signifier 'sanctions' suggests a compromise wording that was able to accommodate different, if not incommensurable, views. The UN Security Council likewise rather vaguely stated its support for the Regional Initiative, but without mentioning, endorsing, or rejecting the regional imposition of comprehensive economic sanctions (UN 1996f). At that time the UN had already problematised comprehensive economic sanctions as their imposition against Iraq had increased the population's hardship instead of effectively changing politics for the better. The UN's ambivalence on the regional declaration of sanctions 'reflected to some extent its nervousness regarding their potentially negative impacts on Burundi's civilian population', as was argued in a study on the humanitarian impact of the regional sanctions (Hoskins and Nutt 1997, p. 8). Some traditional interveners even begun to explicitly dispute them. Belgium called the sanctions 'premature'. The US Secretary of State for Foreign Affairs Warren Christopher urged the regional forces to relax sanctions (Wohlgemuth 2005, p. 130). These articulations indicate that the international community was unwilling to rally behind the signifier and to follow the politics of intervention crafted by the Regional Initiative. International hesitance to endorse economic sanctions can be comprehended as a first sign that the regional forces were not able to hegemonise the field of the interveners. They rather articulated a counter-hegemonic position.

The Regional Initiative's decision to impose sanctions and their subsequent implementation were often interpreted as signifying that the region was able to act in unison. In this sequence, Tanzania, Kenya, Ethiopia, Uganda, Rwanda, Zaire, and Zambia issued national declarations on sanctions in the immediate aftermath of the summit. As all adjacent states joined the sanction regime, the major trading routes to Burundi were blocked (Wohlgemuth 2005, p. 130). One scholar described sanctions as 'perhaps one of the first major efforts to genuinely introduce an "African solution to an African problem"' (Wohlgemuth 2005, p. 126). This signification of the sanctions can also be reconstructed in an interview given by Nyerere:

> INTERVIEWER: The African governments in the region, you've been working with the leaders there, and they have imposed sanctions on Burundi. Has this had any effect?
> NYERERE: Leaders of the region are absolutely united on this one, and the significance of this is sometimes lost in the outside world. The outside world regards Africa as military rule and – and dictatorships by single-party system.... But they don't realize the significance of what has

taken place in East Africa. These leaders who met in Arusha were really saying to the military regime in Burundi we can no longer accept military rule on our borders.
INTERVIEWER: And this is a major change.
NYERERE: This is a major change on the continent, and I really hope that the significance will be [noticed by] the allies outside Africa.

(Nyerere 1996a)

In this interview, the chief facilitator underlined unity of action. The US special envoy reported that the Kenyan government likewise understood sanctions as a welcome opportunity to prove the region's capacity to act in unison, especially in light of the revival of the EAC (Wolpe 2011, p. 23). The signifier 'sanctions' thus became overdetermined. It did not only signify the blocking of trading routes to Burundi, but regional unity and ultimately region-wide, progressive change. Sanctions came to represent a collective regional subjectivity that began to actively shape regional politics.

Yet, this signification did not become stabilised, but was challenged. 'Sanction' became a floating signifier, that is, it was claimed by different discourses. It is worthy repeating Laclau and Mouffe here:

Only the presence of a vast area of floating elements and the possibility of their articulation to opposite camps – which implies a constant redefinition of the latter – is what constitutes the field permitting us to define a practice as hegemonic.

(Laclau and Mouffe 2001 [1985], p. 136)

The struggle over the meaning of 'sanctions' can be interpreted as one element in the emergence of a regional counter-hegemony, as I will reconstruct in the following section. Initially the overdetermination of sanctions as regional unity and progressive change was primarily disputed from within Burundi. The Buyoya government, in an anti-sanctions campaign, most explicitly questioned the plausibility of the argument that regional sanctions enabled real change in Burundi (for details, see Grauvogel 2015). By September, the Buyoya government complied with two of the three demands attached to the sanctions – namely the restoration of parliament and unbanning of political parties. But the Burundian government continued to reject the regionally sponsored negotiations, which the Regional Initiative (1996c) considered as the most important condition for lifting the sanctions (see also Regional Sanctions Coordinating Committee 1996). Instead, the Buyoya government participated in an alternative negotiation process, sponsored by the Community of Sant'Egidio in Rome, thereby undermining the regional argument that only regional intervention was able to enact real, progressive change. Thereafter, the Regional Initiative (1997a) had to readjust the conditions attached to the lifting of sanctions. Sanctions would be suspended 'once there is movement in the negotiations'. Doubts about the equation of sanctions with change thus entered the statements and communiqués of the Regional Initiative. Against this questioning of the regional signification of sanctions, the Regional Initiative (1996c, 1997a) began to emphasise the 'cohesion' of the regional intervention.

From April 1997 onwards, other interveners more openly questioned the regional signification of sanctions. The OAU Secretary-General Salim, who had enacted the Regional Initiative into the position of an intervener, publicly disclosed:

> I am going to try to influence [the Regional Initiative] to look into ways of removing some of these sanctions which in actual fact are affecting more on common men and women than the government of Major Pierre Buyoya.
> (Salim 1997)

Although the OAU Secretary-General did not demand their complete removal but more exemptions (like medical goods and food supplies), this official statement spoke of the dwindling OAU support for the regional position. In May 1997, the OAU (1997) welcomed the Regional Initiative's easing of sanctions 'as well as the declared readiness of the leaders of the region to suspend all sanctions ... once the negotiations have been initiated'. Considering the then ongoing negotiations in Rome, the OAU statement rather reads like a diplomatic demand to suspend sanctions immediately. In November 1997, the Common Market for Eastern and Southern Africa (COMESA) explicitly demanded the lifting of sanctions. This was a severe affront to the regional overdetermination of sanctions with regional unity: five out of the twenty members of COMESA had previously joined the Regional Initiative in declaring sanctions on Burundi (Wohlgemuth 2005, p. 134). By distancing themselves from their previous support for sanctions, the COMESA decision thus dislocated the claim of regional unity and substantiated the counter-claim that the sanctions were a product of the hard-liners in Tanzania and Uganda (ICG 1998a, p. 6), not of a mythical regional unity. This counter-claim was further substantiated by developments at the Regional Initiative's summit in February 1998. In the official communiqué, the Regional Initiative (1998) once more endorsed sanctions against Burundi. Shortly thereafter, however, it was reported that the communiqué was not agreed with the Regional Initiative's council of ministers, who – on the contrary – had recommended the lifting of the sanctions (ICG 1998a, p. 7). The overdetermination of sanctions as an expression of regional unity was almost fully undermined when the Burundian government negotiated an agreement with Frodebu, the main political opposition party. The negotiations sponsored by the Community of Sant'Egidio had failed and instead the government initiated a national dialogue from April to June 1998, which culminated in a Partenariat (a partnership agreement), that created a coalition government between Uprona and Frodebu. Most African and Western governments recognised the Patenariat as genuine. Not so the Tanzanian authorities who maintained that the agreement was a sham – 'a partnership between jailer and prisoner' (cited by Mthembu-Salter 1999, p. 9). In the light of these divergent assessments, 'sanction' as a metaphor for regional unity fully disintegrated. The signifier could no longer suggest a mythical unity.

The OAU openly disputed the regional policy when the Burundian government finally committed to regional peace negotiations. From 15 to 21 June 1998, the Burundian parties met in Arusha. In the opening address, Tanzanian President Mkapa rearticulated the last condition attached to the lifting of sanctions: 'When all the parties to the conflict have demonstrated a real willingness to engage in negotiations in good faith and when there is an irreversible progress in discussions', sanctions would be lifted (cited by ICG 1998b, p. 3). It took the OAU half a year to respond to this re-articulation. However, this time, it was unambiguous:

> Noting that the inter-Burundi talks did commence on 15 June 1998 in the presence of the heads of State of the region and under the mediation of Mwalimu Julius Nyerere,
> Also noting that the Government of Burundi has implemented all the conditionalities demanded by the heads of State of the subregion,
> Considering that the parties to the Burundi conflict have already held three sessions of negotiation in Arusha in a serene atmosphere underpinned by the irreversible political will of the protagonists to resolve the crisis through political dialogue,
> Taking into account the fact that the said sanctions mostly affect the most vulnerable categories of the population and undermine development achievements, as well as impede the peace process,
> Makes an urgent and brotherly appeal to the heads of State of the sub-region to lift the sanctions immediately.
> (OAU 1998)

With this statement, the OAU openly disputed the regional intervention policy – as did the donor governments. The donors conditioned the further funding of the regional facilitation on the lifting of sanctions (Wohlgemuth 2005, p. 138). The Regional Initiative was no longer able to sustain the position that sanctions were necessary to enact real change. On 23 January 1999, the Regional Initiative officially suspended the sanctions.

In sum, the claims and counter-claims around the signifier 'sanctions' disclosed a gap among the interveners. Prior to the sanctions, the regional intervention was a subject position delineated elsewhere. By declaring sanctions without consulting the UN or the OAU, the Regional Initiative trespassed outside its position. 'Sanctions' began to testify regional unity and change – an overdetermination that was however soon disputed and undermined. 'Sanctions' was a floating signifier that was subject to incompatible significations. By resisting to deviate from this signification of sanctions as regional unity and change for two and a half years, the Regional Initiative performed a counter-hegemonic potential. Their insistence on this signification lay bare a gap between them and other intervention forces. In the following, it will become obvious that these regional statements on sanctions can be comprehended as a larger counter-hegemonic moment against intervention routines.

The region: from passive entity to agent of change

No other signifier was as omnipresent as 'region' or 'regional' in the text corpus. In this section I will reconstruct how this signifier was filled and how it functioned within the regional discourse on Burundi, arguing that the filling of the signifier 'region' manifested another counter-hegemonic moment in the regional politics of intervention.

When the Regional Initiative (1995) convened for the first time in Cairo, they published a declaration 'on the Great Lakes region'. At least initially, the Great Lakes Region was comprehended as a space with 'persistent tensions, hostilities, insecurities and recent genocide' (Regional Initiative 1995, see also Mkapa 1996d, 1998a, Nyerere 1996c). The signification was in accordance with the hegemonic representation of the African continent and especially of the Great Lakes as being plagued by violence and conflict. Consequently, the regional governments, being themselves part of this problem, considered themselves as *passive*. The problems were to be solved by the international community, whose responsibility it was to mobilise financial resources 'so as to bring economic and social development in the region' (Regional Initiative 1995). In November 1995, those governments that were involved in the Regional Initiative thus saw themselves as recipients of interventions rather than interveners.

It has to be remembered that the figure of the intervener is commonly understood as the embodiment of agency. Mitchell (2014, p. 3), for instance, wrote that 'intervention is a way of imagining action, predicated on a simple belief: that humans can change the course of events by interposing themselves in it'. In November 1995, the Regional Initiative did not comprehend itself as an intervener. The emergence of the Regional Initiative was a result of broader discursive shifts being articulated by others. Their becoming a regional intervention resembled what Chandler (2009, p. 22) called a 'desire to divest policy responsibility', that is, a subordination under a hegemonic discourse articulated elsewhere. At this point, it is helpful to quote Butler on the relation of the power of subjection and the power of agency.

> Power not only *acts on* a subject but, in a transitive sense, *enacts* the subject into being. As a condition, power precedes the subject. Power loses its appearance of priority, however, when it is wielded by the subject, a situation that gives rise to the reverse perspective that power is the effect of the subject.
>
> (Butler 1997, p. 13, emphasis in original)

In other words, as soon as the subject of the Regional Initiative was enacted by a powerful discourse that preceded its existence, the Regional Initiative found itself in a subject position that is commonly associated with agency. After becoming a subject, the Regional Initiative itself had the agency to re-articulate the discourse, as the discourse no longer constituted it as a mere recipient of politics crafted elsewhere.

After being enacted as an intervener, the Regional Initiative identified with new attributes. In July 1996, Tanzanian President Mkapa (1996b) argued that the region had entered the 'dawn of a new era of peace, stability and cooperation'. He lauded the Regional Initiative for helping the Burundian people and for being very persistent in pursuing 'the path of peace' (Mkapa 1996c, 1996d). In retrospect, a member of the facilitation team explained that 'never before in the short history of the countries in the Great Lakes Region had [they] taken such a proactive action' (Butiku 2004, p. 65). Hence, with enacting the Regional Initiative into being, the respective governments became able to (partially and temporarily) emancipate themselves from the oppressive representation of passivity.

This transformation of subjectivity involved a re-identification and a new name for the territory in which the regional interveners were located: East Africa. In order to reconstruct this transformation, it is worthwhile repeating a paragraph, which I have already quoted.

> Leaders of the region are absolutely united on this one, and the significance of this is sometimes lost in the outside world. The outside world regards Africa as military rule and – and dictatorships by single-party system.... *But they don't realize the significance of what has taken place in East Africa.* These leaders who met in Arusha were really saying to the military regime in Burundi we can no longer accept military rule on our borders.
>
> (Nyerere 1996a, emphasis mine)

Chief facilitator Nyerere depicted East Africa as a place of avant-garde politics. The regional interveners became the pioneers of progressive change who finally could dislocate the negative representation of African politics held by the outside world. In this quote, *the regional intervention on Burundi shapes the subjectivity of the regional interveners.* By condemning the Burundian *coup d'état* of 1996, the subjectivity of the regional interveners transformed itself; they were finally able to distance themselves from their own past.

Nyerere made this statement at a time when the Kenyan, Tanzanian, and Ugandan Government were working on the revival of the East African Community. This re-ordering of the regional space also shone through when Ugandan President Museveni (1998a) complained that the Regional Initiative 'cannot assist directly the people of Burundi because of these "sovereign ropes"'. He concluded: 'The problem takes much longer than the case would be if East Africa would be one political unit.' Once being enacted as an intervener, the Ugandan President began to question the limits of this subject position. Cynthia Weber (1992, p. 215) argued that 'for intervention to be a meaningful concept, sovereignty must exist because intervention implies a violation of sovereignty'. In his statement, the Ugandan President stretched his subject position by scrutinising the binary sovereignty–intervention. The statement indicates an alternative signification of interveners that, in the hegemonic representation, are considered as forces temporarily interposing themselves into a foreign body politic. It can be argued that the statement added a floating dimension to the subject position. Museveni's articulation spoke to the broader discourse on Pan-Africanism and East African integration that likewise aimed at transcending the 'sovereign ropes' associated with colonialism. Therefore, the treaty of the East African Community signed in 2000, speaks of the establishment of a political federation.[10] Yet, this alternative filling of the subject position of the regional intervener did not gain momentum among fellow regional interveners. In the treaty of the East African Community, peace and security integration was marginalised.[11] While intervening in Burundi, the Tanzanian and Kenyan government reportedly blocked any substantive security cooperation within the East African Community as they disapproved of Uganda's military intervention into the Democratic Republic of Congo (1996–1997, 1998–2003) (Mair 2001, p. 14). Thus, the binary intervention–sovereignty continued to separate the regional interveners from the Burundians.

Being an intervener also involved the claim to be the best match for this position. Tanzanian President Mkapa (1998b) explained that 'at the regional level we understand each other better – sharing, as we do, history, cultural values and temperaments'. In contrast to 'other countries [who] can afford to shut their eyes to this problem … as neighbours we cannot have that detachment' (Mkapa 1996a, see also 1998a, 1999b, Regional Initiative 1996a). 'As their neighbours we wish them well' (Mkapa 1996b). These statements clearly contribute to establish the regional intervention as the best alternative, a necessary strategy for becoming the hegemonic agent of change.

The hegemonisation of the regional forces in the field of intervention can also be reconstructed in their relation to the OAU. The Regional Initiative (e.g. 1996b) often referred to itself as a 'sub-region', thereby suggesting a certain hierarchical structuring on the African continent and beyond. This representation was, however, also explicitly countered by regional forces. The Tanzanian President argued that 'it is easier for few regional leaders to sit down together and hammer out solutions anchored in the region and supported by our continental body and the international community at large' (Mkapa 1998b). Here, the Regional Initiative becomes the hegemonic force that shapes the intervention. However, at the first summit of the Regional Initiative (1995) in Cairo, the participants declared the intervention to be 'an African initiative', thereby creating a sense of inclusiveness towards the continent. Intervention politics on Burundi also became a 'practical expression to the OAU desire that we, ourselves, should take a leading role to prevent, manage, resolve conflicts in our beloved continent' (Mkapa 1996a). The search for a new significance of the continent replaced the representation of a neglected location where conflict, strife, and refugees prevailed. 'African solutions to African problems' became a shared nodal point for both the OAU and the Regional Initiative (Mkapa 1996a, 1996b, Mandela 2000b). The regional intervention into Burundi thus filled 'African solutions to African problems' with meaning. In 2000, this signifier chain became the leitmotiv of the African Union.

Instead of comprehending the Regional Initiative as one intervention force among many, the last section revealed some regional differences to the hegemonic subject position. Once the regional forces became interveners, they made use of their new agency by trying to transform themselves, that is, their 'region'. In the statements of the regional interveners, the 'region' became a space for progressive politics. The differences to the hegemonic subject position were thus constituted primarily by re-articulation of their regional subjectivity, not the subject position of the interveners as such. However, through trying (but ultimately failing) to reorganise the region as a territory without 'sovereign ropes', the regional interveners touched the limits of the subject position of the intervener. The subject position relies on a frontier between an internal and external that renders certain articulations an intervention rather than normal politics. In this sense, the Regional Initiative also performed a potential difference that was not actualised.

Searching for lessons learnt: the anti-apartheid struggle

The difference from other interventions was also constituted through frequent references to the anti-apartheid struggle. The anti-apartheid struggle functioned as a historical template for how to intervene against an oppressive regime. It has to be recalled that the Regional Initiative, including the facilitation, had been enacted as interveners for the first time, lacking any sedimented knowledge of that position. They could not draw on a past in order to define the politics of the present. For instance, nowadays the AU is able to craft their intervention on the basis of lessons learnt, the latter being stabilised and authorised interpretations of the past. The Regional Initiative could not draw on such lessons learnt. But they could draw on the anti-apartheid struggle. The life of the chief facilitator on Burundi was deeply entangled with the anti-apartheid struggle. As early as 1959, Nyerere – then prime minister of British-administered Tanganyika – acted as a principle speaker at the launch of the boycott movement, later re-named the anti-apartheid movement (see Nyerere 1959). In 1961, the British Commonwealth discussed the request of the South African Government to be recognised as a republic rather than a dominion that would have given the latter full membership in the Commonwealth. Nyerere however successfully opposed this request stating that independent Tanganyika would not join an organisation which showed no respect for racial equality. A Commonwealth diplomat recalled that 'this has seriously rattled the British establishment ... and above all, shook the South African Government' (Anyaoku and Cassam 2010, p. 66). In the years that followed, the Tanzanian Government hosted the OAU Liberation Committee and co-founded the South African Development Coordination Committee that aimed at reducing the neighbourhood's economic dependence on apartheid South Africa. He also lobbied international organisations to mobilise support for armed resistance against the apartheid regime. Nyerere's political and personal past was thus deeply interwoven with organising the anti-apartheid struggle. In this sense, it was not surprising that the anti-apartheid struggle functioned as a template for signifying the regional intervention politics towards Burundi.

From 1995 to 1998, it was Nyerere especially who evoked this past in order to make sense of the Burundian present. In 1996, he built an analogy between 'the Tutsis' in Burundi and 'the whites' in South Africa, as both 'minorities' seemed to dominate a 'majority', fearing the day they had to relinquish their grip on the state institutions (Nyerere 1996b). In 1985, he argued regarding the whites of South Africa:

> There are a lots of whites in South Africa – most of them English-speaking – who have accepted the system because ... it was protecting their wealth, their standard of living.... That's why they supported it, not because they believed in it as a philosophy.
>
> (Nyerere 1985, p. 7)

By articulating an analogy with the whites of apartheid South Africa, Nyerere comprehended the signifier 'Tutsi' as marking a structural position in the Burundian social and political terrain. Tutsis, so the reasoning went, had not many reasons to resist the regime. Reading Burundi with the South African past encouraged a particular knowledge about the violent crisis, namely that the Tutsi oppression, rather than dysfunctional state institutions (Ndikumana 1998) or structural poverty (Oketch and Polzer 2002, p. 86), was the major obstacle to peace. Under this analogy, both whites and Tutsis were plagued by similar fears. Afrikaner nationalists in apartheid South Africa had reportedly feared that, with apartheid ending, their physical survival was no longer guaranteed (Giliomee 1997, p. 119). Their survival depended, so the reasoning went, on the perpetuation of apartheid. Similarly, the Tutsi in Burundi are said to have feared an event like the Rwandan revolution of 1959, during which the Tutsi government was overthrown, thousands massacred, and around 100,000 people forced into exile (Ndikumana 1998, p. 34). In a similar manner to Afrikaner nationalists, the Tutsi elite in Bujumbura are said to have cultivated the understanding that democratic majority rule would threaten their own physical survival.

This analogy renders two complex and historically different constellations similar. In 1996 (the year when Nyerere articulated the analogy), apartheid South Africa was already history. The meaning of apartheid was on its way to being stabilised and its demise began to function as a *lesson learnt* – 'a key model for resolving intractable conflicts', as scholars later argued (Bentley and Southall 2005, p. 163, see also Curtis 2007). By contrast, the Burundian present was in flux. By chaining the South African past to the Burundian present, a certain field of intervention became visible: the analogy uncovered a path for the regional intervention that otherwise might have remained in the dark. For chief facilitator Nyerere, change in South Africa was enacted through sanctions:

> [I] want simply recall that the imposition of sanctions was successful in the case of South Africa, a country much more robust than Burundi.... Leaders like Frederik De Klerk ... had no choice but to realise that there was no other alternative than to negotiate with their adversaries.
>
> (Nyerere 1996c, translation mine)

The demise of apartheid is attributed to many factors (for an overview, see Lipton 2007), but economic sanctions are generally considered one of them. For a long time, Nyerere had campaigned for sanctions against apartheid South Africa. When economic sanctions against South Africa became widely accepted in Western capitals by the mid-1980s, it was clear that sanctions would not only affect the economy of South Africa but also its neighbourhood, including Tanzania. It is worthy quoting an interview with Nyerere from 1985:

> A few days ago ... we had another meeting of the frontline states and we discussed sanctions and there was again unanimous agreement of all of us that sanctions will hurt, but sanctions must be applied because sanctions will end apartheid much quicker.
>
> (Nyerere 1985)

Throughout his political career, the Burundian chief facilitator was personally committed to enabling the imposition of sanctions against apartheid South Africa. He even accepted that economic sanctions against South Africa would harm the well-being of those people living close to the apartheid state. It is very plausible to assume that Nyerere really comprehended sanctions as having activated positive change in South Africa. Thus, by articulating a chain of equivalence between South Africa and Burundi, the imposition of sanctions against the Burundian regime became almost a necessity.

The detailed logic was articulated as following: sanctions had enabled South African President De Klerk 'to oppose the extremists of his camp with the following argument: "What can we do but to accept the dialogue demanded by the international community?"' (Nyerere 1996b). The sanctions helped to convince the core Afrikaner constituency to accept that they could no longer oppose change and that the best way forward was to negotiate an agreement with the ANC (Wolpe 2011, p. 15). With the help of this analogy, Burundian President Buyoya was able to approach the Tutsi extremists with the same arguments, convincing them that a negotiated agreement was the only and best solution. In short, the stabilised signification of the demise of apartheid became a template for structuring the Burundian field of intervention. 'Much of [Nyerere's] approach towards Burundi has been based on the lessons he learned in militant opposition to the apartheid regime in South Africa' (ICG 1998a, p. 9). Indeed, at least for him and his facilitation team, apartheid South Africa functioned as a stabilised nodal point that structured the field of intervention.

Unlike Nyerere, none of the high-profile South Africans in the Burundian field of intervention articulated similar analogies. During the peace negotiations, as one facilitator reported, 'there was caution against the blind adoption of foreign models by applying them wholesale to Burundi' (Mwansasu 2004, p. 163). Having said this, Mandela's former legal advisor chaired the committee on democracy and good governance and was responsible for drafting the power-sharing agreement at Arusha. The legal advisor argued that the Burundian peace process was 'an opportunity to look at the latest institutional technologies'

(Haysom 2007). He was personally involved in the negotiations of the post-apartheid constitution in South Africa. It is plausible that he considered the latter as the 'latest institutional technology'. Yet, publicly he distanced himself from the chain of equivalence arguing that

> the remedies, which have been so easy for us in South Africa simply would not work in Burundi.... People would say, 'well, we are not going to be protected against a genocide by a supreme court.' In South Africa, there was a real belief that you could guarantee non-discrimination, cultural and linguistic rights through robust courts.
>
> (Haysom 2007)

Despite his personal entanglements in the South African constitution-making process, he was thus careful not to openly articulate the latter as the lesson learnt. Yet, does this mean that the South African understanding of the Burundian field of intervention was not structured by its own past? At the beginning of the peace negotiations, the committee on democracy and good governance referred to the Burundian 1992 constitution for inspiration (see above). However, after the final deadline set by the new chief facilitator Mandela, 10 per cent of the final text was still contested. It was the facilitation under Mandela who proposed a draft for the remaining 10 per cent. Thus, at the end, the facilitation had quite some space to draft the power-sharing formula. It is plausible that they saw the power-sharing formula in South Africa as a historical template for the draft (cf. Bentley and Southall 2005, Curtis 2007).[12]

The regional interveners thus contextualised their subject position. Rather than radically re-articulating the subject position of the intervener (as Museveni tried to), the regional intervention filled this position with new elements that previously had not been attached to this position. The subject position thus became re-constituted as a position of African agency. The anti-apartheid struggle functioned as a coordinate system, pointing the new interveners to what to do. Under these analogies, the Burundian complexity is rendered similar. Instead of lessons learnt nowadays fixed in countless reports, the anti-apartheid struggle was a lived lesson that some of the African/regional/South African interveners seemed to have 'owned'. Yet, this moment of a reinvented subjectivity soon faded, as I argue in more detail in the following.

Signifying the African/regional/South African intervention: who are we?

'The region' functioned as a marker of this reinvented subjectivity. In the statements of the regional interveners, 'regional' or 'the region' became synonymous with a progressive agent of change. The regional entanglements in the Second Congo War however seriously dislocated this representation. In the First Congo War in 1996, the Rwandan and Ugandan Governments had helped an armed movement under the leadership of Laurent-Désiré Kabila to overthrow the long-time authoritarian regime under Mobutu Sese Seko. Yet, soon after Kabila becoming president, the alliance broke and a new war commenced, lasting from 1998 to 2003. In his first speech as chief facilitator, Nelson Mandela pointed to the Second Congo War:

> It is not possible to establish regional peace unless component parts of a region establish domestic foundations for a stable democratic order. Peace in Burundi will give hope for the Democratic Republic of Congo and other countries in the region.
>
> (Mandela 2000a)

In this statement, the signifier 'region' no longer signified peace, progress, and agency. Instead, the previous constitution of the regional space returned to the discursive surface: the region was understood as a place full of violence and conflict. The Ugandan and Rwandan entanglement in the Second Congo War rendered the representation of the region as a place of peace and progress implausible. Instead, Burundi again became a small glimmer of hope for a region plagued by instabilities (see also Mamabolo 2008a). It seemed as if history had repeated itself. At the outset of the regional intervention, Burundian politics functioned as a model for the rest of Africa, particularly for its immediate neighbourhood. The latter, by contrast, was trapped in a representation of passivity. Yet, the *old* representatives of the Regional Initiative opposed this bleak subjectivation. In reflecting about the regional entanglements in the Second Congo War, the chair of the Regional Initiative replied that 'the region is not [only] Rwanda and Uganda. There is [also] Tanzania' (Museveni 2000). This relatively self-critical statement was not shared by all Ugandans. According to Uganda's special envoy for the Great Lakes Region, 'the role Uganda has played through our president has been tremendous' (Ugandan Parliament 2001). Instead of understanding Burundi as a glimmer of hope for a region in despair, the special envoy argued: 'Some of us talk about our problems and we think we really have problems, but the problems in Burundi certainly go beyond [ours]' (Ugandan Parliament 2001). Hence, 'the region' became a floating signifier that was subjected to incommensurate fillings. Becoming floating testifies to the struggles over the transforming subjectivities on the African continent. The transformation of subjectivity towards more agency not only broke open gaps of signification between reactionaries and reformers but also between those willing to make Africa a better place.

'The region' became a floating signifier at a moment when the South Africans entered the Burundian intervention scene. Therewith, the subjectivity of the intervention could no longer be reduced to the signifiers 'Great Lakes' or 'East Africa'. By being appointed as chief facilitator, Mandela, and other South African Government staff, had the ability to re-articulate the subject position. Once enacted by discursive shifts as a subject, the subject becomes able to transform this discourse. The signifier 'regional', which had previously functioned as a marker of difference from other interventions, was no longer fitting. Instead, the intervention politics became an expression of the new agency of the continent as a whole (Zuma 2002a, 2002b). Between May 2001 and July 2002, the continental organisation rapidly transformed into the AU. Some South African officials regarded the AU as a core mechanism for changing the negative representations of Africa in international relations. A better image seemed to be the precondition for attracting more foreign investment and position South Africa as a global trading nation (Tieku 2004, p. 253). South African President Mbeki introduced the policy of African Renaissance – basically a metaphor that imagined a continent proactively addressing its crises and walking into a prosperous future.[13] The intervention politics towards Burundi became one expression of this African Renaissance (Mbeki 2001, South African Parliament 2001a), a reading that was also widely shared within South Africa. South African parliamentarians argued that Burundi was 'a positive sign that Africa is tired of wars and is ready to work and compete with other continents on an economic level' (South African Parliament 2001a, p. 119). The South African facilitator Nqakula likewise argued that it is 'the responsibility of the leaders on the African continent to ensure that the Burundi peace process received the full attention of the African leaders so that in the end the solution for Burundi is an *African solution*' (Nqakula 2006, emphasis mine, see also 2007b, Mamabolo 2008a). Thus, during the South African engagement in Burundi, 'Africa' replaced 'the region' as a marker of collective subjectivity.

Within South Africa, the intervention was not predominantly ascribed to a collective 'African' subjectivity but to its national self. The then South African President understood Burundi as 'a practical manifestation of *our government's and country's* commitment to three matters central to the objective of a better life for the peoples of our continent, including ourselves – peace, democracy and development' (Mbeki 2001, emphasis mine, see also South African Parliament 2001a, pp. 189–190). He thus reduced the intervention to a South African performance. The exceptionalism of South Africa was also echoed by others: 'South Africa has a historical role to play in the region and therefore it needed to intervene to ensure the maintenance of peace in the country of Burundi' (South African Parliament 2001b). The intervention politics thus again began to shape the subjectivity of the intervener: this time the intervention confirmed the South African exceptionality. The South African Foreign Minister argued that 'the Burundi Mission is a wonderful example of the New South Africa and what we stand for, nationally, continentally, and globally' (Dlamini-Zuma 2004, see also Dlamini-Zuma and Salomão 2008). Intervening in Burundi thus became a performance of the New South Africa. Like the Regional Initiative, the South African Foreign Minister associated the intervention with a progressive agency.

The discursive replacement of 'regional' with 'African' or 'South African' solutions went hand in hand with the weakening of the Regional Initiative in the field of intervention. In contrast to Nyerere, who had relied on the Regional Initiative to apply direct pressure, Mandela distrusted the heads of state in the Regional Initiative and thus sought to reduce their hold on the peace process by including people from outside the immediate neighbourhood: for example, the

Gabonian President, who temporarily joined the South African facilitation team (Bentley and Southall 2005, p. 74). At the UN, chief facilitator Mandela (2000b) praised the 'support of so many leaders from the African continent'. He however forgot to explicitly mention all those 'East African' heads of state, who had previously dominated the discourse. The chief facilitator reportedly aimed to build a broader coalition between forces from different scales, arguing that this would enhance the legitimacy of the peace process and, ultimately, put more pressure on Burundian parties (Bentley and Southall 2005, pp. 174–175, Khadiagala 2007, p. 169). He thereby implied that a solely regional intervention could not generate the same legitimacy internationally.

While South African authorities seriously questioned the grip of the neighbourhood on the intervention politics, the then still operative OAU (2000b, 2001a, 2001b) encouraged the regional (East African) forces to continue facilitating the implementation of the Arusha Agreement. The regional forces began to fight for their subjectivation as interveners: 'The regional leaders will continue to provide their support for the peace process in Burundi' (Regional Initiative 2001). In another instance, Museveni warned the still active armed movements that they had not met 'the expectations of the region', nor did he mention the AU, South Africa, or the international community at large (Museveni 2002a). He therewith underpinned the notion that the 'region' was still the hegemonic agent of change in the Burundian field of intervention. The Tanzanian President argued that the implementation of the Arusha Agreement would fail 'unless a new "catalyst" was found to push the process in a positive direction'. He continued: 'Examples of such a potential new catalyst could include increasing the involvement of the region' (UN 2001, p. 11). Hence, the regional forces tried to reclaim their former function as the nodal point in the field of intervention, a path that finally opened up when chief facilitator Zuma was urged to resume work within the existing framework provided by the Regional Initiative. In Zuma's first speech before the UN Security Council, he pointed to decisions taken by the Regional Initiative and explicitly lauded its chair (Zuma 2002b, see also Khadiagala 2013).

In the last years of the intervention, the Regional Initiative re-stabilised as a nodal point. According to chief facilitator Nqakula, his facilitation 'relied on [their] leadership and guidance' (Nqakula 2006, see also 2007a, 2007b, 2008, Mamabolo 2008b). The South African special envoy argued that 'the region is responsible for bringing peace to Burundi and it has appointed a number of facilitators/mediators ... on behalf of the region' (Mamabolo 2008a).

Thus, with the dislocation of the region as a place of progressive politics as well as with the increasing centrality of the African scale, the Regional Initiative temporarily lost its function as a nodal point in the field of intervention. After Nyerere's death, the interveners seemed to be more fragmented, identifiable as either 'African', 'regional', or 'South African'. The Regional Initiative was not able to continue the reinvention of themselves as progressive agents of change. That said, the representatives of the Regional Initiative tried to counter the subjectivation of the region as the bigger problem. Against this backdrop, the African/regional/South African intervention could no longer perform the agency normally associated with interveners. This fading of agency became clear after the Arusha Agreement when the interveners occasionally threatened to sanction the remaining armed movements.

Threatening with sanctions: the fading of agency

After the lifting of sanctions in January 1999, the signifier 'sanction' soon reappeared in the discourse of the African/regional/South African intervention. As I reconstructed it further above, between 1996 to 1999 the signifier was overdetermined, testifying to a united regional response vis-à-vis a violent crisis. However, this overdetermination of the signifier was lost in the period after the Arusha Agreement: 'sanctions' no longer functioned as a metaphor for the regional emancipation from the subject position delineated for them by others. By threatening sanctions, the regional interveners tried to draw on past agency, yet thereby only performing a caricature of their former selves – as I will reconstruct in the following paragraphs.

Referring to the reluctance of some armed movements to accept the Arusha Agreement, the chief facilitator rejected the continuation of violence as no longer justified. Prior to the Arusha Agreement, the armed movement fought a deaf system of domination, that would not listen to popular demands. Yet after the Arusha Agreement, so the argument went, legitimate demands could only be raised within the framework of the Arusha Agreement (Mandela 2000b). After Arusha the object of intervention was thus re-shifted towards those continuing the violence.[14] The OAU likewise no longer sympathised with the demands of the armed movements and urged them to sign the agreement, to stop the violence and to 'enter into substantive negotiations with a view of concluding a ceasefire agreement' (OAU 2000b, see also 2001a, 2001b). Many interveners thus constituted the remaining armed movements as an obstacle to peace in Burundi.

However, the Regional Initiative was not able to articulate a 'united' position on the armed movements – analogous to the united position against the *coup d'état* of 1996. A report of the Security Council mission to the Great Lakes revealed the regional disagreements on the armed movements.[15] Ugandan President Museveni told the UN Security Council mission that the

> sanctions had forced President Buyoya to join the peace process, and ... that, in the same vein, sanctions should be imposed on the rebel groups in Burundi and on those who supported them if they failed to adhere to the Arusha process.
>
> (UN 2001, p. 14)

The Ugandan President thus drew an analogy with the previous sanction regime, evoking the agency these sanctions signalled. Yet at that time differences among the regional interveners were too big to be easily transcended. The Tanzanian President insisted that the armed movements had (legitimate) political demands and should therefore not be sanctioned (UN 2001, p. 11). There was thus no regional agreement on who was responsible for the protracted implementation of the Arusha Agreement. In this moment, the Burundian antagonisms also penetrated the regional discourse. Instead of reanimating their collective subjectivity that was already dislocated by the Congo wars and Nyerere's death, regional differences reinforced themselves.

The possibilities for a united performance of agency changed after Buyoya left office in November 2001, with Frodebu taking over. From a Tanzanian view, the primary embodiment of continuing Hutu oppression had thus resigned. Thereafter, the Tanzanian Government reportedly began to view intervention politics as a means to safeguard the legacy of Nyerere as the man who brought peace to Burundi and who laid the foundation for the Arusha Agreement (ICG 2002, p. 21). By re-signifying the intervention as a practice aiming at preserving Nyerere's legacy, the Tanzanian Government finally rallied behind the constitution of the remaining armed movements as a problem. After all, the armed movements undermined the legacy of the father of the Tanzanian nation. After some armed factions signed a ceasefire agreement in 2002, the Regional Initiative warned the remaining CNDD-FDD faction under Pierre Nkurunziza and Palipehutu-FNL under Agathon Rwasa to enter into negotiations within the following month. Otherwise the regional intervention would enact 'appropriate measures against the recalcitrant party' (Regional Initiative 2002, see also Zuma 2002a). The CNDD-FDD did not miss the deadline, but Palipehutu-FNL did. Yet, instead of imposing sanctions immediately, the regional interveners continued to enunciate threats – without a follow-up. Chief facilitator Zuma announced that Palipehutu-FNL would 'face robust sanctions' (Zuma 2002b). The AU (2003a, 2003b, 2003c, 2003d), which in the meantime had succeeded the OAU, repeated the warning. The Regional Initiative specified:

> In the case of a categorical refusal to join the negotiation process, the Burundi people, the Regional Initiative on Burundi and the African Union will consider it [Palipehutu-FNL] to be an organization that is against peace and stability in Burundi and will treat it as such.
>
> (Regional Initiative 2003)

Through these statements the signifier 'sanctions' again acted as a nodal point in the discourse. It held together a heterogeneous crowd of interveners, otherwise drifting apart. This time however the signifier was no longer floating, that is, subjected to incompatible fillings. None of the African/regional/South African interveners filled the signifier with potentially counter-hegemonic elements that could spark resistance. The signifier 'sanctions' also no longer functioned as a marker of difference, announcing regional unity of action. Instead of utilising the signifier to articulate a different and better self, the African/regional/South African forces tried to perform a minimum of the agency generally associated with interveners by warning the last remaining armed movement of something that was never really practised – as will also become clear in the next paragraph.

In June 2004, the Regional Initiative (2004a) imposed restrictions on movement for leading figures of Palipehutu-FNL, a decision that was also endorsed by the AU (2004a, 2004b). Yet, these targeted sanctions had reportedly little effect as Palipehutu-FNL forces primarily operated within Burundi (ICG 2004a, p. 12). In August, the Regional Initiative (2004b) formally declared Palipehutu-FNL a terrorist organisation. At the end of 2004, the UN Security Council reiterated that 'appropriate measures' should 'be taken against those individuals who threaten the peace and national reconciliation process in Burundi' (UN 2004) – yet these 'appropriate measures' were never enacted. The International Crisis Group was therefore able to argue that 'it is impossible not to notice the lack of pressure from both regional leaders and the international community on the [Palipehutu-]FNL to bring them to the negotiating table' (ICG 2004a, p. 12). In a nutshell, instead of testifying to united action, these warnings of sanctions signified the 'lack of pressure' of the interveners. The signifier no longer signalled agency.

Changing practices and discourses within Burundi also outpaced regional intervention politics. After the CNDD-FDD joined the Arusha consensus, they – together with the Burundian army – waged an intensive war against their former brothers in arms (van Eck 2004, p. 2).[16] This war strongly reduced Palipehutu-FNL's ability to continue fighting (ICG 2004b, p. 8) and therewith rendered less plausible the African/regional/South African representation of Palipehutu-FNL as a threat against peace and stability in Burundi. The elections of 2005 further dislocated African/regional intervention politics. In post-election Burundi, the attention soon shifted towards the increasingly authoritarian politics of the new CNDD-FDD government that seemed to undermine the Arusha framework.[17]

'We are not like them': reconstructing antagonisms and counter-hegemony

With being enacted as intervener, the regional forces were enabled to articulate a new subjectivity that, however, was precarious and open to dislocations. In the last section, the African/regional/South African subjectivity became visible as *different* – not only to their own past but also to the rest. In the remainder of this chapter, I will scrutinise this difference in more detail. It will become more and more clear that the enactment of a 'progressive' regional intervention relied on an antagonistic differentiation against other forces in the field of intervention; especially against the Burundians themselves.

Burundi as a regional aberration: the military regime of Pierre Buyoya

Some years after the democratic election of President Ndadaye, regional forces still spoke of the Burundian summer of 1993 as 'the envy of Africa as far as democracy is concerned' (Ugandan Parliament 1995, p. 17). Tanzanian President Mkapa (1996b) called the first democratically elected president of Burundi 'the personification of hope for the institutional evolution of multiparty democracy and unity in Burundi'. A UN Commission of Inquiry (1996, p. 20) likewise characterised Ndadaye's presidency as a time of 'unprecedented harmony and prosperity to the country'. The fall from grace is well articulated by a member of the Ugandan Parliament (1995, p. 17): 'In fact, by that time, they [Burundi] had even built a monument of unity, a promised land. Now, today, Burundi has gone to the dogs.' In 1998, the International Crisis Group reported that the Regional Initiative considered Burundi as a 'stereotype of old-fashioned African leadership' (ICG 1998a, p. 8). Are these articulations markers of difference or even antagonism? And how did these (positive/negative) fillings of Burundi relate to the subjectivity of the regional interveners?

The signification of mass violence as the ultimate Other is deeply embedded in modern philosophy. In this sense, it is not surprising that, already at the foundational meeting in Cairo, the Regional Initiative named those it held responsible for mass violence in Burundi.

> The Heads of State and delegations were convinced that the problems of Rwanda and Burundi were basically a consequence of a confluence of negative interests of colonialism and *local opportunists* who have fostered the ideology of exclusion that generates fear, frustration, hatred and tendencies to extermination and genocide.
> (Regional Initiative 1995, emphasis mine)

The name for the Burundian subject held responsible was still rather imprecise and open to multiple projections: 'local opportunists' – or subsequently 'all Burundian parties', as articulated by the Regional Initiative (1996a) and the OAU (1996a, 1996b). The emerging regional interveners did not yet constitute an Burundian opposite but opposed another genocide. In June 1996, the chief facilitator argued that 'the international community must not sit again with its hands folded, as we did in Rwanda' (Nyerere 1996b). The OAU (1996c) explained that the regional intervention was 'a fraternal and genuine concern to prevent yet another African tragedy'. The spectre of genocide and the still incipient regional politics of prevention forestalled a more detailed contouring of the subject considered responsible for the violence.

Immediately after the coup of July 1996, this vagueness, however, disappeared. By historical coincidence, a UN report on Ndadaye's assassination in 1993 was published just on the eve of the coup, thereby contributing to stabilise the signification of past violence (UN Commission of Inquiry 1996). Referring to this report, the Tanzanian President argued that the moment of hope was briskly interrupted by Ndadaye's assassination, for which 'the army of which Buyoya is part' has to be held responsible (Mkapa 1996c). This statement is remarkable, since the UN report concluded that the coup including the assassination was planned 'by officers highly placed in the line of command of the Burundian Army'; however, no perpetrator could be named with certainty (UN Commission of Inquiry 1996). And Buyoya? At that time, Buyoya still enjoyed the reputation of a politician who had initiated democratic reform in the late 1980s and accepted electoral defeat in 1993. However, by accepting the army's request to return to the presidency by force, this representation crumbled.

> [Buyoya] handed his political enemies an easy argument: that the coup of 25 July showed him in his true colours and that, secretly, he had not accepted the results of [the 1993] elections, that he had been involved in the killing of Ndadaye in 1993 and had supported the violent Tutsi army putsch and systematically destroyed all other political parties. By seizing power on 25 July, he was de facto accepting responsibility for a regime which had killed the first democratically elected President of Burundi and had abandoned a power-sharing agreement (the Government Convention of September 1994 to July 1996) in favour of a dictatorial military regime.
> (ICG 1998a, p. 17)

A new signification of Buyoya as the meta-perpetrator became possible.[18] The Tanzanian head of state concluded that the coup of 1996 was initiated 'by the army and [the] UPRONA party in October 1993, to emasculate a democratically elected government, and eventually return to power the very man who lost in a free and fair election' (Mkapa 1996c).[19] Thus, the name of Pierre Buyoya began to replace the vagueness that had previously surrounded the regional articulations on violence in Burundi.

The articulation of Buyoya as the meta-perpetrator most explicitly expressed itself in the imposition of sanctions in the aftermath of the coup. In this context, the Regional Initiative (1996b, 1998) began calling the new government the 'Buyoya regime' or 'Bujumbura regime' (see also Regional Foreign Ministers 1996), thereby refusing to recognise Buyoya as the legitimate Burundian President[20] and marking him as well as his government as the major obstacle to peace. During the whole sanctioning period (1996–1999), the Regional Initiative (1997a, 1997b) directed its demands towards the Buyoya government – to, for instance, disband the 'regroupment' camps; to release the speaker of the parliament and a former president; as well as to halt all trials until all negotiating parties agreed how to deal with such crimes.[21] By contrast, similar appeals were not directed to other Burundian subjects in the field of intervention. It was generally Buyoya who was made responsible for the lack of progress. A member of the facilitation team reported that Buyoya's delegation blocked any progress in the negotiations (Hyera 2004, pp. 55–57). In 1997, the regional heads of state publicly expressed their 'disappointment over the refusal of the government of Burundi to take part in the first session of all party negotiations in Arusha' (Regional Initiative 1997b). As the regionally sponsored negotiations were non-negotiable from the point of view of the Regional Initiative (see above), the gap separating the Regional Initiative from the Buyoya government temporarily widened (cf. Wodrig and Grauvogel 2016).

Can this temporal gap be comprehended as the empirical articulation of an ontological antagonism? At this point, it is worth repeating that an ontological antagonism marks the radical limit of our own discourse, that is, the system of signification, in which we are embedded. The antagonism blocks the full realisation of this system of signification, but it also constitutes the discourse by disclosing what the latter is radically not (Laclau 1990, p. 21, for IR in general, see Campbell 1998). The ontological antagonism 'is a symbol of my non-being and, in this way, it is overflowed by a plurality of meanings which prevent it being fixed as full positivity' (Laclau and Mouffe 2001 [1985], p. 125). Thus, an ontological antagonism that constitutes/blocks a structured discourse does not manifest itself empirically without ambiguity: as soon as one scrutinises the supposedly empirical manifestation of the antagonism, inconsistencies come into view as well.

Certainly, the friction between the Burundian Government and the Regional Initiative is hardly comparable to the violent practices around the ethnically stabilised antagonism within Burundi. Yet, this does not mean that the Burundian Government could not function as a empirical surface for constituting/blocking the discourse of the Regional Initiative – as will become more explicit in the following. Above all, staging a *coup d'état* and reinstating Buyoya helped the Regional Initiative to articulate a new agency and to comprehend themselves as progressive subjects. Yet, the coup and the new government under Buyoya also blocked the full realisation of this new representation of the region. These two dimensions express themselves in quotes I already cited in a different context: Nyerere (1996c) stated in the name of all Africans '[we] do not accept military regimes anymore' (translation mine). The enactment of sanctions were 'a declaration of principle – that the era of *coups d'état* was over' (Mkapa 1996c). And, in the most explicit way: 'Burundi is a political aberration: it is the only one under military rule' (Nyerere 1998, p. 150). Thus, in the words of the chief facilitator, Burundi became a regional aberration that marked a radical difference from the rest of the region. Past scholarship has also pointed to a common pattern among interveners to pathologise the society under intervention: 'ripe for intervention', as Kai Koddenbrock (2016, pp. 28–55) called it (see also Hughes and Pupavac 2005). Chandler argued:

> Discussions of humanitarian atrocities from Rwanda to Srebrenica focused on evil 'others', particularly evil individuals and elites, held to bear direct individual moral responsibility for war crimes.
>
> (Chandler 2014, p. 442)

By constituting Burundi as a regional aberration, the Regional Initiative rendered their intervention politics plausible and, one might add, necessary. Pierre Buyoya was not the embodiment of evil, but he personified a military regime that belonged to the old order on the African continent.

This empirical antagonism only temporarily stabilised. After the Buyoya government finally committed to regional peace negotiations, the representation of Buyoya as the major obstacle to peace lost some of its plausibility. Buyoya became a responsible leader, one who was committed to the art of compromise (Mandela 2000b). He and other signatories of the Arusha Agreement were subsequently comprehended as 'a new class of leadership' and 'men of peace' (South African Parliament 2001a, Zuma 2002b). However, the Tanzanian interveners were not as quick to let go of the representation. After the Arusha Agreement, the Tanzanian President insisted on the representation of Buyoya and his party as an obstacle to peace (ICG 2001, p. 5, UN 2001, p. 11), thereby indicating a stronger attachment to this antagonistic frontier. This stronger attachment to the antagonism solidified during the 1990s. From 1996 to 1999, the Tanzanian and Burundian Governments were entangled in accusations and counter-accusations. The refugee camps located in Tanzanian territory had emerged as recruiting grounds for Hutu armed movements. The Buyoya government complained that Tanzanian authorities were complicit in recruiting, training, and arming these movements (Wolpe 2011, p. 11). In 1997, the Tanzanian Government (1997) complained about 'acts of provocation by Burundian armed forces'. In 2001, Burundian President Buyoya argued that the Burundian–Tanzanian borderlands were in an 'open state of war' (UN 2001, p. 10, see also Mthembu-Salter 2002, Wolpe 2011, pp. 17–19). Thus, for the Tanzanian authorities the antagonism had become *real*: that is, the contingency of its articulation was lost. Such strong attachment to an empirical projection provides 'rigid templates with which to "read" events, pushing aside all ambiguity and ambivalence which may enable alternative readings' (Glynos 2008, pp. 279–280). Even after the representation of Buyoya as an obstacle to peace lost much of its plausibility, the strong Tanzanian attachment with this representation hampered a volte-face.

In short, the name Pierre Buyoya temporarily became a mark of radical difference. He became the empirical embodiment of an ontological antagonism. The majority of the African/regional/South African interveners were not attached to this antagonism, but the Tanzanian authorities were. In this sense, Buyoya temporarily represented what the Regional Initiative no longer wanted to be. Having said this, this empirical antagonism should not be understood as an element of a regional counter-hegemony: articulating a radical (and negative) difference to the recipients of intervention seems to be a hegemonic mode of crafting interventions instead. At least, it is not specific to regional interventions.

Negative forces and terrorists: changing markers of antagonism

As soon as Pierre Buyoya was no longer regarded as an obstacle to peace, other Burundian figures inherited this function. The negative attention shifted towards those armed movements which refused to agree to the compromise of the Arusha Agreement. Initially, the chief facilitator and others reached out to the armed movements, by prompting them to join the negotiations (OAU 1999, 2000a, Mandela 2000a).[22] The language chief facilitator Mandela used signalled appreciation for, rather than confrontation with, them. However, after these armed movements refused to sign the agreement, the language and signifiers changed. At the UN, Mandela argued that there cannot be *any justification* for continuing violent attacks on the civilian population when a political agreement has been reached and the way opened for them to bring their concerns to the negotiating table. We call upon them once again to demonstrate the quality of their leadership by announcing a ceasefire and halting the slaughter of innocent women, men and children, including the disabled.

(Mandela 2000b, emphasis mine)

This statement aimed to send a signal to the armed Hutu movements that violence and war was no longer justified, thereby articulating a rupture from appreciating them as freedom fighters to considering them as negative forces (ICG 2000b, p. 32). The Regional Initiative also began to direct their demands to the 'Burundian belligerents' (Museveni 2002a). The next chief facilitator emphasised that 'the only road to stability and order in Burundi is through negotiations and not through the barrel of a gun' (Zuma 2002a). Their continuous fighting thus was no longer considered as political. In this line of reasoning, the armed movements were ultimately considered as 'rebels without a cause' (Zuma 2002b). The Rwandan President Kagame (2002) even considered the armed movements as a threat to Rwandan national security. Thus, most of the African/regional/South African interveners agreed on an understanding of the armed movements as negative forces and ultimately rebels without a cause. The Tanzanian President, however, openly objected to understanding the armed Hutu movements as negative forces: 'The issue with the negative forces was not so simple and even some of the Arusha signatories could be perceived as containing "negatives forces", including the government'. Ultimately, the continued fighting were 'military expressions of political intent' (UN 2001, p. 11). Therewith, the Tanzanian President refused to signify the armed movements as 'rebels without a cause'. Although most prominent figures of the regional intervention distanced themselves from the remaining forces of violence, the Tanzanian President was not the only one sustaining the previous solidified antagonism (South African Parliament 2001a, p. 80).

The representation of the remaining armed movement as an antagonistic force undermining the peace intervention further stabilised after the CNDD-FDD signed a ceasefire agreement. Even the Tanzanian President conceded that 'to say that we should have a fresh start and assume that nothing has happened in Burundi over the past several years is not right' (Kikwete 2006), thereby rejecting Palipehutu-FNL's demand to re-negotiate the post-conflict order. Thereafter, the continuing fighting of Palipehutu-FNL was considered as a 'self-exclusion' that 'will not impede Burundi's progress towards its renewal' (Mbeki 2003). The chief facilitator argued that Palipehutu-FNL 'does not present an obstacle to the peace process, taking into account that the majority of parties are part of the process' (Zuma 2003). Thus, Palipehutu-FNL stopped being an obstacle to peace and instead became a force excluding itself.

After the peace agreement, the African/regional/South African intervention tried to introduce closure by marginalising violent critique. Most of the African/regional/South African interveners rejected any understanding of continued

90 *Regional forces in Burundi*

violence as political. This shift was not inevitable. Many members of the South African and Ugandan Governments considered themselves former freedom fighters, with these former freedom fighters having previously been supported by Nyerere – a man who, under certain conditions, considered violence to be a legitimate means of countering oppression (cf. Frazer and Hutchings 2007). Against this backdrop, it would have been likewise plausible to understand the continued fighting as an expression of legitimate demands that remained to be negotiated. Yet, the aforementioned turmoil in eastern Congo fatally undermined the representation of armed movements as freedom fighters. Instead armed movements became associated with greedy and ultimately apolitical violence. By marginalising the remaining armed movements, the African/regional/South African intervention arguably conformed to routine practices of liberal peacebuilding: 'What liberal peacebuilding represents is a closure and diminishing of debate over the nature and path toward peace' (Peterson 2013, p. 323). Thus, empirical antagonism cannot be understood as an expression of a counter-hegemony, but – on the contrary – conforms to hegemonic practices of intervention.

Burundi, or particular subjects within Burundi, remained markers of radical difference to the interveners. After the electoral victory of the CNDD-FDD in 2005, a new empirical manifestation of radical difference was found. Chief facilitator Nqakula warned:

> The political landscape had been poisoned by a number of very bad judgement calls on the part of the Government and the leadership of the ruling [CNDD-FDD]. President Nkurunziza was also engaged in a standoff with the political opposition.
>
> (Nqakula 2007b)

A new obstacle to peace was found. This constant re-articulation of Burundi as a political aberration suggests that it functioned as a means to sustain the African/regional/South African authority in the field of intervention. Rather than fostering 'local ownership' or agonistic dialogue, the interveners authoritatively decided whom to consider as the new obstacle to peace. These constant re-articulations also distracted from the still pending promise of the regionally sponsored peace bringing real, democratic change. Thus, ultimately, representing one Burundian force or another as an obstacle to peace helped the African/regional/South African interveners to stabilise their position as peacebuilders.

Crafting a fragile counter-hegemony: regional interveners and the usual suspects

The usual suspects enacted the regional intervention into being. This discursive structuring does not conform to how political discourse theorists normally imagine the breeding ground of a counter-hegemony which is considered to arise from the excluded (Laclau 2005, pp. 139–141). For instance, the hegemony of liberal peacebuilding is considered to have excluded local rationalities and representations. Therefore, it was expected that the local turn would represent 'a dangerous and wild place where Western rationality, with its diktats of universality and modernisation, is challenged in different ways' (Mac Ginty and Richmond 2013, p. 763). We already know that the African/regional/South African intervention has not functioned as such 'a dangerous and wild place' that questioned the prevailing rationality of interventions. Yet, by identifying with this new subject position, the regional interveners were able to question 'the "natural" right of the North to intervene in the political formations of the South' (Mac Ginty and Richmond 2013, p. 764). Can the regional intervention into Burundi thus be understood as a counter-hegemony?

Already at the Cairo summit in November 1995, the Regional Initiative had began to distance itself from those forces that enacted it into being. It should be remembered that the participants of this summit still conceived of themselves as a passive entity waiting for external help. The Regional Initiative was not yet the semi-institutionalised expression of a new regional agency. The wait for external help did not stop the emerging Regional Initiative (1995) from understanding the Burundian crisis as a consequence of the 'negative interests of colonialism'. In the following years, this distancing from representatives of the colonial past was repeated several times. The chair of the Regional Initiative argued that Burundi and other regional crises were 'not African problems, they are European problems in Africa' (Museveni 2002b). Rwandan President Kagame (2009) clarified that 'the international community are linked with [our current problems] historically'. Even the Arusha Agreement stated that 'the colonial administration, first German and then Belgian ... played a decisive role in the heightening of frustrations'[23] (Arusha Agreement 2000, Protocol 1, art. 2). One could argue that this distancing is merely rhetorical since colonialism had long disappeared. Yet, this interpretation concealed how the regional intervention substantiated their agency against the contemporary representatives of colonialism, a structure that becomes especially explicit the following statement:

> Some of the governments of the West, and including the United States, have really been very bad on our continent. They have used the Cold War and all sorts of things to back up a bunch of corrupted leaders on our continent. I think they should stop now and let the people of Africa sort out their own, their own future.
>
> (Nyerere 1996a)

In this statement, 'the West' becomes the representative of hegemony, which for centuries had dominated the African continent. The call for African solutions only makes sense by countering this century-old hegemony. The constitution of radical difference towards the usual suspects was reinforced by Ugandan President Museveni, who considered the Regional Initiative as a metaphor for doing interventions 'without the help of outsiders' (cited by ICG 2000a, p. 19). Thus, distancing from the usual suspects was constitutive for the regional intervention. It functioned as the *raison d'être* for African solutions.

From day one, the usual suspects were ambiguous subjects: they embodied the radical difference that blocked/constituted the regional intervention, but they also empowered and funded African solutions. This ambiguity became explicit in various statements. In November 1995, the Regional Initiative (1995) called upon the international community to mobilise resources for facilitating economic and social development – not just in Burundi, but in the neighbourhood as well. In July 1996, the OAU (1996c) demanded financial, logistical, and other material assistance for the regional security assistance force. During the peace negotiations, the Regional Initiative (1999) commended the donors' 'unflinching ... material support' (see also Mandela 2000a). In the aftermath of the peace negotiations, the Regional Initiative (2001) even publicly acknowledged its financial dependency on the usual suspects: 'Without this generous support, the progress of the negotiations would have been seriously handicapped.' This function attributed to the usual suspects awkwardly clashed with antagonistic projections. In these initial years, the representation of the usual suspects as the antagonising force was plausible and persistent. Shortly after the constitutive summit of the Regional Initiative, the EU and the US dispatched special envoys to Burundi and adjacent territories.[24] According to the report of the facilitation team:

> It is not always productive to strategize with [the special envoys] considering that they have their own interests. Being representatives of large countries, they have a tendency to want to dominate and control the process.... It was suggested that the Nyerere Foundation begin to seek funds from the sub-regional countries and other countries in Africa including the OAU so as to minimize the potential for disruptive influence from external donors.
> (Facilitator's report of the first session, quoted by Khadiagala 2003, p. 234)

As this statement suggests, the special envoys blocked the full realisation of African solutions. The chief facilitator refers to their tendency to want to control the process, thereby challenging the hegemony of the regional interveners in this field. The facilitation team imagined it could transcend the obstacles to its own fullness by erasing ambiguity and funding its own intervention politics: an imagining which soon disintegrated in the light of sedimented structures of economic capital. Thereafter, the Regional Initiative, including the facilitation team, were careful not to explicitly name the constitutive antagonism.

Instead, the Tanzanian President tried to dissolve the ambiguity:

> Conflict resolution and peace-keeping are expensive undertakings which our fledgling economies cannot be expected to finance on our own. The case has, therefore, been made for the international community to lend a helping hand to African initiatives for peace.... We have created an agenda and a momentum for peace. All we ask of the international community is continuous and solid support to make it work and sustain it.[25]
> (Mkapa 1998c)

In mid-1998, Tanzanian President Mkapa refrained from representing the usual suspects as antagonistic forces by trying to articulate a new common ground – but on African/regional terms. The donors should limit themselves to providing funding, whereas the regional intervention was creating the agenda for peace. This proposal is miles away from the subject position initially projected upon the regional interveners, which envisioned them as implementing intervention politics crafted elsewhere. That said, the statement does also signal that the counter-hegemonic impetus – in terms of regional agency despite international resistance – lost momentum. Theoretically,

> every subversion of a hegemonic space depends upon the resources of marginalised spaces, and the defence of the possibilities which are opened up through subversion depends in turn upon the construction and reinforcement of alternative spaces.
> (Smith 1998, pp. 234–235, translation mine)

In other words, the regional intervention lacked the resources to defend the alternative space of intervention. By articulating a new common ground, the Tanzanian President renounced the claim to articulate a regional counter-intervention but tried to integrate regional practices into the international community.

This discursive shift became more pronounced after Mandela was appointed the new chief facilitator. In January 2000, he argued before the UN Security Council: 'Apart from the financial and humanitarian assistance, the international community also has a part to play *politically*' (Mandela 2000a, emphasis mine). Instead of comprehending the usual suspects as helping with the expenses, they are empowered to also craft the intervention politics. After the conclusion of the agreement, the chief facilitator even said that 'international interest and participation were crucial for moving the peace process forward' (Mandela 2000b). Mandela reportedly understood that the contemporary representatives of colonialism would guard their position in the field of intervention with vigour. Therefore, it was better to make them 'part of the solution rather than the problem' (Rautenbach and Vrey 2010, p. 16). Zuma continued to represent the intervention as a common project: 'We cannot achieve the results we seek if we work alone. We need the wholehearted support of the international community' (Zuma 2002b). At that time, no empirically stabilised antagonism penetrated the discursive surface. The Mbeki administration reportedly refrained from trying to radically change the international status quo. Rather, the South African Government tried to enact change by initiating reforms and place African concerns on the international agenda (Habib 2009, p. 147).

When Mandela and Zuma eventually reduced their involvement in Burundi, the gap separating the African/regional/South African forces from the international community became visible again. Rather than speaking of a shared human responsibility towards Burundi, the late South African facilitator claimed to represent the 'Regional Initiative of the African Union'. He continued: 'if the international community helps us, then indeed there is a lot that we will be able

94 *Regional forces in Burundi*

to achieve for ourselves' (Nqakula 2007b). In the latter quote, the international community was once more imagined as providing assistance, rather than politically crafting the intervention. In 2007, it was no longer necessary to articulate African solutions against the contemporary representatives of colonialism. The African Union had already institutionalised the previously counter-hegemonic space, in which the Regional Initiative had started to articulate intervention politics. Within the African peace and security architecture, the EU had already committed itself to fund African peacekeeping and related capacity building via the African Peace Facility (cf. Cilliers and Pottgieter 2010, p. 130). Thus, at that time, regional interventions were already integrated into hegemonic peacebuilding. The regional intervention into Burundi is thus an example of a fragile and elusive counter-hegemony that soon lost momentum.

Notes

1 An exception in this regard is the Tanzanian overthrow of the Ugandan Government of Idi Amin in 1979 (see Wheeler 2000, pp. 111–138).
2 For the transition from Nyerere to Mandela, see Khadiagala 2003, p. 236, Bentley and Southall 2005, p. 72.
3 Before Nyerere embraced democracy, sporadic demands for democratisation from below had been officially ignored or intimidated into silence (Shivji 1991, p. 83).
4 The speech is republished in part at http://mobile.monitor.co.ug/News/-/691252/ 1096080/-/format/xhtml/-/bdlr0e/-/index.html (accessed 26 April 2013).
5 On broad-based politics in Uganda, see Lindemann 2011.
6 With the polarisation of public space, alternative ethnic categories such as the small minority of Twas disappeared from the general debate. The historically important princely elites, who held the power in traditional Burundi and were not subsumed under the categories of Hutu nor Tutsi, had long become 'virtually assimilated into the Tutsi frame of reference' (Lemarchand 1994, p. 15).
7 The other successful *coups d'état* in Burundian history took place in 1965, 1976 and 1987.
8 These strong statements of principle can so far only be attributed to Tanzanian forces. This is not to say that other regional heads of state rejected the new declaration of principle per se. It is first and foremost a problem of data as I lack any useful text by, for instance, Museveni from that period.
9 The regional preparations to dispatch a security assistance force – although previously requested by the Burundian Government – had been met with vigorous protest within Burundi. Influential officers within the army, especially, regarded the security assistance for as a means to deprive them of their privileges. Due to the protests, the technical committee which the Regional Initiative had dispatched had to cancel their preparatory mission to Bujumbura. Resistance within the military increased to such a degree that the coup appeared as a way to escape military intervention. The spectre of a regionally sponsored military force directly fostered the decision to stage a coup within the army. Insisting on military intervention in the aftermath of the coup was thus not a real option, as the main opponents to regional military intervention were back in government (ICG 1998a, p. 4, Hyera 2004, p. 58).
10 The EAC Treaty aimed at accomplishing political federation in stages: first a customs union, followed by a common market, a monetary union, and, lastly, a political federation that enabled the member states to transcend their sovereign separation (see Adar 2011). The EAC was more ambitious than comparable regional organisations on the continent. It was even suggested the unification process could be fast-tracked by

implementing the stages in parallel instead of in sequence. This desire to accelerate the integration process contrasts, however, with the member state's weakness to implement decisions (Reith and Boltz 2011).
11 According to the EAC Treaty, one of the many objectives is to promote peace, security and stability 'within', and good neighbourliness 'among', the members (Art. 5). In Article 124, the signatories agreed that 'peace and security are pre-requisites to social and economic development'. The article calls on the members to prevent, better manage, and resolve disputes and conflicts 'between them'. The treaty cites regional disaster management, refugees, cross border crime (Art. 124, 3–5), as well as defence (Art. 125) as special areas of cooperation.
12 The International Crisis Group reported that Mandela 'has often proved inflexible, stubborn and impervious to any advice or any external influence on his management of the peace process, probably trusting too much his own experience when he managed the South African minority/majority dossier' (ICG 2000b, p. 16).
13 At a session of the South African Parliament, Mbeki introduced his vision of the African Renaissance. He argued that the persistent violent crises in Burundi and other African countries frustrated 'the regeneration of our continent'. Therefore, he demanded, the 'collective mind of Africans' should be preoccupied to find solutions to these violent situations (Mbeki 1998).
14 The armed movements rejected their pathologisation, arguing that the peace agreement had not fundamentally altered the practices of rule in Burundi, but that it had primarily given jobs to those people who participated in the negotiations (Wolpe 2011, p. 58).
15 The UN Security Council delegation talked to various regional heads of state, among them Yoweri Museveni, Benjamin Mkapa, and Nelson Mandela. In the report, the positions of the respective interlocutors are usually paraphrased, but at times the authors of this report also indirectly quoted the respective heads of state.
16 The advisor to the facilitation Jan van Eck argued that the CNDD-FDD already understood Palipehutu-FNL as a potential competitor for mobilising votes.
17 These changing practices in Burundi did *not* render an agreement with the Palipehutu-FNL completely unnecessary. In 2005, the Tanzanian Government took the lead in facilitating a ceasefire between the new CNDD-FDD government and Palipehutu-FNL, leading to various agreements from September 2006 to December 2008 (Mahiga 2005).
18 This does not mean that the new representation superseded the old one. Among the international community as well as among OAU staff, Buyoya continued to enjoy the reputation of a moderate (ICG 1998a, p. 48).
19 Chief facilitator Nyerere (1996b), by contrast, acknowledged that Buyoya was not the author of the *coup d'état*.
20 The Tanzanian authorities, especially, denied Buyoya recognition. In November 1997, the Tanzanian Government allowed the Burundian political and military opposition to make use of the embassy offices in Dar es Salaam, thereby underlining that the Tanzanian state did not consider the Buyoya government the legitimate representative of Burundi (ICG 1998a, p. 45). Having said this, *neither* Tanzanian authorities *nor* the Regional Initiative urged Buyoya to resign and reinstate the former Frodebu president – as was demanded by the UN Security Council; a demand that the latter, however, never repeated (UN 1996f).
21 The OAU (1997, 2000b), however, was reluctant to issue similar statements. Only twice, the OAU urged the Buyoya government to dismantle the regroupment camps.
22 When the Arusha peace negotiations started in mid-1998, all Burundian parties were invited to participate. However, by that time, both the CNDD as well as Palipehutu had fragmented. The political representatives in Arusha soon lost their control over their respective military arms FDD (therefore CNDD-FDD) and FNL (therefore Palipehutu-FNL). At the beginning of the Arusha peace negotiations, the participants

signed a ceasefire agreement but, as the two major armed movements remained outside of the process due to the internal splits, this agreement had no effect (Wolpe 2011, p. 46).
23 According to a member of the facilitation team, none of the Burundian forces questioned this wording (Mpangala 2004, pp. 124–125). By contrast, the Belgian Government reportedly protested against these 'unfounded accusations' (ICG 2000b, p. 4 n. 10).
24 Reportedly, the US and EU nominated the special envoys in order to 'strengthen Nyerere's hands' (Wolpe 2011, p. 26).
25 Donors financially supported the regional peace negotiations with US$15 million (Bentley and Southall 2005, p. 65).

References

Adar, K.G., 2011. *The East African community*. Moncalieri, Italy: International Democracy Watch Report.

Ameir, S.J.K., 2008. Tanzania's role in Burundi's peace process. Master's thesis: University of Witwatersrand. Available from: http://wiredspace.wits.ac.za/handle/10539/7367 (accessed 18 March 2013).

Anyaoku, E., and Cassam, A., 2010. Nyerere and the Commonwealth. In: C. Chachage and A. Cassam, eds., *Africa's liberation: The legacy of Nyerere*. Kampala: Fountain Publishers, 66–71.

Arusha Agreement 2000. *Arusha Peace and Reconciliation Agreement for Burundi* of 28 August. Available from: http://peacemaker.un.org/sites/peacemaker.un.org/files/BI_000828_Arusha%20Peace%20and%20Reconciliation%20Agreement%20for%20Burundi.pdf (accessed 1 November 2016).

AU [African Union] 2003a. Communiqué of 14 January. Addis Ababa: Mechanism for conflict prevention, management and resolution, Central Organ/MEC/AMB/Comm. (LXXXVIII).

AU 2003b. Communiqué of 3 February. Addis Ababa: Mechanism for conflict prevention, management and resolution, Central Organ/MEC/AHG/Comm.(VII).

AU 2003c. Communiqué of 2 April. Addis Ababa: Mechanism for conflict prevention, management and resolution, Central Organ/MEC/AMB/Comm.(XCI).

AU 2003d. Decision on Burundi of 8 July. Addis Ababa: AU executive council, EX/CL/42(III)d.

AU 2004a. Decision on Burundi of 3 July. Addis Ababa: AU executive council, EX.CL/106(V).

AU 2004b. Communiqué of 4 July. Addis Ababa: AU peace and security council, PSC/MIN/Comm.(XII).

Bah, M., 2003. Interview. *IRIN*, 12 December.

Bentley, K.A., and Southall, R., 2005. *An African peace process: Mandela, South Africa and Burundi*. Cape Town: Human Sciences Research Council Press.

Binningsbø, H.M., 2013. Power sharing, peace and democracy: Any obvious relationships? *International Area Studies Review*, 16 (1), 89–112.

Bomani, J., 2004. Foreword. In: G. Mpangala and B.U. Mwansasu, eds., *Beyond conflict in Burundi*. Dar es Salaam: Mwalimu Nyerere Foundation, v–xii.

Butiku, J.W., 2004. The facilitation of the Burundi peace negotiations. In: G. Mpangala and B.U. Mwansasu, eds., *Beyond conflict in Burundi*. Dar es Salaam: The Mwalimu Nyerere Foundation, 63–118.

Butler, J., 1997. *The psychic life of power: Theories in subjection*. Stanford: Stanford University Press.

Campbell, D., 1998. *Writing security: United States foreign policy and the politics of identity*. Manchester: Manchester University Press.

Chandler, D., 2009. *Hollow hegemony: Rethinking global politics, power and resistance*. London: Pluto Press.

Chandler, D., 2014. Beyond good and evil: Ethics in a world of complexity. *International Politics*, 51 (4), 441–457.

Chrétien, J.-P., 2000. Le Burundi après la signature de l'accord d'Arusha. *Politique Africaine*, 80 (4), 136–151.

Cilliers, J., and Pottgieter, J., 2010. The African standby force. In: U. Engel and J. Gomes Porto, eds., *Africa's new peace and security architecture*. Farnham: Ashgate, 111–141.

Curtis, D., 2007. South Africa: 'Exporting' peace to the Great Lakes region. In: A. Adebajo, A. Adebajo, and C. Landsberg, eds., *South Africa in Africa: The post-apartheid era*. Scottsville: University of KwaZulu-Natal Press, 253–273.

Daley, P., 2006. Ethnicity and political violence in Africa: The challenge to the Burundi state. *Political Geography*, 25 (6), 657–679.

Dlamini-Zuma, N., 2004. Speech of 3 June. Available from: www.dirco.gov.za/docs/speeches/2004/dzum0603.htm (accessed 15 July 2013).

Dlamini-Zuma, N., and Salomão, T., 2008. Media briefing of 13 August. Johannesburg: South African Department of International Relations and Cooperation. Available from: www.polity.org.za/article/sa-dlamini-zuma-transcript-of-southern-african-development-community-summit-media-briefing-13082008-2008-08-14 (accessed 26 February 2013).

Frazer, E., and Hutchings, K., 2007. Argument and rhetoric in the justification of political violence. *European Journal of Political Theory*, 6 (2), 180–199.

Furley, O., and Katalikawe, J., 1997. Constitutional reform in Uganda: The new approach. *African Affairs*, 96 (383), 243–260.

Gibson, J., 2010. Land redistribution/restitution in South Africa: A model of multiple values as the past meets the present. *British Journal of Political Science*, 40 (1), 135–169.

Giliomee, H., 1997. Surrender without defeat: Afrikaners and the South African 'miracle'. *Daedalus*, 126 (2), 113–146.

Glynos, J., 2008. Ideological fantasy at work. *Journal of Political Ideologies*, 13 (3), 275–296.

Grauvogel, J., 2015. Regional sanctions against Burundi: The regime's argumentative self-entrapment. *Journal of Modern African Studies*, 53 (2), 169–191.

Habib, A., 2009. South Africa's foreign policy: Hegemonic aspirations, neoliberal orientations and global transformation. *South African Journal of International Affairs*, 16 (2), 143–159.

Hara, F., 1999. Burundi: A case of parallel diplomacy. In: C.A. Crocker, F.O. Hampson, and P. Aall, eds., *Herding cats: Multiparty mediation in a complex world*. Washington DC: United States Institute of Peace Press, 139–158.

Haysom, N., 2007. Interview of 15 September. Available from: www.constitutionnet.org/video/interview-nicholas-haysom-political-affairs-director-executive-office-unsg (accessed 8 August 2013).

Hoffman, B., and Robinson, L., 2009. Tanzania's missing opposition. *Journal of Democracy*, 20 (4), 123–136.

Hoskins, E., and Nutt, S., 1997. *The humanitarian impacts of economic sanctions on Burundi*. Thomas J. Watson Jr. Institute for International Studies, Brown University, Occasional Paper no. 29. Providence RI: Thomas J. Watson Jr. Institute for International Studies.

Hughes, C., and Pupavac, V., 2005. Framing post-conflict societies: International pathologisation of Cambodia and the post-Yugoslav states. *Third World Quarterly*, 26 (6), 873–889.
Hyera, A., 2004. Background of the Burundi peace negotiations. In: G. Mpangala and B.U. Mwansasu, eds., *Beyond conflict in Burundi*. Dar es Salaam: The Mwalimu Nyerere Foundation, 49–62.
ICG [International Crisis Group] 1998a. Burundi under Siege. Lift the sanctions; relaunch the peace process. *Burundi Report* no. 1.
ICG 1998b. Burundi's peace process. The road from Arusha. *Burundi Report* no. 2.
ICG 2000a. The Mandela effect. Prospects for peace in Burundi. *Central Africa Report* no. 13.
ICG 2000b. Burundi: Neither war nor peace. *Africa Report* no. 25.
ICG 2001. Burundi: One hundred days to put the peace process back on track. *Africa Report* no. 33.
ICG 2002. Burundi after six month of transition: Continuing the war or winning peace? *Africa Report* no. 46.
ICG 2004a. End of transition in Burundi: The home stretch. *Africa Report* no. 81.
ICG 2004b. Elections in Burundi: The peace wager. *Africa Briefing*, 9 December.
Kagame, P., 2002. Interview. *Africa Confidential*, 18 October.
Kagame, P., 2009. Interview. *The Guardian*, 30 March.
Khadiagala, G.M., 2003. Burundi. In: J. Boulden, ed., *Dealing with conflict in Africa: The United Nations and regional organizations*. New York: Palgrave Macmillan, 215–251.
Khadiagala, G.M., 2007. *Meddlers or mediators? African interveners in civil conflict in eastern Africa*. Leiden: Martinus Nijhoff.
Khadiagala, G.M., 2013. Burundi, 2002–2012. In: J. Boulden, ed., *Responding to conflict in Africa: The United Nations and regional organizations*. New York: Palgrave Macmillan, 101–119.
Kikwete, J., 2006. Tanzania says no 'fresh start'. *Reuters*, 11 July.
Koddenbrock, K., 2016. *The practice of humanitarian intervention: Aid workers, agencies and institutions in the Democratic Republic of the Congo*. Abingdon: Routledge.
Laclau, E., 1990. *New reflections on the revolution of our time*. London: Verso.
Laclau, E., 2005. *On populist reason*. London: Verso.
Laclau, E., 2007 [1996]. *Emancipation(s)*. London: Verso.
Laclau, E. and Mouffe, C., 2001 [1985]. *Hegemony and socialist strategy*. 2nd edn. London: Verso.
Lemarchand, R., 1994. *Burundi: Ethnocide as discourse and practice*. Cambridge: Cambridge University Press.
Lemarchand, R., and Martin, D., 1974. *Selective genocide in Burundi*. London: Minority Rights Group.
Lemay-Hébert, N., 2011. The 'empty-shell' approach: The setup process of international administrations in Timor-Leste and Kosovo, its consequences and lessons. *International Studies Perspectives*, 12 (2), 190–211.
Lindemann, S., 2011. Just another change of guard? Broad-based politics and civil war in Museveni's Uganda. *African Affairs*, 110 (440), 387–416.
Lipton, M., 2007. *Liberals, Marxists, and nationalists: Competing interpretations of South African history*. New York: Palgrave Macmillan.
Mac Ginty, R., and Richmond, O.P., 2013. The local turn in peace building: A critical agenda for peace. *Third World Quarterly*, 34 (5), 763–783.
Mahiga, A.P., 2005. Speech of 6 December. New York: UN Security Council.

Mair, S., 2001. *East African Co-operation: Regionale Integration und Kooperation südlich der Sahara*, Part 1. Berlin: SWP-Studie.

Makara, S., Rakner, L., and Svåsand, L., 2009. Turnaround: The National Resistance Movement and the reintroduction of a multiparty system in Uganda. *International Political Science Review*, 30 (2), 185–204.

Mamabolo, K., 2008a. Media briefing of 6 March. Pretoria: South African Department of International Relations and Cooperation. Available from: www.dirco.gov.za/docs/speeches/2008/mama0307.html (accessed 23 March 2012).

Mamabolo, K., 2008b. Media briefing of 8 June. Johannesburg: South African Department of International Relations and Cooperation. Available from: www.dirco.gov.za/docs/speeches/2008/ndarwa0609.html (accessed 15 July 2013).

Mandela, N., 2000a. Speech of 19 January. New York: UN Security Council. Available from: http://reliefweb.int/report/burundi/president-mandelas-security-council-speech-burundi (accessed 20 March 2012).

Mandela, N., 2000b. Speech of 29 September. New York: UN Security Council. S/PV.4201.

Maundi, M.O., 2004. The international dynamic of the peace process. In: G. Mpangala and B.U. Mwansasu, eds., *Beyond conflict in Burundi*. Dar es Salaam: The Mwalimu Nyerere Foundation, 304–335.

Mbeki, T., 1998. The African Renaissance. Speech of 13 August. Available from: www.unisa.ac.za/contents/colleges/docs/1998/tm1998/tm980813.pdf (accessed 16 September 2014).

Mbeki, T., 2001. Our obligations to peace and development in Africa. *ANC Today*, 1 (42).

Mbeki, T., 2003. Africans come together to build a new future. *ANC Today*, 3 (40).

Mitchell, A., 2014. *International intervention in a secular age: Re-enchanting humanity?* Abingdon: Routledge.

Mkapa, B.W., 1996a. Speech of 25 June. Arusha: Regional Peace Initiative on Burundi summit.

Mkapa, B.W., 1996b. Speech of 8 July. Yaoundé, Cameroon: OAU summit.

Mkapa, B.W., 1996c. Speech of 21 August. Windhoek, Namibia.

Mkapa, B.W., 1996d. Speech of 24 August. Maseru, Lesotho: SADC summit.

Mkapa, B.W., 1997. Speech of 6 January. Dar es Salaam.

Mkapa, B.W., 1998a. Speech of 9 January. Dar es Salaam.

Mkapa, B.W., 1998b. Speech of 23 January. Arusha: Workshop on conflict resolution in Africa.

Mkapa, B.W., 1998c. Speech of 6 May. Dar es Salaam: Visit of UN Secretary General.

Mkapa, B.W., 1999a. *Peace-making and conflict resolution in Africa: A Tanzanian view*. Lecture of 1 September. University of Uppsala.

Mkapa, B.W., 1999b. Interview of 16 March. Dar es Salaam.

Mngomezulu, B.R., 2006. An assessment of the role played by political leaders, nationalisms and sub-nationalisms in the establishment and collapse of the East African Community, 1960–1970. Master's thesis: University of South Africa.

Mpangala, G.P., 2004. The nature of conflict in Burundi. In: G. Mpangala and B.U. Mwansasu, eds., *Beyond conflict in Burundi*. Dar es Salaam: The Mwalimu Nyerere Foundation, 119–135.

Mthembu-Salter, G., 1999. *An assessment of sanctions against Burundi*. London: ActionAid.

Mthembu-Salter, G., 2002. Burundi's peace agreement without peace. *Track Two*, 11 (5–6), 21–35.

Muhumuza, W., 2009. From fundamental change to no change: The National Resistance Movement and democratization in Uganda. *Les Cahiers*, 41, 21–42.

Museveni, Y.K., 1998a. Towards a closer co-operation in Africa. Speech of 10 July. Kampala.
Museveni, Y.K., 1998b. Speech of 21 January. Arusha: Workshop on individual and institutional mediators on African conflicts. Available from: www.metafro.be/grandslacs/grandslacsdir300/0844.pdf (accessed 14 November 2011).
Museveni, Y.K., 2000. Interview. *IRIN*, 20 May.
Museveni, Y.K., 2002a. Speech of 5 August. New York: UN Security Council, S/2002/894.
Museveni, Y.K., 2002b. Speech of 14 May. Washington DC: Woodrow Wilson Centre.
Muyangwa, M., and Vogt, M., 2000. *An assessment of the OAU mechanism for conflict prevention, management and resolution, 1993–2000*. New York: International Peace Academy.
Mwansasu, B.U., 2004. Democracy and good governance. In: G. Mpangala and B.U. Mwansasu, eds., *Beyond conflict in Burundi*. Dar es Salaam: The Mwalimu Nyerere Foundation, 136–186.
Mwenda, A.M., 2007. Personalizing power in Uganda. *Journal of Democracy*, 18 (3), 23–37.
Ndikumana, L., 1998. Institutional failure and ethnic conflicts in Burundi. *African Studies Review*, 41 (1), 29–47.
Nindorera, W., 2008. Burundi: The deficient transformation of the CNDD-FDD. In: J. De Zeeuw, ed., *From soldiers to politicians: Transforming rebel movements after civil war*. Bolder: Lynne Rienner, 103–130.
Nqakula, C., 2006. Media briefing of 29 May. Pretoria: South African Department of International Relations and Cooperation. Available from: www.gov.za/c-nqakula-finalisation-outstanding-questions-regarding-peace-burundi (accessed 15 July 2013).
Nqakula, C., 2007a. Media briefing of 15 October. Pretoria: South African Department of International Relations and Cooperation. Available from: www.gov.za/c-nqakula-burundi-peace-process-developments (accessed 15 July 2013).
Nqakula, C., 2007b. Speech of 28 November. New York: UN Security Council, S/PV.5786.
Nqakula, C., 2008. Media briefing of 14 October. Pretoria: South African Department of International Relations and Cooperation. Available from: www.dirco.gov.za/docs/speeches/2008/ntsa1015.html (accessed 15 July 2013).
Nyang'oro, J.E., 2011. *A political biography of Jakaya Mrisho Kikwete*. Asmara, Eritrea: Africa World Press.
Nye, J.S., 1965. *Pan-Africanism and East African integration*. Cambridge, MA: Harvard University Press.
Nyerere, J.K., 1959. Letter on boycott of South Africa of 5 October. Available from: www.anc.org.za/content/julius-nyerere-boycott-south-africa (accessed 6 August 2013).
Nyerere, J.K., 1985. Interview. *Africa Report*, 1 November.
Nyerere, J.K., 1996a. Interview. Available from: www.juliusnyerere.info/index.php/resources/j.k.nyerere_talks_with_charlayne_hunter-gault/ (accessed 10 February 2011).
Nyerere, J.K., 1996b. Peace may hinge on one man. *Christian Science Monitor*, 19 June.
Nyerere, J.K., 1996c. La junte burundaise doit négocier une solution politique. *Le Monde*, 28 August.
Nyerere, J.K., 1998. Africa today and tomorrow. *Review of African Political Economy*, 25 (75), 149–152.
OAU [Organisation of African Unity] 1996a. Resolution of 26–28 February. Addis Ababa: Council of ministers, CM/Res.1619 (LXIII).

OAU 1996b. Resolution of 1–5 July. Yaoundé: Council of ministers, CM/Res.1649 (LXIV).
OAU 1996c. Resolution of 10 July. Yaoundé: Assembly of heads of state and governments, AHG/Res.257 (XXXII).
OAU 1996d. Statement of 25 July. Addis Ababa: Mechanism for conflict prevention, management, and resolution. UN Security Council documentation: S/1996/594.
OAU 1996e. Communiqué of 5 August. Addis Ababa: Mechanism for conflict prevention, management and resolution. Available from: http://reliefweb.int/report/burundi/communiqué-burundi (accessed 11 July 2013)].
OAU 1997. Decision of 27–31 May. Harare: Council of ministers, CM/Dec.330–363 (LXVI).
OAU 1998. Resolution on the regional sanctions of 17–18 December. Ouagadougou: Mechanism for conflict prevention, management and resolution. UN Security Council documentation: S/1998/1229.
OAU 1999. Decision on the report of the secretary-general on Burundi of 8–10 July. Algiers: Council of ministers, CM/Draft/Dec.451 (LXX).
OAU 2000a. Decision of 6–8 July. Lomé: Council of ministers, CM/2164 (LXXII)-b.
OAU 2000b. Communiqué of 2 October. Addis Ababa: Mechanism for conflict prevention, management and resolution, Central/Organ/MEC/AMB/COMM (LXX).
OAU 2001a. Communiqué of 19 May. Lomé: Mechanism for conflict prevention, management and resolution.
OAU 2001b. Communiqué of 22 August. Addis Ababa: Mechanism for conflict prevention, management and resolution, Central Organ/MEC/AMB/Comm.(LXXV).
Oketch, J.S., and Polzer, T., 2002. Conflict and coffee in Burundi. In: J. Lind and K. Sturman, eds., *Scarcity and surfeit: The ecology of Africa's conflicts*. Pretoria: Institute for Security Studies, 85–156.
Ould-Abdallah, A., 2000. *Burundi on the brink 1993–95*. Washington DC: United States Institute of Peace Press.
Paris, R., 1997. Peacebuilding and the limits of liberal internationalism. *International Security*, 22 (2), 54–89.
Peterson, J.H., 2013. Creating space for emancipatory human security: Liberal obstructions and the potential of agonism. *International Studies Quarterly*, 57 (2), 318–328.
Prunier, G., 2009. *Africa's world war: Congo, the Rwandan genocide, and the making of a continental catastrophe*. Oxford University Press.
Rautenbach, G., and Vrey, W., 2010. South Africa's foreign policy and Africa: The case of Burundi. In: H. Boshoff, W. Vrey, and G. Rautenbach, eds., *The Burundi peace process: From civil war to conditional peace*. Pretoria: Institute for Security Studies, 11–34.
Regional Foreign Ministers 1996. Press release of 16 August. Kampala. Available from: http://reliefweb.int/report/burundi/regional-foreign-ministers-meeting-press-release (accessed 21 June 2013).
Regional Initiative [Regional Peace Initiative on Burundi] 1995. Cairo declaration on the Great Lakes region. New York: UN Security Council, S/1995/1001.
Regional Initiative 1996a. Communiqué on 1st summit of 26 June. Arusha. Available from: http://reliefweb.int/report/burundi/press-communique-arusha-regional-summit-burundi (accessed 23 May 2013).
Regional Initiative 1996b. Communiqué on 2nd summit of 31 July. Arusha. UN Security Council documentation: S/1996/620.
Regional Initiative 1996c. Communiqué on 3rd summit of 12 October. Arusha. Available from: www.metafro.be/grandslacs/grandslacsdir300/0209.pdf (accessed 23 May 2013).

Regional Initiative 1997a. Communiqué on 4th summit of 16 April. Arusha. Available from: http://reliefweb.int/node/30092 (accessed 22 February 2012).
Regional Initiative 1997b. Communiqué on 5th summit of 4 September. Dar es Salaam. Available from: http://reliefweb.int/report/burundi/joint-communique-fifth-regional-summit-burundi-conflict (accessed 20 March 2012).
Regional Initiative 1998. Communiqué on 6th summit of 21 February. Kampala. Available from: http://reliefweb.int/report/burundi/communique-sixth-regional-summit-burundi-conflict (accessed 22 March 2012).
Regional Initiative 1999. Communiqué on 8th summit of 1 December. Arusha. Available from: www.metafro.be/grandslacs/grandslacsdir0/1671.pdf/base_view (accessed 21 June 2013).
Regional Initiative 2001. Communiqué on 15th summit of 23 July. Arusha.
Regional Initiative 2002. Communiqué on 18th summit of 7 October. Dar es Salaam. UN Security Council documentation: S/2002/1217.
Regional Initiative 2003. Communiqué on 20th summit of 26 November. Dar es Salaam. UN Security Council documentation: S/2003/1112.
Regional Initiative 2004a. Communiqué on 21st summit of 5 June. Dar es Salaam. UN Security Council documentation: S/2004/471.
Regional Initiative 2004b. Communiqué on 22nd summit of 18 August. Dar es Salaam. Available from: http://reliefweb.int/report/burundi/communique-22nd-summit-great-lakes-regional-peace-initiative-burundi (accessed 21 June 2013).
Regional Sanctions Coordinating Committee 1996. Recommendations of 25 September. Kigali. Available from: http://reliefweb.int/node/27285 (accessed 22 February 2012).
Reith, S., and Boltz, M., 2011. The East African Community: Regional integration between aspiration and reality. *KAS Auslandsinformationen*, 9 (10).
Republic of South Africa 1996. *Constitution of the Republic of South Africa*. Available from: www.gov.za/documents/constitution/constitution-republic-south-africa-1996-1 (accessed 1 November 2016).
Reyntjens, F., 1993. The proof of the pudding is in the eating: The June 1993 elections in Burundi. *Journal of Modern African Studies*, 31 (4), 563–583.
Richmond, O., and Tellidis, I., 2014. Emerging actors in international peacebuilding and statebuilding: Status quo or critical states? *Global Governance*, 20, 563–584.
Salim, S.A., 1997. Relaxation of sanctions on Burundi. *Pan-African News Agency*, 15 April.
Shivji, I.G., 1991. The democracy debate in Africa: Tanzania. *Review of African Political Economy*, 50, 79–91.
Smith, A.M., 1998. Das Unbehagen der Hegemonie. Die Politischen Theorien von Judith Butler, Ernesto Laclau und Chantal Mouffe. In: O. Marchart, ed., *Das Undarstellbare der Politik: Zur Hegemonietheorie Ernesto Laclaus*. Vienna: Turia und Kant, 225–237.
South African Parliament 2001a. Proceedings of 31 October. Cape Town: National assembly and national council of provinces.
South African Parliament 2001b. Proceedings of 14 November. Cape Town: Joint standing committee on defence and select committee on security and constitutional affairs.
Tanzanian Government 1997. Statement on Burundi and the incident of 27 October 1997. New York: UN Security Council, S/1997/850.
Tieku, T.K., 2004. Explaining the clash and accommodation of interests of major actors in the creation of the African Union. *African Affairs*, 103 (411), 249–267.
Tieku, T.K., 2013. Exercising African agency in Burundi via multilateral channels: Opportunities and challenges. *Conflict, Security and Development*, 13 (5), 513–535.

Ugandan Parliament 1995. Hansard of 11 July. Kampala.
Ugandan Parliament 2001. Hansard of 1 August. Kampala.
UN 1996a. Resolution of 29 January. New York: UN Security Council, S/RES/1040 (1996).
UN 1996b. Report on Burundi of 1 February. New York: UN Secretary Council, S/1996/116.
UN 1996c. Resolution of 5 March. New York: UN Security Council, S/RES/1049 (1996).
UN 1996d. Press release of 18 July. New York, HR/4299.
UN 1996e. Statement by the UN Security Council President of 29 July. New York: UN Security Council, Statement, S/PREST/1996/32.
UN 1996f. Resolution of 30 August. New York: UN Security Council, S/RES/1072 (1996).
UN 2001. Report of the Security Council mission to the Great Lakes region, 15–26 May 2001. New York: UN Security Council, S/2001/521.
UN 2004. Resolution of 1 December. New York: UN Security Council, S/RES/1577 (2004).
UN Commission of Inquiry 1996. Inquiry concerning the assassination of the President of Burundi on 21 October 1993 and the massacres that followed. New York: United Nations, S/1996/682.
Uvin, P., 2009. *Life after violence: A people's story of Burundi*. London: Zed Books.
van Eck, J., 2004. *Challenges to a durable peace in Burundi*. Johannesburg: Institute for Security Studies, Situation Report, 15 April.
Vandeginste, S., 2009. Power-sharing, conflict and transition in Burundi: Twenty years of trial and error. *Africa Spectrum*, 44 (3), 63–86.
Weber, C., 1992. Reconsidering statehood: Examining the sovereignty/intervention boundary. *Review of International Studies*, 18 (3), 199–216.
Wheeler, N.J., 2000. *Saving strangers: Humanitarian intervention in international society*. Oxford: Oxford University Press.
White House 1973. *Burundi problem: The response of African leadership*. Memorandum. Washington DC: National security council.
Wodrig, S., 2014. Crafting a region while intervening? Regional discourses on Burundi. *Journal of Intervention and Statebuilding*, 8 (2–3), 214–239.
Wodrig, S., and Grauvogel, J., 2016. Talking past each other: Regional and domestic resistance in the Burundian intervention scene. *Cooperation and Conflict*, 51 (3), 272–290.
Wohlgemuth, L., 2005. African sanctions: The case of Burundi. In: P. Wallensteen and C. Staibano, eds., *International sanctions: Between words and wars in the global system*. London: Frank Cass, 126–143.
Wolpe, H., 2011. *Making peace after genocide: Anatomy of the Burundi process*. Washington DC: United States Institute for Peace Press.
Žižek, S., 2000. Da capo senza fine. In: J. Butler, E. Laclau, and S. Žižek, eds., *Contingency, hegemony, universality: Contemporary dialogues on the left*. London: Verso, 213–262.
Zuma, J., 2002a. Speech of 8 October. Dar es Salaam: Summit of the Regional Peace Initiative on Burundi.
Zuma, J., 2002b. Speech of 4 December. New York: UN Security Council. Available from: www.polity.org.za/article/zuma-un-security-council-on-burundi-ceasefire-negotiations-04122002-2002-12-04 (accessed 14 July 2013).
Zuma, J., 2003. Speech of 4 December. New York: UN Security Council. Available from: www.polity.org.za/article/j-zuma-statement-to-un-security-council-on-burundi-peace-process-04122003-2003-12-04 (accessed 21 March 2012).

Zuma, J., 2004. Message of 19 July. Johannesburg: South Africa-Burundi women's dialogue. Available from: www.dirco.gov.za/docs/speeches/2004/zuma0720.htm (accessed 26 August 2013).

Zuma, J., 2011. Media briefing of 11 August. Bujumbura. Available from: www.gov.za/media-statement-president-jacob-zuma-conclusion-official-talks-president-pierre-nkurunziza-during (accessed 18 March 2013).

5 Regional forces in Zimbabwe
'Will we become like them?'

The beginning of regional intervention politics into Zimbabwe is blurred and cannot easily be reduced to one date. In 1998, at a conference in the Zimbabwean capital Harare, the then Deputy President of South Africa Thabo Mbeki tried to facilitate between the Zimbabwean and the British Governments who had taken increasingly conflicting positions on land reform and colonial legacies. Those of us who have not paid special attention to politics in Zimbabwe might first have heard of the crisis in 2000 when land occupations became more frequent on large-scale farms that, at that historical juncture, were mostly in the hands of white farmers.[1] The surge of violent land occupations coincided with a failed referendum about a new constitution that for many signalled the declining hegemony of the ruling Zimbabwe African National Union–Patriotic Front (ZANU-PF). Although the ruling party under Zimbabwe's long-time President Robert Mugabe won the parliamentary elections in June 2000, the margin was narrow and the ruling party was accused of having intimidated the opposition. Although the violence associated with the land occupation and the election was relatively limited compared to Burundi, what was going on in Zimbabwe was met with international outrage. The behind-the-scene interventions of the South African President soon became known to the public as 'quite diplomacy' – a term which was full of criticism for Mbeki, who at this point already acted as president. This public and vocal criticism escorted regional intervention politics for the next decade, disclosing sedimented antagonisms that criss-crossed southern African societies. This chapter reconstructs how these sedimented antagonisms have made impossible the articulation of a common transformative position despite the existence of a regional organisation.

The Southern African Development Community (SADC) could have drawn on the Organ on Politics, Defence and Security Cooperation (SADC Organ) that was created in 1996 to, among other things, formalise regional conflict mediation. For the subsequent years, however, the functioning of SADC Organ was paralysed by divergent interpretations on its arrangement (Malan 1998, p. 2). A compromise was only found in early 2000 – on the eve of the regional intervention in Zimbabwe. Yet, instead of making use of this institution, SADC set up a Task Force on Zimbabwe in August 2001, which convened only a few times and then stopped meeting. Instead of SADC asserting its authority in the field of intervention, agency was initially claimed by other forces: the US Congress passed the Zimbabwe Democracy and Economic Recovery Act in 2001 that functioned as the legal basis for the enactment of sanctions in 2002/2003. The EU followed the US example and likewise imposed targeted sanctions. The British Commonwealth also set Zimbabwe repeatedly on the agenda. In 2003, after being suspended, Zimbabwe however formally withdrew from this organisation.

After a violent presidential election in March 2002, the South African Government continued with its 'quiet diplomacy', facilitating direct talks between the ruling ZANU-PF and the opposition party Movement for Democratic Change (MDC). Some years later, Mbeki (2006a) revealed that the parties actually agreed upon a new constitution which had functioned as a principle bone of contention. Before the constitution was adopted, however, the facilitation collapsed in 2004. SADC did not assume formal responsibility for the regional intervention until March 2007, at which point SADC member states formally mandated Mbeki to mediate between the Zimbabwean Government and the opposition. The former South African Deputy Foreign Minister explained that the facilitation was 'not South Africa only'. Rather, 'Africa is totally involved' (Pahad 2008d). After the violent presidential elections of 2008 Mbeki sponsored the Global Political Agreement signed in September 2008 that established power-sharing between ZANU-PF and MDC. At that time, Mbeki was ousted from president and, in early 2009, from the mediation process. He was replaced by the new South African President Jacob Zuma. The SADC facilitation ended in 2013 after the general elections in Zimbabwe at the end of July.

The facilitation was initially performed by the presidency. Mbeki regularly dispatched those members of the administration to Harare whom he trusted most: especially the then Foreign Minister Nkosazana Dlamini-Zuma and her deputy, Aziz Pahad (Gumede 2007, p. 220). After being officially mandated by SADC, Mbeki and later also Zuma appointed facilitation teams that performed the official intervention. The members of the facilitation teams generally did not comment on their interventions (Mufamadi 2008a, Zulu 2010). The relative silence of the official mediation team contrasted with the polyphony of popular criticism directed against their intervention.

The subsequent sections will also give voice to the numerous, non-official interveners like national oppositions and members of civil society, whose objections revealed the heterogeneity of and divisions among the regional interveners. Unlike the regional intervention in Burundi, southern African forces failed to identify common signifiers that were able to structure politics on Zimbabwe. In the first section, I show how regional forces differed in their sense-making of Zimbabwe. Some regional forces, especially South African opposition and civil society, comprehended the crisis in Zimbabwe in terms of an increasingly authoritarian government. They hoped, by implication, that regional intervention would push for a democratic opening. They thus embraced an allegedly universal template of peacemaking to make sense of the intervention. By contrast, the regional governments, especially, were keen to argue that unequal land redistribution and sedimented racism were at the heart of the crisis. By putting emphasis on inequality and liberation, they thus differed from the discourse usually shaping peacemaking interventions. In the second section, I show how the regional authorities failed to reinvent themselves as a progressive force that was able to represent itself as acting with regard to Zimbabwe. Instead, the crisis in Zimbabwe seemed to infect the neighbouring societies as well. In the third section, it becomes clear that the intervention scene remained complex. It was criss-crossed by controversies about who had to be considered as the problem and who should act.

Lost in difference: the difficult quest for common ground

In Zimbabwe the then latest societal demand for democracy grew out of a constitutional reform movement that formally established itself in 1997.[2] This movement (the National Constitutional Assembly) campaigned for a participatory reform process of the Lancaster House Constitution, which was written during the British-mediated transition from White-minority rule to independent Zimbabwe in 1979. They considered the Lancaster House Constitution as an obstacle to broader democratisation (Matombo and Sachikonye 2010, p. 115).[3] In an attempt to co-opt the constitutional reform movement, the government launched a parallel process in 1999 and put forward a draft that was not acceptable to the constitutional reform movement. The government-sponsored draft did not include a presidential term limit and, in the light of increasingly vocal demands for land redistribution among the people, the government added the last-minute clause to the constitutional draft that 'obliged' the British Government to pay for the land reform.[4] Thereupon, the constitutional reform movement campaigned to reject the draft, which a majority did at the referendum in February 2000. For many engaged in the constitutional reform movement, the rejection of the government-sponsored draft signalled a democratic awakening of the people who had raised their voice against the rule of the former liberation movement (Kagoro 2004, p. 249). It was this constitutional reform movement, from which the opposition party MDC emerged.

The Zimbabwean Government countered the constitutional reform movement by reactivating the long-unfulfilled demand for land. Land occupations became more frequent after the rejection of a constitutional draft. In April 2000, the Zimbabwean Commercial Farmers Union spoke of 6,000 to 7,000 land occupiers on 500 farms (Alexander 2003, p. 102 n. 46). The police no longer expelled the occupiers from the land as the hard-pressed ruling party rediscovered them as a relevant constituency. Violence varied ranging from cattle theft and mutilation to looting property, attacking game guards (Chaumba Scoones, and Wollmer 2004, p. 542), and eventually killing some white farmers as well as black farm workers.[5] In the light of this violent demand for land redistribution, the government initiated the fast-track land reform programme, in the course of which a total of 11 million hectares including the best arable land were redistributed. About 4,000 mostly large-scale white commercial farmers were expropriated and about 300,000 small farmers received land. 'This was the largest, and most controversial, property transfer in Zimbabwe's post-independence history' (Sachikonye 2003, p. 227).

Around 2000, the demand for land reform and the demand for more democracy became markers of antagonistic political projects. The MDC claimed to bring real democratic change. The government, by contrast, claimed to serve a long-unfulfilled demand. In the light of this antagonism dividing Zimbabwe, the regional interveners could not finding a common answer. Instead they were themselves lost in difference. In the following, I will reconstruct how the regional forces became entangled into the discursive order set in Zimbabwe. They could not escape the categories 'land' and 'democracy'.

Making sense of the 'crisis' in Zimbabwe

Analysing the politics of Zimbabwe illustrates the contingency of constituting violence as an international crisis. Compared to Burundi and other places, 'violence was kept at a low boil' (ICG 2004a, p. 79). However, this did not imply that the violence in Zimbabwe was not constituted as an international crisis: 'the murder of several white farmers sparked sharp international press reaction' (ICG 2004a, p. 79). The international and especially the British press were electrified (cf. Willems 2005). A journalist tried to explain the British concern over the killing of the white Zimbabwean farmers by suggesting that the victims of the violence and those reading the newspapers in Britain had similar family names (interview with journalist, 30 August 2012) – which was, of course, a legacy of settler colonialism in former Rhodesia. The British public seemed to be unsettled that 'their' people were becoming targets of violence. Drawing an analogy between 'their' names and 'our' names transcended the spatial distance (and arguably indifference) (cf. Edkins 2002, p. 244), turning Zimbabwe into a state for British political intervention. Yet, it was not only the former colonial power, in which 'Zimbabwe' became a synonym for crisis. The US President argued that 'the actions and policies of certain members of the Government of Zimbabwe ... constitute an unusual and extraordinary threat to the foreign policy of the United States' (US President 2003). Diverse international forces constituted what was going on in Zimbabwe as a rupture with normal politics. Even for those regional forces that eventually became interveners, it became difficult to escape this representation and to conceive of Zimbabwe in terms of non-crisis.

The South African President initially considered what was going on in Zimbabwe as a 'land question': 'the land question, a direct production of the colonialization of Zimbabwe, essentially and substantially, remained still to be addressed' (Mbeki 2000b). The regional organisation SADC (2001a) likewise discussed the Zimbabwean 'land question'. Accordingly, the phrase 'land question' did not herald a recent rupture that called for an extraordinary response. Instead the phrase described a historical legacy that needed to be addressed. These statements, after all, did not testify to a sense of urgency to act from a distant that often precedes the politics of intervention (Fassin and Pandolfi 2010, p. 16). Understanding the events as related to the 'land question' demanded a careful approach to facilitating reform rather than the fundamental external transformation of the politics in a completely dislocated space. By speaking about a 'land question', a quiet-diplomacy approach appeared an obvious choice. But for the regional elites it was difficult to withstand the politics of crisis. In February 2001 the ruling African National Congress (ANC) already attested that Zimbabwe had a problem: 'the root of the problem is that ... [the Zimbabwean Government] is seeking a solution to the question of land reform and redistribution' (South African Parliament 2001, p. 84). It was the British Commonwealth (2001), including the many southern African member states, that constituted Zimbabwe as a land crisis: 'Land is at the core of the crisis in Zimbabwe' (repeated in British Commonwealth 2002). Although the southern African ruling elites were hesitant to constitute Zimbabwe as a crisis, they eventually accepted that there was at least a limited dislocation of normal politics.

Associating Zimbabwe with a 'land crisis' was still far from those humanitarian emergencies where multiple 'types of evils coexist and exacerbate each other' (Ophir 2010, p. 71), that is, where a place is seen as being subjected to multiple social crises that are in need of external closure. Some South Africans however also saw Zimbabwe in these terms, as a place of multiple evils. In the parliament Zimbabwe was represented as being on 'a tragic course'. It was 'an urgent crisis', experiencing a 'breakdown of social order'. One parliamentarian even described what was going on in Zimbabwe as 'a dirty war' (South African Parliament 2000a, pp. 3, 153, 163, 2001, pp. 78, 79, 97). The leader of the South African opposition looked at Zimbabwe as someone 'who sees his neighbour's house on fire' (Leon 2000). He outlined a future, in which Zimbabwe might sink 'into a wasteland of conflict, famine, disease and dictatorship' (Leon 2000). Parliamentarians empathised with the 'hard-pressed and long-suffering Zimbabwean citizens' (South African Parliament 2001, p. 164, see also p. 97). In these statements, Zimbabwe became an almost obvious object of intervention in urgent need of external closure. These statements played with vocabulary typically used to signify collapsing African states (Chaumba, Scoones, and Wollmer 2004, p. 534).

For those seeing an organic crisis happening in Zimbabwe, the signification of Zimbabwe as a 'land crisis' manifested itself as a lie. According to the then South African opposition leader: 'Land is the smokescreen. Avoiding democracy and suppressing opposition is the reality' (Leon 2000, see also 2005, South African Parliament 2001, p. 80, Trollip 2010a). He accused the South African Government of remaining 'wilfully blind to the fact that land reform was never the issue in Zimbabwe. It was political power, pure and simple' (Leon 2003).

As a response, SADC (2003a) accused 'those opposed to Zimbabwe' of having shifted the agenda 'from the core issue of land by selective diversion of attention on governance and human rights issues'. Especially within South Africa, it was clear that Zimbabwe was a place in need of external intervention. Mbeki, as the principle figure in the Zimbabwean intervention scene, initially hesitated to consider Zimbabwe as such a place, as has already become clear. Yet, over time, those voices constituting Zimbabwe as a place in need of comprehensive intervention became louder. In 2002, the then Botswanan President Festus Mogae (2002) publicly called the situation in Zimbabwe a 'drought of good governance', thereby disclosing the heterogeneity of SADC. At a later stage, the coalition partners in the South African Government also objected to the filling of the signifier 'crisis' with land: 'The hastily launched land reform programme was less about land reform, and more about seeking to consolidate the ZANU-PF apparatus and its electoral base' (SACP 2004). It was 'a well-timed electoral gimmick by a leadership that had run out of ideas' (COSATU 2008a). Countering the constitution of Zimbabwe as a land crisis thus paved the way for constituting Zimbabwe as a more fundamental crisis and a state in need of intervention. In December 2003 the then South African President complained that 'the land question has disappeared from the global discourse about Zimbabwe' (Mbeki 2003a). This illustrates how the signifier 'land' only initially functioned as a relevant nodal point in the regional intervention politics towards Zimbabwe (see also Alden and Anseeuw 2009, p. 72). It never managed to empty itself so as to function as a common reference point, as will be argued in more detail in the following.

Beyond the liberal peace: land reform as a moment of ambivalence

In 1993, Mandela (1993, p. 97) declared: 'South Africa's foreign policy will be based on our belief that human rights should be the core concern of foreign policy', hence distancing the ANC from its past as a socialist liberation movement and facilitating the transition from apartheid to democracy one year later. Mandela became the embodiment of liberal peace beyond the West who was imagined as spreading democracy to other parts of the continent. Yet, soon, the South African foreign policy with 'a naïve almost crusading human rights flavour' (Habib 2009, p. 148) encountered objections and resistances. Mandela's public threat to sanction Nigeria's then military regime under Sani Abacha is often quoted as such a moment of open resistance, as efforts to get SADC and the then Organisation of African Unity to impose sanctions led to nothing but to the isolation of the South African Government on the issue (Landsberg 2000, pp. 110–111, Kagwanja 2006, p. 163). Upon assuming office in 1999, President Mbeki abandoned the unilateralism of the past and instead outlined a multilateral approach towards the continent. Yet, the South African opposition leader hung on to this foreign policy position, arguing that the abuse of human rights by the Zimbabwean Government demanded an external and, if necessary, unilateral intervention. The criticism of the South African opposition leader built on the earlier identification of human rights as the core concern of South Africa's post-apartheid foreign policy. He thus aimed to position Zimbabwe within the logic of liberal peace – a move that was, however, countered by many forces within South Africa. On the contrary, in the controversy about Zimbabwe a position different from the hegemonic liberal peace became visible. How was this difference from the liberal peace articulated? I argue that in the debate around the signifier 'land', a filling of intervention was proposed that did not really intertwine with liberal peacebuilding.

It was in the context of the South African Parliament discussing the situation in Zimbabwe in April 2000[6] that the ANC tabled a motion noting 'that the dispossession of the people of Zimbabwe of their land by war, trickery and oppressive colonial wars was the root cause of the two wars of liberation' (South African Parliament 2000a, p. 6). Another motion by the ANC noted that 'continued landlessness among large numbers of Zimbabweans, 20 years after independence, poses a serious threat to peace and stability in that country' (South African Parliament 2000a, p. 9). Almost a year later, the ANC chief whip again emphasised that 'today too much remains in the hands of too few' (South African Parliament 2001, p. 84). In these statements the land crisis was an effect of the violent history of settler colonialism that had established and solidified a structure of unequal land distribution. During settler colonialism and later in Rhodesia, the most fertile and productive farming lands were privately owned by white settlers, whereas the black population had to shift to the Native Reserves, administered under customary law. During the liberation war, landless peasants supported the armed liberation movements, hoping to recover the 'lost lands' (Ranger 1985). Independence however dashed these hopes. The negotiated transition and the dominance of other economic rationalities impeded the major redistribution of land (see Palmer 1990). In the early 1980s, the reclamation of lost land began to express itself in land occupation. Squatters frequently occupied white-owned land but were eventually evicted (Alexander 2003, pp. 83–92). Only in 2000, did these land occupations become visible beyond the local scale. The ANC politicians quoted above thus integrated these land occupations into a history of inequality that had not yet addressed the demand for land.[7] They acknowledged an unfulfilled demand for land, thereby endorsing a signifier for redistribution that was, according to Moyo (2001, pp. 311–314), long marginalised and rather invisible at the international level. It is this identification with the demand for land redistribution that most clearly marks the difference of this regional intervention from hegemonic liberal peacemaking.

The signifier 'redistribution' is not necessarily incompatible with liberal peace. That said, the discursive order within Zimbabwe suggested such incompatibility: with the emergence of the opposition, the ruling ZANU-PF reinvented itself as the representative of the unfulfilled demand for land, rejecting the MDC as representative of white interests. Instead of countering this discursive order, the regional intervention became entangled in the Zimbabwean discourse, either endorsing or rejecting the demand for land. The then South African opposition leader clearly ignored land redistribution as an important demand when he complained that '[white farmers] will lose their property and livelihood to land seizure without compensation from the state' (Leon 2000). Unlike other regional forces, the oppositional Democratic Alliance (DA) condemned 'the violent occupation of farms' without acknowledging the unfulfilled demand for land (South African Parliament 2000a, p. 3). Instead of redistribution, the signifier 'property rights' functioned as a nodal point in the statements and commentaries of the South African opposition. The opposition leader called upon the South African Government to defend 'respect for property rights' (Leon 2000). Referring to

Zimbabwe's legalisation of land expropriation without compensation, he even appealed to 'the international community' to declare the policy a 'clear violation of international law regarding property rights' (Leon 2000). Here, the Zimbabwean politics of redistribution manifested themselves especially as the infringement of property rights.

The South African Government was ambivalent as to how to respond to this discursive order within Zimbabwe. The ANC chief whip in parliament called upon the Zimbabwean Government 'to enforce the rule of law in that country to ensure that the landless majority has access to land' (South African Parliament 2000a, p. 6). By demanding both the rule of law as well as land for the landless masses, the parliamentarian tried to transcend the *either/or*. The South African Government however lost no opportunity to acknowledge the unfulfilled demand for land, whose non-fulfilment they ascribed to Britain's failed obligations: 'Britain undertook a solemn obligation to assist the government of Zimbabwe to solve the issue of landlessness' (South African Parliament 2000a, p. 6). Britain's responsibility for land reform in Zimbabwe is often explained by the negotiations between the Rhodesian white minority government and the liberation movement that eventually culminated in the signing of the Lancaster House Agreement of 1979 and, subsequently, in independent, majority-ruled Zimbabwe. The Zimbabwean liberation movement had previously mobilised against the unequal distribution of land, which was mostly in the hands of white Rhodesians. At Lancaster, the Rhodesian delegation, however, dismissed the demand for land for the masses, thus jeopardising the negotiations. As a compromise the British Government proposed a willing seller/willing buyer scheme, which obliged the next government, conceivably the former liberation movement, to wait until land was on the market and, if so, to pay full compensation. The British chief negotiator Lord Carrington reassured the liberation movement by promising that the British Government would cover any additional costs arising from the compensations – without, however, fixing this promise in any written form (Tendi 2010, pp. 76–77). At the end of 1997 this outstanding promise became reactivated, when the then British Secretary of State for International Development, Clare Short, wrote a letter to Zimbabwean President Mugabe, denying that Britain had any special responsibility to pay for the land redistribution. In the name of the new Labour government, Short offered to support a land reform if it contributed to poverty eradication, thereby dismissing the then latest Zimbabwean plan for land reform as inadequate (Short 2007). The Zimbabwean Government interpreted Short's letter as a sign that the British Government would not honour its obligations (Tendi 2010, p. 74).

After the 1997 letter, the South African Government turned its attention to Britain and their outstanding promise. The regional intervention thus emerged by attaching a particular meaning to the signifier 'land redistribution'. Instead of perpetuating the antagonistic difference between redistribution and property rights, the official regional intervention held the British Government accountable for not living up to their promise. SADC (2007) appealed to Britain 'to honour its compensation obligations with regards to land reform made at Lancaster

House'. Referring to the 1998 conference that was convened to find a compromise on land reform in Zimbabwe, Mbeki argued:

> The British government could not find a mere £9 million to buy 118 farms, which purchase had been agreed at the [1998] international conference. These would have been used to resettle the war veterans who had begun to occupy farms owned by the white 'kith and kin', continuing a struggle for the return of the land to the indigenous majority, which had started at the end of the 19th century.
>
> (Mbeki 2003a)

In these and comparable statements, Mbeki linked together various points in history (the indigenous displacement and disenfranchisement by British settlers, the promise at Lancaster House, and the 1998 conference). This chain of equivalence enacted the British–Zimbabwean bilateral relations as an object of treatment and, hence, South African intervention politics: 'Our view is, ... the British and Zimbabwe governments need to get together to deal with this question' (Mbeki 2000a). This object of intervention was also affirmed by the short-lived SADC Task Force on Zimbabwe, which was 'concerned about the slow pace of dialogue between Zimbabwe and Britain which had not resulted in the anticipated flow of financial resource' (SADC 2001b). The SADC Task Force continued 'urging' the parties to intensify dialogue (see also SADC 2001a).

By constituting historical injustices as an object of intervention, the South African Government circumvented the difficult question whether redistribution had to be understood in antagonistic difference to liberal politics. The regional intervention did not articulate 'redistribution' as a moment of outright counter-hegemony to liberal peace, which supports Richmond and Tellidis' (2014) diagnosis that the BRICS countries have no alternative model of peace on offer. But the regional interveners identified 'redistribution' as a relevant signifier within the field of intervention. Thereby, this regional intervention deviated from many other interventions like Burundi, where interveners privileged liberal statebuilding while marginalising economic inequalities. Initially, this regional intervention was able to differ from the hegemonic liberal peace discourse, only to return to its categories at a later stage. I will reconstruct this return to a vocabulary associated with the liberal peace in the remainder of this section.

An alternative filling of 'democracy' – and its fall apart

The South African Government had long refused to represent Zimbabwe as a bleak place in need of urgent external transformation – as was suggested by others (e.g. South African Parliament 2001, p. 74). These dramatic diagnoses almost necessarily led to calls like *We need to do something!* By contrast, the South African Government emphasised that the Zimbabwean Government was democratically elected: 'We cannot only believe in the ballot box when it suits us. Let us leave the internal politics of our neighbours to the people of those countries' (South African Parliament 2001, p. 87). This statement underlines how, at least initially, the South African Government did not identify Zimbabwean democracy as an object of intervention. The complex lines of signification however, which the South African Government associated with and attached to 'democracy in Zimbabwe' in 2001, only became visible a few years later after a confidential discussion paper South African President Mbeki had drafted was leaked to the public (Mbeki 2001a). This thirty-seven-page long Mbeki Mugabe Paper was intended for internal ANC consumption and hence its argumentation frequently makes reference to the politics of liberation (see Moore 2010).

As the document stands out in length and complexity, it seems useful to start with a lexicometric frequency analysis, as the frequency of certain signifiers illustrates some of chains of signification: From a total of 8,606 words, the most frequent word is 'revolution*' (220 times), followed by 'party' (189 times), 'democra*' (128 times), 'nation*' (106 times), 'state' (91 times), 'people' (66 times), 'masses' (51 times), and 'public' (32 times). It is illuminating that the most frequent word in the document is neither 'crisis' (only 19 times) nor 'democra*' nor 'opposition' but 'revolution*' followed by 'party'. It is likewise noteworthy that 'opposition' is only mentioned fourteen times but diverse signifiers can be understood as synonyms for 'the people', amounting to a total of 169 references. These are more references to 'the people' than to 'democracy'.

The discussion paper begins by arguing that 'Zimbabwe is confronted by a number of problems that require urgent solutions'. This initial sentence already departs from the government's public statements that refrained from constituting Zimbabwe as a place in need of urgent solutions. In the following pages, Mbeki analysed these problems beginning with 'the first revolution': that is, the moment when the 'revolutionary party' ZANU-PF liberated the country from white minority rule. Based on the ideology of the National Democratic Revolution,[8] Mbeki argued that the 'revolutionary party' had the duty to entrench democracy, which ZANU-PF had done at the beginning but stopped doing so by the mid-1990s: 'Rather than advance the objective of the further involvement of the masses of the people', ZANU-PF had abandoned 'one of its most fundamental tasks, the construction of a genuinely popular democracy' (Mbeki 2001a, p. 19). By then, the masses alienated from the 'party of revolution' and 'the forces opposed to ZANU-PF [were] successfully being presented as the true representative of the democratic order' (Mbeki 2001a, p. 21). Aside from the utilisation of the signifier 'revolution', the analysis proposed a rather common reading of the Zimbabwean crisis of democracy: ZANU-PF no longer functioned as the force representing democracy. However, from this Mbeki did not infer that new representatives would emerge as soon as 'the people' no longer felt represented. Instead he argued that the 'party of revolution' had to reassert itself as the 'the leading party of democracy' (Mbeki 2001a, p. 20) in order to further the revolution. The conclusion was stated at the very beginning of the discussion paper:

> Our view is that this task [to address the problems in Zimbabwe] must be carried out by the party of revolution – ZANU-PF – which has the capacity

both to understand the challenges facing all sectors of Zimbabwe society, and the ability to play the vanguard role in addressing the interests of all these sectors.

(Mbeki 2001a, p. 1)

In a nutshell, the South African President filled the signifier 'democracy' with the politics of revolution in southern Africa, thereby significantly altering the meaning of 'democracy'. Within the Zimbabwean field of intervention, 'democracy' could no longer be understood as automatically referring to a liberal concept but stood for the continuation of liberation politics. In other words, 'democracy' – the signifier most closely associated with liberal peace – became an almost invisible marker of difference no longer alluding to formal institutions but to the furtherance of the politics of (economic) liberation. The discussion paper also outlined the politics of intervention:

Immediately, our objective must be to re-confirm the party of revolution as the leading party of democracy. Among other things, this mean that the party of revolution must:

- distance itself from the violence and intimidation of the 'war veterans' and related forces and practices; and
- re-emerge as the greatest and most principled defender of the democratic institutions and processes it has itself put in place during the last two decades.

(Mbeki 2001a, p. 22)

It is striking that the South African President did not publicly reaffirm the objective of helping to re-enact ZANU-PF as the representative of democracy. This public silence is revealing of the structure of the discursive surface within South Africa. The president was not able to inscribe an alternative filling to the signifier 'democracy' nor to openly utter the signifier 'revolution'. At the beginning of the 2000s, the signifier 'revolution' rather signified a past than a future. People no longer associated 'revolution' with 'radical democracy'. In post-apartheid South Africa, the revolutionary terminology of the former liberation movement was replaced by 'reconciliation' and 'empowerment', limiting the totalising horizon of change linked to the signifier 'revolution'. The South African Government instead frequently called upon the Zimbabwean Government to address the land occupations, the violence, and the breaching of the rule of law (Mbeki 2000b, 2001b, 2001c) as well as to enable free and fair elections (ANC 2000, Pahad 2000, South African Parliament 2000b, p. 2, Mbeki 2002a). These demands appeared 'normal' and thus sayable. They could be read as statements in defence of a 'liberal peace'. Yet, against the backdrop of the confidential discussion paper, the statements could also be read as helping to 're-confirm the party of revolution as the leading party of democracy'. Such traces of meaning can also be reconstructed in a public statement Mbeki articulated before

116 *Regional forces in Zimbabwe*

the 2002 presidential elections. Here he appealed 'to all our brothers and sisters [in Zimbabwe] to *reaffirm* their commitment to democracy ... when they choose their President' (Mbeki 2002b, emphasis mine). In light of the internal discussion paper, 'reaffirm' can be read as the 'reaffirmation of the status quo'. It is plausible to read this statement as an invitation to freely and fairly reaffirm ZANU-PF as the leading force of democracy in Zimbabwe.

Instead of articulating a different filling of 'democracy' in public, alternative understandings only became visible between the lines and in the above analysed confidential discussion document. Understanding 'democracy' as the continuation of the revolution thus never became a marker of a regional counter-hegemony.

This alternative, yet confidential filling of 'democracy' was further marginalised after the 2002 presidential elections. As one of the two ANC alliance partners in government, the South African Communist Party (SACP), argued: 'The 2002 presidential election, which our own South African alliance had fervently hoped would lay the basis for a resolution of the crisis (regardless of the winner), has itself become fuel to the fire' (SACP 2004). The 2002 presidential elections dislocated the argument that normality would return without much intervention. The elections furthered the divisions not just within Zimbabwean society but also among the interveners. After naming the elections 'legitimate' (South African Observer Mission 2002) and so coming to a different conclusion than other observer missions,[9] the intervention politics of the South African Government were sharply criticised for not being even-handed but enthusiastically endorsing the ruling ZANU-PF (Sachikonye 2005, pp. 579–580). Whereas some academics countered that 'powerful western countries' have used election observation 'to impose their hegemony and undermine the sovereignty of the concerned African states' (Matlosa 2002, p. 130), the South African Government did not use the fluidity of the moment to articulate a fully counter-hegemonic position. Instead it appropriated internationally accepted terminology. After the 2002 presidential elections Mbeki began to mediate between ZANU-PF and MDC, announcing that the formation of a government of national unity was on the agenda (Mbeki 2003b, Sachikonye 2005, pp. 579–580). No other intervention forces had yet publicly discussed a power-sharing deal for Zimbabwe. However, as I outlined with respect to Burundi, 'power-sharing' was a popular signifier among interveners, considered as being able to bring democracy to deeply divided societies. Instead of articulating a potentially counter-hegemonic position (such as outlined in the Mbeki Mugabe Paper), the embracing of power-sharing as the conception of order thus prepared the ground for the regional hegemony in the Zimbabwean field of intervention – as will be reconstructed in detail below.

Some years before 'power-sharing' emerged as a shared nodal point in the Zimbabwean field of intervention, other forces within the South African Government already rallied behind the signifier. In a discussion paper, the ANC alliance partner concluded that 'there is no solution to the Zimbabwe crisis, at least within any foreseeable future, without ZANU-PF ... (or, for that matter, without the MDC)' (SACP 2004). Therefore, the regional intervention should sponsor 'some kind of patriotic, nationally unifying developmental project that addresses the all-round crisis' with 'far-sighted groupings' from the ruling party and the opposition (SACP 2004). Around the year 2004, 'power-sharing' thus became a visible possibility in the field of intervention, facilitated by the dislocatory 2002 parliamentary elections. Yet, hopes of Zimbabwe being transformed for the better persisted, preventing a rather unambitious power sharing deal to structure the politics of intervention. As Laclau (1990, pp. 39–40) wrote, 'the more dislocated a structure is, the more the field of decisions not determined by it will expand'. At this point, many forces still hoped that Zimbabwe would quickly recover or that the crisis would even be the harbinger of a more prosperous future: 'We look forward to the day that Zimbabwe will once again become prosperous, peaceful and one of the real diamonds of Africa' (South African Parliament 2007, p. 33). These hopes still structured the possible decisions for the regional interveners.

The emergence and demise of 'power-sharing' as an empty signifier

A moment which further dislocated the intervention as practised up to that point was in March 2007 when the MDC organised a rally that was crushed by the police, who arrested many of the activists, among them the Zimbabwean opposition leader Morgan Tsvangirai – the face of the opposition. Two days later, a picture of Tsvangirai's face, badly beaten, circulated on the internet, facilitating renewed international media attention on Zimbabwe (Zondi and Bhengu 2011, p. 9). The then US Foreign Minister called for the 'immediate and unconditional release of those individuals detained by the government of Zimbabwe after its brutal attack' on the rally (quoted by Pleming 2007). It was not necessarily statements by prominent international figures like Condolezza Rice that facilitated a re-structuring of the regional politics of intervention. More importantly, shortly after the beating of Tsvangirai the then Zambian President Levy Mwanawasa publicly criticised the Zimbabwean Government:

> One SADC country has sunk into such economic difficulties that it may be likened to a sinking Titanic whose passengers are jumping out in a bid to save their lives. The nationals of the said country are abandoning it in hundreds on a daily basis and crossing its borders in search of any means of survival in all the neighbouring states or beyond.
> (Mwanawasa 2007)

This statement was a disruption of diplomatic practices among heads of government in southern Africa who had refused to see Zimbabwe as a multidimensional crisis. At a special debate in the South African Parliament about the deteriorating situation in Zimbabwe, a South African Government official also broke with the hitherto normalised vocabulary on Zimbabwe:

> The latest political developments in Zimbabwe, including the arrests, detention and assaults of senior opposition leaders, are a major cause for concern.

118 Regional forces in Zimbabwe

> The South African government wishes to stress its concern, its disappointment and its disapproval of the measures undertaken by the security forces in dealing with the political protests. The current Zimbabwean situation is a manifestation of the absence of open political dialogue, which is regrettably sinking the country into a deeper political and economic crisis.
> (South African Parliament 2007, p. 7)

The South African opposition leader 'noticed a new realism on the part of some members of the ANC' (South African Parliament 2007, p. 15) as they would finally 'realise' the extent of the crisis in Zimbabwe. Another member of parliament argued that 'the scenes of Zimbabwean opposition supporters and leaders being brutally beaten have disturbed many of us' (South African Parliament 2007, p. 18).

The picture of Tsvangirai's beaten face, taken in March 2007, began to symbolise the deteriorating situation. It signalled a rupture, making it more difficult to continuing as before. March 2007 was the temporal moment when diverse regional forces attuned to the call: *We have to do something more!* (Mwanawasa 2007, SADC 2007, South African Parliament 2007). The dislocations thus constituted a field of intervention in which new nodal points could emerge. Yet, as Laclau rightly warned those expecting radical turnarounds:

> To avoid any misunderstanding, we must once again emphasize that the dislocation of a structure does not mean that *everything* becomes possible or that *all* symbolic frameworks disappear, since no dislocation could take place in that psychotic universe.
> (Laclau 1990, p. 43, emphasis in original)

Although part of the structure always remains fixed, dislocations widen the field of the possible. After a period of controversy, the widened field of the possible was sutured again with the emergence of 'a government of national unity' as a nodal point that thenceforth structured the politics of regional intervention.

In the aftermath of the beating of Tsvangirai, diverse signifiers floated in the field, each capable of determining the future of intervention politics. A debate in the South African Parliament reflected this fluidity in the field of intervention. One member of parliament directly called for a 'government of national unity' (South African Parliament 2007, p. 14) and others made related proposals, such as to facilitate an 'all-inclusive dialogue' (South African Parliament 2007, p. 8), to bring 'the two sides to the negotiating table' (South African Parliament 2007, p. 16), to persuade 'the Zimbabwean leaders to meet and find a solution to their country's problems' (South African Parliament 2007, p. 23), and to initiate 'a meeting with both the ruling and opposition party members of parliament with the aim of persuading both to realise the urgency of dialogue' (South African Parliament 2007, p. 31). South African parliamentarians thus already widely identified with the policy to facilitate a dialogue. Yet, others articulated demands that could not easily be subsumed under the signifier 'dialogue': the opposition leader called for 'smart sanctions' (South African Parliament 2007, p. 17). A member of another opposition party suggested that 'Zimbabwean leaders who now reside in South Africa should be assisted to form a proper opposition to the regime in Zimbabwe, thereby assisting in restoring democracy' (South African Parliament 2007, p. 33). Another member of parliament argued that 'the removal from office of the man with the heart of a lion is the only solution left' (South African Parliament 2007, p. 22). Thus, the field was still relatively fluid; sponsoring a government of national unity was one possibility among many.

By then, the Congress of South African Trade Unions (COSATU), another ANC alliance partner in government, also began to publicly position itself on this matter. In a press release issued in August 2007, COSATU (2007b) was very critical of the South African President, who had not yet made 'any progress' in his role as mediator. The ANC alliance partner continued to call upon the SADC governments 'to take a much tougher line with the ZANU-PF government' (COSATU 2007b). A few months later, the Secretary-General of COSATU even reiterated an argument that had hitherto only been articulated by the South African opposition:

We [the South African Government] should have given him [Mugabe] very, very stern indications some time ago that we must act like democrats, allow people to have views, to demonstrate to exercise their basic freedoms or else we will have to *teach you a lesson.*

(Vavi 2007, emphasis mine)

This statement clearly transcends the meaning attachable to the signifier 'dialogue', rather suggesting a more forceful approach. It was at this point that the ANC alliance partner COSATU publicly emerged as the main internal opposition to the official regional intervention politics (Booysen 2011, p. 3). Thus, other possibilities still remained conceivable. A negotiated power-sharing deal had not yet sutured the widened field of possibilities entirely; however, at least 'dialogue' became a more accepted nodal point for regional intervention.

The moment of fluidity stopped around the 2008 general elections. The signifier 'government of national unity' quickly emerged as the only possible solution. Many regional forces shaping intervention politics had lost hope well before the 2008 general elections that things would get better: 'So the environment is so bad I doubt you will have free and fair elections' (Vavi 2007, see also COSATU 2008a). The first round of the general election was on 29 March and the Zimbabwean opposition officially won – yet not without a twist. The Zimbabwe Electoral Commission failed to release the final results for more than a month, closing the space so that a government of national unity became the only possible way forward – as will be analysed below. On 2 May, the electoral commission announced that the MDC had won 47.9 per cent of the vote, missing the absolute majority and making a second round of elections necessary. The second round of elections was scheduled for 27 June but on 22 June Tsvangirai announced: 'We believe a credible election is impossible. We can't ask the people to cast their vote on June 27 when that vote will cost their lives. We will no longer participate in this violent sham of an election' (quoted in Glendinning and Jones 2008). Without the opposition running, Mugabe received 85.5 per cent of the vote and declared his re-election as president. At this time, so insiders argued, the MDC realised its inability to translate an electoral victory into state power (Raftopoulos 2010, p. 708). Even for the Zimbabwean opposition, the 2008 elections thus came to signify the hopelessness of electoral change, a sentiment which they shared with many of the regional forces: 'The intensified nationwide campaigns of violence and intimidation in Zimbabwe have totally put paid to any possibility of a free or fair election' (South African Parliament 2008, p. 10).

A power-sharing deal thus emerged as the only credible horizon for change (cf. Laclau 2007 [1996], p. 102). The South African Government interpreted the results of the first electoral round (MDC: 47.9 per cent; ZANU-PF: 43.2 per cent) as a sign that 'clearly the Zimbabwean electorate want the leadership of the country to work together for the reconstruction and development of their country' (Pahad 2008b). The South African Government official added that 'all political parties in Zimbabwe have indicated that they are in favour of some form of government of national reconciliation' (Pahad 2008c). A sort of power-sharing deal was considered as the only way forward: shortly before the first round of elections, the South African Government partner COSATU (2008a) identified a government of national unity as the only possible solution. At a debate shortly before the second round of elections, a parliamentarian argued: 'The obvious need now is for the formation of a transitional government that will include all parties to take the country through a period of stabilization and recovery before holding new elections' (South African Parliament 2008, p. 10).

Those regional forces pioneering a government of national unity substantiated their position with a myth. According to Laclau (1990, p. 61), a myth refers to 'a space of representation which bears no relation of continuity with the dominant "structural objectivity"'. In other words, the dominant structural objectivity of Zimbabwe was in organic crisis and deep polarisation. A myth, by contrast, imagined a future which was radically different from the present: 'The "work" of myth is to suture that dislocated space through the constitution of a new space of representation' (Laclau 1990, p. 61). According to the official representatives of the regional intervention, a government of national unity could definitely suture the dislocated space. Mbeki expected the government of national unity to do it all:

> Rebuild the state machinery, enable it to meet the needs of the people, overcome the current socio-economic crisis, end the threat of the explosion or implosion of Zimbabwe, end all manifestations of repression, intimidation and violence; and guarantee the democratic and human rights of all Zimbabweans, including their political and other formations.
>
> (Mbeki 2008b)

The signifier thus came to signify a future of order, reversing the chaos of crisis. Mbeki's successor in the presidential office, Kgalema Motlanthe, likewise argued that

the delay in the formation of such an inclusive government only serves to prolong the possibility of such human rights abuses taking place whereas once there is an inclusive government all of that would come to an end
(Motlanthe 2008, see also 2009)

The myth attached to the signifier 'government of national unity' thus concealed the complex origins of the crisis and instead offered renewed hope of a radically different future than the present. This is not to deny more sceptical voices, for instance, among the regional heads of state. The Tanzanian President Jakaya Kikwete (2009) recognised that the formation of a government of national unity was a 'difficult task' as politicians 'with different stands and with a history of hostilities' had to work together. However, he also considered the government of national unity as 'the beginning of a new era in the history of this country', therewith repeating the myth of a different future that is not comparable with the present.

With the increasing acceptance of the necessity of a government of national unity, the signifier itself became the surface for different projections, thereby emptying itself to a certain degree of its particular meaning. As political discourse theory argues, a (relatively) empty signifier 'serves as the container for shifting significations' (Žižek 2000, p. 224). The umbrella trade union COSATU managed to endorse the signifier in principle but at the same time criticising how the South African Government actualised it. For COSATU a government of national unity should build a 'unity for the people' (COSATU 2008a). However, the 'SADC process' had failed to bring 'concrete deliverables' and to ensure a 'transparent and all-inclusive [dialogue] for the all-round participation of the Zimbabwean people' (COSATU 2008a). With a future under a mediated power-sharing becoming more visible, COSATU together with regional civil society organisations became even clearer: 'We reject any elitist power-sharing agreement that fails to address the inadequacy of the current constitutional regime' (COSATU et al. 2008). As an alternative, these organisations proposed a transitional authority led by an individual who would neither be member of ZANU-PF nor of the MDC. They demanded that this transitional authority would include members from a broad sector of Zimbabwean society and would work under a limited mandate tasked with the drafting of a new constitution and, thereafter, the holding of elections under this new constitutional framework (COSATU et al. 2008). Yet this filling did not enter into the Global Political Agreement of September 2008 that institutionalised power-sharing for Zimbabwe. For one electoral period ZANU-PF and MDC would share power; however, they would retain Mugabe as president. Despite these different projects onto the signifier, COSATU (2008g) gave its 'cautious support' to the agreement, albeit remarking that 'the demands raised by civil society and supported by COSATU have not been met'. This support is indicative of the hegemonisation of the signifier: at this point, it was very difficult to think beyond some sort of power-sharing, even though one did not identify with its current actualisation.

The difficultly of thinking beyond some sort of power-sharing was openly addressed by the then-Botswanan President Ian Khama:

> [The formation of a government of national unity] was the only thing that was on the table. Our plea and request for a re-run of that election was never ever an issue. It was never taken up. It was never agreed to. And we made it several times. And even today, we still think that would have been the best thing, to have a re-run of that election.
> (Khama 2009a, see also 2008)

The exclusion of other possibilities was thus very political. In light of the deep gaps of signification criss-crossing the field of intervention it is nevertheless remarkable that a signifier was able to emerge as a common nodal point, structuring the coming politics of regional intervention.

Although many regional and continental forces accepted the necessity of forming a government of national unity, the new regional hegemony was met with resistance within Zimbabwe. The Zimbabwean parties obstructed the actual implementation of the power-sharing deal for almost half a year. Only in February 2009 did Mugabe appoint Tsvangirai as prime minister. In the meantime, the field of intervention changed. Once the signifier 'government of national unity' functioned as the common ground for the regional intervention, they defended this ground. In a rather unusual intonation, SADC (2008) '*decided* that the inclusive government be formed *forthwith* in Zimbabwe' (emphasis mine).

With the institutionalisation of the government of national unity and, hence, the actualisation of the myth, the hopes projected upon the tendentially emptied signifier slowly turned into disappointment. Only for a short time, the signifier 'government of national unity' could empty itself of its actual possibilities, bonding together otherwise divergent positions. In the direct aftermath of the swearing in of the new Zimbabwean Government, the then recently elected South African President and new chief mediator Zuma (2009c) declared its formation as a sign that the 'Zimbabwean political leadership was ready to collectively tackle the political and the socio-economic challenges facing that country' (see also Ntsaluba 2009a, Zuma 2009a). It 'appears to be the opportunity, perhaps their only opportunity, to pull the country out of the abyss' (Ntsaluba 2009c). A South African Government official however insinuated that such power sharing deal was 'more than anybody had expected' (Ntsaluba 2009b). In this latter statement, the formation of a government of national unity no longer represented a better, post-crisis future still to come. Instead, the mere actualisation of such a government was more than everybody had expected. It is a rather pragmatic view without any vision of radical transformation. Such a rather disillusioned way of looking at the power-sharing was also facilitated by SADC (2009c), which had to continue warning the Zimbabwean Government 'not [to] allow the situation to deteriorate any further'. Chief facilitator Zuma likewise continued to remind the Zimbabwean Government and especially ZANU-PF to enact institutional reforms as agreed in the Global Political Agreement (Zuma 2011). Throughout the power-sharing period from 2009 to 2013,

Mugabe instead pushed for early elections – reportedly in order to prevent any of the institutional reforms agreed upon in the Global Political Agreement (Raftopoulos 2013, p. 18). Yet, Zuma (2011) opposed Mugabe's plan to hold early elections: 'The fact that Zimbabwean parties are in an electioneering mode, and are agitating for the holding of elections ... is counterproductive.' The chief facilitator thereby held on to the horizon of some kind of departure from crisis-as-usual. This hope for some kind of change was, in the end, projected into the constitutional reform process – as discussed in the last part of this section.

The constitutional reform process as the last hope for change

After the myth was dislocated by actuality, regional intervention focused on the constitutional reform process. The Global Political Agreement delineated a process led by a parliamentary select committee empowered to coordinate the constitution-making process. The agreement mandated the committee to consult with the wider public, with all stakeholders, and with the Zimbabwean Parliament, before writing a final draft, which in turn had to be accepted by the Zimbabwean electorate. This implementation of this process became the last hope that power-sharing could change something for the better.

Unlike the signifiers 'land' and 'democracy', signifiers referring to constitutional politics had not become subjects of regional debate in Zimbabwe until 2008. And yet the struggle around the constitution-making at the end of the 1990s marked the beginning of the crisis. Constitutional politics remained invisible to most of the regional forces shaping the discourse on Zimbabwe, although the South African President retrospectively disclosed that he had facilitated a compromise on a constitutional reform between 2002 and 2004 (Mbeki 2006a, 2007a), which was however never enacted (see ICG 2006, pp. 3–5). After SADC began to officially drive regional intervention politics in March 2007, chief facilitator Mbeki again pressed for a comprehensive constitutional reform. Once more this process did not culminate into a fundamental reformation of the constitution (see ICG 2007, p. 5, Petretto 2007, p. 2). In short, official regional intervention had addressed the signifier 'constitution' all the way through. Yet unlike 'land' and 'democracy' the signifier 'constitution' did not activate a controversy among regional forces. From a regional angle the constitution did not signify a horizon of change able to suture the crisis in Zimbabwe. Constitutional engineering seemed to be a detail in the wider politics of change.

Yet in 2008 the Zimbabwean constitution-making process suddenly became the subject of divergent regional projections. During the 2008 election chaos, many Zimbabwean civil society organisations began to raise their voices again, rejecting an elite-driven constitution-making process as envisioned by the official regional intervention. For instance, the speaker of the SADC facilitation team suggested that the draft constitution facilitated in 2007 could be taken 'straight to parliament or to the population in order to get a popular mandate for that' (Mufamadi 2008b), not even considering a more people-driven, participatory process. The Zimbabwean civil society organisations demanded in contrast that the drafting of a new constitution should not be the preserve of political parties but of the 'Zimbabwean people' (NCA 2008, WOZA 2008, ZLHR 2008). This demand strongly resonated among regional civil society organisations including COSATU that called for the constitution to be a product of a people-driven, participatory process (COSATU *et al.* 2008). For a short while the Zimbabwean constitution-making process thus became a floating signifier in the regional discourse. This floating element was however soon grounded when the Global Political Agreement determined the constitution-making process to be a people-driven approach, as I explicated above.

In 2008 the signifier did not yet function as a nodal point signalling the last hope for change. This changed after the formation of the government of national unity. Thereafter, regional articulations focused on one element only: that a new constitution should be enacted before the next election. The myth of change, attached to the sponsoring of the government of national unity initially, became reduced to this one element only. This reductive vision of change can be seen in SADC facilitation's repeated criticisms on the 'insufficient progress' and 'delay' in the constitutional reform process as outlined in the agreement (SADC 2011a, 2012a, 2012b, 2012c, 2013, Zuma 2011). SADC was widely acknowledged as having been instrumental in keeping the constitution-making process on course (Dzinesa 2012, p. 4, Sachikonye 2013, p. 181). Other regional interveners including the major South African opposition party by and large reinforced this position: The SADC facilitation should 'use the mechanisms at its disposal to ensure that elections do not go ahead in Zimbabwe until key democratic reforms have been made' (Trollip 2011, see also Mubu 2011). Thus, at the end, the regional intervention was able to identify a common albeit limited horizon for change in Zimbabwe.[10]

At the end of the regional intervention, most of the regional forces shaping the discourse on Zimbabwe endorsed signifiers like 'power-sharing' and 'constitutional engineering', generally associated with liberal peacebuilding. These signifiers promised to bridge the regional differences that came to the fore in the first years of the intervention. The signifier 'power-sharing' was emptied so as to no longer refer to any post-conflict order in particular but change. Official regional intervention promised that power-sharing would suture the dislocated space. Yet this myth soon crumbled. The implementation of the constitutional reform process as delineated in the Global Political Agreement thereafter functioned as the last remaining hope for change. This return to liberal peacebuilding terminology also signalled the marginalisation of all those signifiers – such as 'land' and 'revolution' – that had previously signified the regional ambivalence towards liberal peacebuilding. Only by marginalising the traces of ambivalence, a common regional position was identified. In the regional discourse the signifiers 'land' and 'revolution' however never functioned as markers of an outright counter-hegemony. Alternatives to the hegemonic liberal peace were rather outlined in lengthy, non-public discussion documents. This reveals the difficulties southern African forces had in articulating an alternative peace to hegemonic liberal peace. These difficulties of official regional intervention in articulating a counter-hegemonic peace become more comprehensible in the next section that reconstructs how the regional interveners failed to invent themselves as interveners in the strong sense.

'Will we become like Zimbabwe?' An atypical subjectivity for interveners

Many hoped that southern African states would act on Zimbabwe. Perhaps they hoped that southern Africa would embrace a similar proactive subjectivity as the Regional Initiative did when faced with the mass violence in Burundi. After all such sense of agency in times of crisis and turmoil seems to be a sentiment normally attributed to interventions. The then opposition leader was thus utterly disappointed when such sentiment did not grip the South African Government:

> We have a duty to act, and yet we do nothing. We have a duty to give leadership, and yet we evade our responsibilities. When that happens, then the dream of an African century will remain just that – a dream, a vision or, at worst, a nightmare. It will consist of poetry, words and sonorous phrases, unmatched by deeds, acts and consequences.
> (South African Parliament 2000a, p. 152)

Surprisingly Zimbabwe's neighbours did not respond with anything comparable to the Regional Initiative in Burundi, despite such a response being expected of them. South Africa, especially, had previously been considered capable of action without waiting to be authorised by anyone else. Post-apartheid South African was not a recipient of interventions but, on the contrary, exported its own liberal peace to the African continent (see above). By the time Zimbabwe emerged as a subject of regional and especially South African politics, the South African Government under Mbeki had begun to promote an African Renaissance, calling for making 'the 21st century an African century': 'The 21st century must, of necessity, be an African century in which Africa rises from its long winter and enjoys a period of renewal and rebirth' (South African Parliament 2000a, p. 146). The African Renaissance thus gave a new name to the image of South Africa as a progressive subject on the continent. The chief whip in parliament continued on the African Renaissance: 'Making this an African century will require us to take practical steps to overcome the obstacles that impede the African Renaissance', listening conflicts as one of these obstacles (South African Parliament 2000a, pp. 146–147). Conflicts such as the one in Zimbabwe were thus already constituted as a field of activity for those progressive subjects bringing about the African Renaissance. It thus came to a surprise that the official regional intervention did not activate this well-delineated subject position. In this sense, the surprising element of the regional intervention politics towards Zimbabwe is the non-performance of a subjectivity typically associated with interveners. Instead of performing agency, regional forces began to self-reflectively ask: *Will we become like Zimbabwe?*

Chains of equivalence between 'us' and 'them': 'land' and 'liberation' north and south of the border

In this section I will reconstruct how the Zimbabwean land and liberation crisis struck a chord in the neighbourhood, preparing the ground for the articulation of a regional subjectivity that did not consider Zimbabwe as an Other but as part of the wider Self. Chains of equivalence between 'us' and 'them' limited the official regional interveners' ability to imagine themselves as knowing how to suture the dislocated polity. Through these chains of equivalence, the Zimbabwean antagonisms travelled into the neighbourhood, rendering easy external solutions implausible. I will begin the reconstruction of these chains of equivalence in May 2000. At that moment the then South African President Mbeki gave a speech in Zimbabwe that he introduced with a personal memory of his temporary imprisonment in Southern Rhodesia, today's Zimbabwe, in 1962:

> Whereas the white minority regime of Southern Rhodesia wanted to deport us back to apartheid South Africa, where we would have been imprisoned for many years, members of this country's liberation movement worked hard and ensured that, instead we were sent back to the then British territory of Bechuanaland.
>
> (Mbeki 2000c)

He used the speech to publicly thank the government and the people of Zimbabwe for having helped to liberate South Africa from apartheid. He concluded that 'as neighbours and peoples who have shared the same trenches in the common struggle for freedom, it is natural that we must now work together to build on the victory of the anti-colonial and anti-racist struggle' (Mbeki 2000c). The speech suggested a continuation of the *common* struggle, making use of the signifier 'common' thirteen times in a text totalling 2,503 words. The speech thus seems to reactivate a solidarity between two liberation movements that once had fought for a common cause. However, as Sabelo Ndlovu-Gatsheni (2011) argued, this solidarity was created retrospectively. This speech and similar statements should better be understood as a re-imagination of a common historical struggle that hardly stands up to a historical test. In the 1960s, the ANC and ZANU (still without the supplement -PF) were not brothers-in-arms. They were entangled in a regional competition. The ANC was rather close to the rival Zimbabwean liberation movement, the Zimbabwean African People's Union (ZAPU). In the introduction to the speech Mbeki failed to mention that the liberation movement that had saved him from imprisonment was not ZANU but ZAPU. Although it might be claimed that this is just a historical detail, not really an important element in the argument. After all the ANC forged a deal with ZANU after the latter had won the first post-independence election in 1980 (Ndlovu-Gatsheni 2011, p. 11). In the following years ZANU under Mugabe emerged as the 'authentic' Zimbabwean liberation movement, even integrating ZAPU in 1987, adding the supplement '-PF' (Patriotic Front) to ZANU. So omitting the rival liberation movement can be read as a historical detail. However, it might also be read as a re-interpretation of the past in order to shape the politics for the future. The omitting of rivalry and heterogeneity among the liberation movements in southern Africa created a chain of equivalence between the intervener and the intervened upon that was built upon an allegedly unchangeable and true history. It was a chain of equivalence that was beyond politics and contingency.[11]

Starting from this historically founded chain of equivalence, it was just a small step to argue that both countries shared the experience of 'extensive land dispossession of the indigenous majority' and that this historical land dispossession continued to be on the respective national agenda (Mbeki 2000c). At the time, the land occupations in Zimbabwe were met with fierce international criticism, the South African Government thus drew an analogy between the Zimbabwean land question and the South African one. This is especially remarkable as the South African Government's land policy tried to circumvent the radical land redistribution looming in Zimbabwe. Land in South Africa had a slightly different meaning than in Zimbabwe. Although land dispossession under the Native Land Act of 1913 that limited black land ownership to the homeland was formative for the South African liberation movement (e.g. the Freedom Charter of 1955), the anti-apartheid movement soon became very urban (interview with scholar, 17 September 2012). Most of the ANC leadership spent either many years in exile or in prison. The exiles and 'inziles', as the ANC prisoners were named, lost interest in land repossession. Hence, land was not a priority during the negotiations on the South African transition (Anseeuw and Alden 2011, p. 13) and thus it is less surprising that the lobby of white commercial farmers was able to ensure a clause in the constitution strongly limiting land redistribution (cf. Republic of South Africa of 1996, Art. 25). Instead, the black urban elite began to economically benefit from the new South Africa under the Black Economic Empowerment framework. Against this backdrop, the first post-apartheid South African Government under Mandela had done 'its best to keep [land reform] off the political agenda' (Lahiff and Cousins 2001, p. 653), enacting a willing seller/willing buyer land redistribution scheme that made available land acquisition grants to poor households enabling them to purchase land as soon as the latter was on the market (Hall 2004, p. 215). The initial land reform thus targeted landless and poor communities. In February 2000, however, the South African land policy changed, aiming at establishing a class of black commercial farmers (Hall 2004, p. 216). Large-scale commercial farms were widely considered as more efficient than small-scale units throughout southern Africa (see Moyo 2000, p. 8, Cousins and Scoones 2010). In this sense, the South African Government adjusted their land redistribution policy to the widely accepted paradigm at a moment when the Zimbabwean Government began to radically question it by promising the landless would receive land. That the South African Government drew an analogy between the Zimbabwean and the South African land question was thus a dangerous undertaking from the very beginning. The analogy constructed a comparability, unveiling the non-necessity of South African land politics.

The South African Government was not the only force that drew an analogy between the Zimbabwean and South African land questions. The Zimbabwean land occupations and fast-track land reform strongly resonated among many societal forces within South Africa, repoliticising the land question there (Lahiff and Cousins 2001, p. 652). Land expropriation and the land injustice had remained important symbolic reference points for the majority of the black population, even after the end of apartheid (Gibson 2010). Edward Lahiff and Ben Cousins (2001, pp. 654–655) argued that Zimbabwean land politics brought 'the possibility of rural conflict close to home'. Many regional land activists in South Africa welcomed the resurge of land politics as an antidote to the previous inaction of the South African Government. A landless movement emerged in South Africa organising land occupations that however never multiplied in the way they did in Zimbabwe. Although relatively small, 'it has been able to touch a raw nerve in South African society – the question of whether South Africa will become "another Zimbabwe"' (Hall 2004, p. 223). The Landless People's Movement proposed that Zimbabwe could be read as 'a way forward for a frustrating and slow law-bounded process of willing seller/willing buyer land reform' (interview with scholar, 17 September 2012). Some traditional leaders and their communities joined them as they hoped to find relief from their dire political and economic circumstances. By contrast, white commercial farmers became increasingly anxious about their own futures (Anseeuw and Alden 2011, pp. 1–2). The chains of equivalence between land politics in South Africa and Zimbabwe multiplied, often forging solidarity between those forces on the other side of the border that were considered as being in an equal position. These multiple chains of equivalence thus ultimately enabled the antagonisms that had solidified within Zimbabwe to travel to South Africa. 'There is validity in raising prickly issues by employing allegories, but in this particular instance the allegory that is being used has not only muddied the waters, but it has also excited rather than allayed anxieties' (South African Parliament 2001, p. 118). Making a comment on Zimbabwe had become a device to address the multiple antagonisms criss-crossing South Africa that after the end of apartheid had disappeared from the discursive surface.

When faced with the fear of renewed polarisation and ultimately violence, the South African Government tried to disarticulate these chains of equivalence by accentuating the difference between the South African and the Zimbabwean land questions. Parliamentarians emphasised that 'ours is a constitution-driven programme of transformation' (South African Parliament 2001, p. 119, see also 2000a, p. 9). Stressing the constitutionality of the South African approach thus became the marker of difference, distinguishing between the South African willing seller/willing buyer scheme on the one hand and the Zimbabwean unconstitutional redistribution process on the other hand. The South African President also tried to accentuate the difference to Zimbabwe when he praised the commercial farmers organisation AgriSA for their positive contribution in addressing unequal land distribution in South Africa (Mbeki 2000b). Organised agriculture also demanded a speedy land reform in South Africa was the message. With this public compliment he suggested that the Zimbabwean land conflict had not infected South African land politics. As a means to dispel the spectre of a Zimbabwean-style land reform in South Africa, a new alliance between the South African Government, organised agriculture, and a small group of black commercial farmers thus emerged (Hall 2004, p. 224).

But the chains of equivalence linking land politics in Zimbabwe and South Africa to each other could not so easily be broken. Soon, the South African Government tried to delegitimise those forces that were perpetuating these chains. 'Because there is an assumption that because we've got a black government in Zimbabwe and you have those land invasions, the same thing will happen here' (Mbeki 2001d). The South African President came to regard the persistence of the chains of equivalence between land politics north and south of the border river Limpopo as a sign of sedimented racism. Those perpetuating the analogy were driven by 'a particular stereotype' (Mbeki 2001d). The South African Government had to constantly reiterate its criticism on the Zimbabwean land reform: 'Thus [we will] convince them [the white minority in South Africa] that we are committed to the guarantee of property rights of white South Africans' (Mbeki 2001e). Those people subjected to racist stereotypes would thus suspect all black governments of violating property rights. The then South African President Mbeki also tried to disarticulate, not without irony, the chains of equivalence with a hyperbole:

> After a short study of our politics, a visitor from Mars might assume that *Zimbabwe is a province of South Africa*. With this understanding, the visitor would come to know that some South Africans are concerned that their country is wrongly handling such matters as land reform, the economy, the rule of law and the independence of the press and the judiciary in its province of Zimbabwe.
>
> (Mbeki 2001e, emphasis mine)

In this hyperbole Mbeki exaggerated the chains of equivalence such that they seemed overdrawn. According to this statement the chains of equivalence would constitute Zimbabwe as a province of South Africa. This metaphor of Zimbabwe as the tenth province of South Africa promised to get to the heart of the problem of the chains of equivalence. Instead of looking at Zimbabwe as a sovereign country, those perpetuating these chains of equivalence would suspend its sovereignty, rendering the crisis a domestic issue.

Despite the various attempts to re-stabilise the difference between South Africa and Zimbabwe, the chains of equivalence persisted. The opposition leader condemned the South African Minister for Agriculture for having 'praised Zimbabwe's disastrous land reform policy, saying that South Africa "had a lot to learn" from Zimbabwe' (Leon 2004a). Even after the Zimbabwean land question had long ceased to attract attention, the then new opposition leader criticised the South African Government for not having decisively distanced itself from the Zimbabwean land reform policies. This had 'opened the door for such dangerous discussions to be initiated in South Africa' (Trollip 2010c). The difference between South African and Zimbabwean land politics was however more seriously undermined by the ANC Youth League. The then president of this ANC sub-organisation, Julius Malema, addressed a Zimbabwean audience as follows:

> In South Africa we are just starting. Here in Zimbabwe you are already very far. The land question has been addressed. We are very happy that today you can account for more than 300,000 new farmers, against the 4,000 who used to dominate agriculture. We hear you are now going straight to the mines. That's what we are going to be doing in South Africa.
>
> (Quoted in Smith 2010)

This statement broke down the difference that the South African Government officials had painstakingly tried to re-establish, and the then president of the ANC Youth League created a new chain of equivalence between the Zimbabwean economic present and the South African economic future.[12] As a youth organisation of the ANC, the latter could not ignore this call to copy from Zimbabwe. The then president of the ANC Youth League was subsequently marginalised within the ANC and eventually expelled (interview with scholar, 15 August 2012). In 2013, Malema however launched a new party, the Economic Freedom Fighters, that became the third largest party in the South African Parliament after the 2014 elections. Thus, the chains of equivalence did not fall apart, thereby blurring the sovereign difference separating the intervener from the intervened upon. The persistent comparison between politics north and south of the border was a spectre for the South African Government which they could not dispel. The chains of equivalence between Zimbabwean and South African land politics turned the relation between intervener and intervened upon upside down: instead of seeing an Other, South African society looked at Zimbabwe as a potential future Self that was either welcomed or utterly feared.

And these analogies did not only refer to the politics of land but also to the politics of liberation and government more broadly. The South African opposition leader proposed another hyperbole, seemingly pointing to the heart of the chains of equivalence: *'Will the ANC do a Mugabe?'* (Leon 2008). Here the name of the Zimbabwean President is turned into a metaphor. Mugabe came to stand for a (horrible) prediction that envisioned how the former liberation movement ANC might turn into an authoritarian party that would secure its power by confronting the opposition with violence. This question – Will the ANC do a Mugabe? – re-articulated the chain of equivalence that the South African Government had once constituted by invoking a common history of oppression and liberation. Long before said hyperbolic question was verbalised, the South African opposition criticised the 'ANC's unswerving loyalty to a fellow liberation movement' (Leon 2003). This criticism, which was repeated various times (see South African Parliament 2001, p. 94, 2003, p. 78, 2007, p. 13, Davidson 2012), still aimed at marginalising the significance of the linked liberation histories for the regional intervention politics instead of turning these linkages upside-down. It was the South African Government which first explicitly established the references to domestic politics:

Questions of press freedom, of the relationship between government and the judiciary and the breakdown of the rule of law have been dangled in front of the people of this country as though these were under threat here, in the new South Africa.

(South African Parliament 2001, p. 84)

As with the 'tenth province of South Africa', the critique of the critique aimed at disarticulating a chain of equivalence by exaggerating it. The ANC parliamentarian established a direct relation between the breakdown of the rule of law in Zimbabwe and a threat of a future still to come in South Africa, yet only to illustrate the chain's absurdity. Yet the exaggeration did not stop the chain of equivalence from multiplying.

The most unsettling variant of the chain of equivalence was proposed from within the South African Government. The Tripartite Alliance of the ANC, COSATU, and SACP was based on the common anti-apartheid struggle and the common liberation from the oppressive regime. The concept 'liberation' thus encapsulated the *raison d'état* of post-apartheid South Africa. The signifier 'liberation' functioned as the foundation for the Tripartite Alliance and as the foundation for the ANC's electoral success. Against this backdrop, any re-interpretation of the signifier had the potential to also alter the foundations of post-apartheid South Africa. The Tripartite Alliance members questioned if ZANU-PF could still legitimately be associated with the signifier 'liberation': 'ZANU PF is less and less a liberation movement confidently fostering a progressive hegemony in its own country and in the region, and more and more a repressive machine focused narrowly on holding on to power' (SACP 2004). Zimbabwe became 'a typical example of a derailed revolution' (Vavi 2004). For COSATU, liberation as a mode of transformation continued to exist, but the union's representatives no longer considered ZANU-PF as the leading party of liberation. Instead, others assumed the role of liberators: 'International solidarity, from Zimbabweans and others, played a key role in the liberation of South Africans from apartheid. Now is our time to repay our debt to *today's freedom fighters* in Zimbabwe' (COSATU 2007a, emphasis mine). These statements questioned a certain stabilisation of the meaning of 'liberation', namely that being a liberation movement was a historical fact for the ANC and ZANU-PF. The Tripartite Alliance members however suggested that the name 'liberation movement' was not once and for all earned during the struggle but that the name must be earned time and again. Being awarded the name 'liberation movement' became a condition: 'Liberation must mean a decent life for all, not a selected few' (Vavi 2004, see also COSATU 2007a, 2008a). These statements did not just address Zimbabwe but also domestic politics within South Africa. 'We need to send a clear signal, not just to Zimbabwe, but to our own mass base about the moral and democratic foundations of our own revolution' (SACP 2004). In 2007, this variant of the chain of equivalence, including the re-articulation of liberation, led to the end of Mbeki's presidency. An alliance within the Tripartite Alliance began to strongly challenge his presidency, accusing him of being elitist and of no longer representing 'the people'. The analogy with Zimbabwe had allowed for the re-articulation of the designation 'liberation movement' as a name to be earned rather than a title forever owned. Remaining a liberation movement thus was conditional upon representing the people or at least the mass base, which Mbeki arguably no longer did. At an ANC congress in December 2007 the delegates failed to confirm Mbeki as party president and instead elected Zuma. Although the defeat at the ANC congress had no formal consequences for his presidency, the ANC National Executive Committee, already dominated by pro-Zuma forces, 'recalled' Mbeki in September 2008. The party committee was not formally authorised to oust a president but Mbeki accepted the decision and resigned (see Gumede 2008, Southall 2009). Thus, in 2007, the Tripartite Alliance partners used the already established analogy between politics north and south of the border to project this 'Zimbabwean' diagnosis upon Mbeki's presidency.

However, the Tripartite Alliance members rejected the chain of equivalence once proposed by the South African opposition, namely that the ANC would necessarily drift into becoming a second ZANU-PF:

> Does this mean that it is inevitable that liberation movement leaders, once they have tasted power, get corrupted and bureaucratised? Is it inevitable that they become aloof from the masses and talking above their heads? We do not believe that the bureaucratisation of democratic movements is inevitable but to keep the democratic movement vibrant and democratic it must retain its link with the people.
>
> (COSATU 2008a)

This statement reinforced the argument that the Tripartite Alliance members did not want to challenge liberation as the foundation of southern African politics – as might have been contemplated by the opposition. Instead they attached a new meaning to this signifier.

By being subjected to such persistent analogies between 'us' and 'them', the South African Government became an atypical intervener. Instead of activating a well-delineated subject position that constituted the new South Africa as a model for the rest, South Africa was busy answering the question: What has Zimbabwe to do with us? In analysing the mass killings by the Norwegian Anders Breivik in 2011, Chandler (2014, p. 444) argued that violent incidents 'are increasingly understood to be reflections upon ourselves and our own societies'. Such self-reflective subjectivity is very different from an intervener who towers above the complexity of things. In the remainder of this section, I will further reconstruct this 'atypical' subjectivity that not only bounded South Africa but also the region as a totality.

A paralysed region

Before Zimbabwe became constituted as an object of intervention, the signifier 'region' seemed to refer to a progressive regional space able to manage its own affairs. After the end of apartheid, a 'climate of hope' (Poku 2001, p. 74) that a better future was approaching seized people in southern Africa. Political, economic, and intellectual elites, especially within South Africa, tended to project this hope upon regional cooperation in general and, in particular, upon the Southern African Development Community, whose institutions were considered able to overcome the balkanisation and marginalisation of southern African economies according to the economic wisdom of that day (Gibb 1998, p. 289, Maclean 1999, p. 947, Nathan 2006, p. 605, Taylor 2011, p. 1235). Yet, one scholar expressed a sentiment shared by many: 'over the subsequent decade the region remained wrecked by a high level of conflict' (Nathan 2006, p. 605). The crisis in Zimbabwe was often represented as having dislocated the better future of a whole region. A South African parliamentarian argued that the crisis in Zimbabwe did an 'enormous damage to all the countries of the southern African region'. He continued: 'They are tarnishing the region's image.... They are destroying the integrity of the region's commitment to uphold democracy, human rights and the rule of law' (South African Parliament 2001, p. 124). In this statement, the representatives of Zimbabwe were represented as contaminating an otherwise fully democratic region. This statement excluded all the tensions within South Africa, let alone the previous crises and wars in Angola, the Democratic Republic of Congo, and Lesotho, imagining the region as a homogenous space instead. The parliamentarian understood Zimbabwe as the biggest obstacle to the fulfilment of a prosperous regional future. He was however not the only one arguing along these lines. Another parliamentarian argued that the crisis in Zimbabwe had the 'worse potential direct consequences for South Africa, even greater than the DRC and the Great Lakes conflict' (South African Parliament 2000a, p. 152). He added that 'no country in this region is insulated from the events that are taking place in Zimbabwe' (South African Parliament 2001, p. 125). These statements imagine a shared regional space in which the fate of all states and societies was necessarily chained together. The crisis in Zimbabwe thus infected all the other regional elements, spreading like a disease with no respect for sovereign borders. It imagines the region as a passive entity that is unable to contain or counter the politics in one of its member states. This regional subjectivity bears resemblance to the passivity of the Great Lakes region at the beginning of the intervention. Yet, contrary to the regional politics on Burundi, southern African forces were unable to find new words for imagining the region.

Before the crisis in Zimbabwe, hopes for a better future were often projected upon an integrated neoliberal region that was to ensure prosperity according to the economic wisdom of the day (Taylor 2011). Subsequently Zimbabwe became a wildcard for a force destroying this liberal dream of prosperity. This can be reconstructed on the basis of numerous statements. A parliamentarian argued that quiet diplomacy would impact 'negatively on overseas confidence in Africa at large, and the SADC region in particular' (South African Parliament 2000a, p. 7, see also pp. 155–156). 'They are destabilising the region's economy' (South African Parliament 2001, p. 124). In these statements, Zimbabwe is described as destroying the prosperous regional future by negatively affecting the image potential investors have of the region. The regional space in southern Africa was thus primarily imagined as the field of economy – at least at the beginning of the regional intervention. In this sense, the regional space as it was represented in the first years of the Zimbabwean crisis is remarkably different from the regional space as it was enacted on Burundi. On Burundi 'the region' became a synonym for revolt against a violent crisis, whereas in the discourse on Zimbabwe the same signifier came to stand for paralysis in view of a hampered region.

The South African Government also perpetuated this regime of representation. The South African President said: 'Our region ... cannot succeed to develop without a strong and successful Zimbabwe, [but likewise] Zimbabwe cannot succeed outside the context of a strong and successful region' (Mbeki 2001a, p. 36). In this statement, regional agency remained paralysed as long as Zimbabwe was constituted as a crisis. By implication, once 'normality' returned to Zimbabwe the region could recover its former subjectivity as an agent. At the end of regional intervention politics, a South African Government official admitted that 'the region really wants to move forward and wants to move forward with a Zimbabwe that constructively contributes to this the region moving forward' (Ntsaluba 2009c). During the intervention, the signifier 'region' did not come to stand for agency. Instead it functioned as a placeholder for the impacts of the Zimbabwean crisis beyond its borders. This regional paralysis stood in stark contrast to the agency claimed by Western governments. However, this Western agency also enabled regional forces to temporarily perform a counter-agency, as I will analyse in the next section.

'We stay united in our opposition to sanctions': the emergence of 'regional' counter-agency

The signifier 'sanctions' was introduced into the Zimbabwean field of intervention by the US Government. In 2001 the US Congress passed the Zimbabwe Democracy and Economic Recovery Act which demanded the US President consult with, among others, EU member states on how to 'implement travel and economic sanctions against those individuals [responsible for the deliberate breakdown of the rule of law, politically motivated violence, and intimidation in Zimbabwe] and their associates and families' (US Congress 2001). The act did not impose sanctions but functioned as the legal basis for their enactment a year later. With the passing of the act, to no one's surprise, the US Congress claimed to be capable of managing the transition to democracy, as in so many other cases before and after. The subjectivity claimed by those imposing sanctions was very different from the subjectivity so far enacted by regional forces that had been entangled in chains of equivalence instead of rising above it all. That said, the SADC heads of state were united in their opposition to the sanctions. Even before the act was ratified, SADC (2000) – unsuccessfully though – urged the US Congress to withdraw the act. In 2003, the US President issued targeted sanctions including an arms embargo despite regional objections.[13] The EU and the British Commonwealth followed suit and issued respective directives.[14] As an immediate response, the South African

Government rejected the EU sanctions, arguing that they would not achieve the intended results. The press release continued: 'on the contrary they may further compound the situation' (DIRCO 2002a).

It is remarkable how SADC found its voice vis-à-vis the Western sanction policies. On other signifiers SADC remained intriguingly silent. Sanctions, by contrast, became a common obstacle for a region otherwise paralysed by the crisis. In this line SADC (2001b, 2003b) argued that sanctions 'would not only hurt citizens of the country, but would also have profound implications for the region as a whole'. The US and EU seemed to have missed the various chains of equivalence between Zimbabwe and its neighbours. The potential enactment of sanctions did not only threaten the power of the Zimbabwean Government. The enforcement of a democratic transition through sanctions also questioned the regional logic of land and liberation. It has to be remembered that the South African Government under Mbeki understood Zimbabwe as a land and liberation crisis, which needed to be sutured from within Zimbabwe, not from without. Sanctions seemed to represent the opposite, not being responsive to the complex structuring of Zimbabwean politics. Instead the sanctioners were far removed from the complexities on the ground. As the then South African President Mbeki (2003b) clarified: 'We are not going to, and we have said this before, be going around the African continent, removing governments.' Sanctions thus became highly overdetermined: they signified regime change and ultimately Western imperialism. By opposing this practice of Western imperialism, the regional interveners began to enact a negative agency – not a *We can do something!* but a *We can oppose something!* 'The region' thus began to become visible as a collective subject primarily by opposing Western intervention policies, thereby positioning their subjectivity in opposition to the West.

Subsequently regional forces tried to deprive the sanctions of any justification. A member of parliament claimed that no 'credible Zimbabwean group' had called for sanctions (South African Parliament 2000a, p. 241). An ANC member reported of a meeting with the MDC leadership at which the latter had said to oppose sanctions as well (South African Parliament 2001, p. 122). The South African President recounted:

> The commercial farmers in Zimbabwe ... said: ... 'Please say to the President that it will not help us, it will not help Zimbabwe, to impose sanctions against Zimbabwe'.... So I reported accordingly, and I said, well, this is what the Commercial Farmers' Union is saying. They are not saying the problem, the land question in Zimbabwe, has been resolved.... So when they say: Please don't make our situation more complicated by imposing sanctions, they are not saying the problem is solved.
>
> (Mbeki 2002c)

All of these statements tried to invoke a regional unity vis-à-vis Western sanctions. In these statements, 'the region' is enacted as a united space in opposition to the ignorant and deaf West whose claim to represent the universal reduced their ability to listen to local and regional voices. The South African Government in particular thus tried to lend weight to their opposition to sanctions by claiming to represent a united region. Yet this claim did not go unopposed, as I will demonstrate below.

Many regional forces including scholars and civil society representatives openly disputed this regional unity vis-à-vis the international sanction regime. Brian Raftopoulos (2013, p. 28) reported how the Zimbabwean opposition party MDC and Zimbabwean civil society organisations had frequently demanded sanctions. The then South African opposition leader was also undermining this representation of regional unity when he demanded that the South African Government also sanction the Zimbabwean Government (Leon 2000, 2001, 2004b, South African Parliament 2001, p. 82). On closer inspection the region was a place of divergent perspectives on sanctions. The regional heterogeneity also became visible when a dockworkers union refused to unload a Chinese ship full of arms destined for the Zimbabwean Government that had docked at the port of Durban. The union explained that the employees were not willing to unload the cargo 'as South Africa cannot be seen to be facilitating the flow of weapons into Zimbabwe at a time where there is a political dispute and volatile situation' (SATAWU 2008). The dockworkers thus enacted temporally and locally limited de facto sanctions. The umbrella union COSATU, in support of the Durban dockworkers, tried to launch an international boycott movement under the slogan 'No to lethal weapons to killing and repression! Return them to Beijing now!' (COSATU 2008b, 2008c, 2008d). After the Chinese government announced that the ship would return without offloading its cargo, COSATU (2008d) declared that 'this is an historic victory for the international trade union movement and civil society'. The umbrella trade union comprehended the enactment of this de facto arms embargo (albeit temporarily very limited) as a performance of agency. Yet in this statement COSATU linked agency not to a regional (civil society) counter-subjectivity but to the 'international trade union movement', thereby abandoning 'the region' as a category for progressive politics.[15]

At the regionally sponsored power-sharing negotiations in the aftermath of the 2008 general elections, the signifier 'sanctions' resurfaced, again exposing the heterogeneity of the region. The signifier proved to be *the* site of struggle during the mediation (Smith-Höhn 2010, p. 1). But the official SADC position was not far removed from the one of the Zimbabwean Government. They both wanted the sanctions to be removed as soon as possible. In view of this discursive power, the Global Political Agreement committed the signatories (read as the MDC) to convince the US and EU to lift the sanctions (Global Political Agreement 2008, Art. 4). This provision in the power-sharing agreement thus functioned as means to re-establish a pseudo-regional unity, stabilising the regional opposition against sanctions (Motlanthe 2009, SADC 2009a, 2009b). However, South African President Zuma (2011) soon admitted that not all the parties implemented the sanctions removal strategy 'as regularly and consistently as was envisaged'. In 2009, SADC (2009a) nevertheless 'mandated all SADC diplomatic missions to stage a deliberate diplomatic campaign to lift the sanctions against Zimbabwe' (see also SADC 2010, 2011c).

In an interview with the magazine *New African*, the then Tanzanian President Kikwete (2007a) reflected upon Western sanctions, arguing that ultimately the EU and the US would expect southern African governments to submit to their interpretation of things. In this statement, the regional opposition against sanctions became a short moment of emancipation. As Laclau (2007 [1996], p. 2) rightly pointed out: 'If we are speaking about *real* emancipation, the "other" opposing the emancipated identity cannot be a purely positive or neutral other but, instead, an "other" which prevents the full constitution of identity.' In Kikwete's interview, imposing sanctions was not a neutral policy but it prevented the full constitution of regional intervention. The Western sanctions questioned the regional authority and undermined the regional politics of change: Many regional forces argued that any effective recovery of the economy depended on the removal of sanctions (Kikwete 2007a, Zuma 2009b, Fransman 2011, see also Eriksson 2011, p. 210, Raftopoulos 2013, p. 25). The regional forces tried to stabilise their emancipated subject position: 'It would be better that the rest of the world acted in support of what the region would try, to contribute to find the solution' (Mbeki 2007a). In this statement 'the region' finally became visible as a stabilised subject position within the Zimbabwean field of intervention, claiming agency over others. In this line South African President Zuma asked:

> What have sanctions done to help the situation? SADC, that they are criticising, has produced an agreement. If I were in the shoes of the big countries I would have said here is an agreement and supported that fully and said let us give SADC the chance. Let us remove all the excuses of many people.
>
> (Zuma 2010)

According to Zuma, the sanctions led nowhere, whereas the regional interveners were capable of transforming Zimbabwe for the better. The statement established a clear hierarchy in the field of intervention, with the demand that the international community lend support for 'the region'.

Meanwhile the regional heterogeneity did not disappear. The Botswanan Foreign Minister suggested that regional sanctions could induce quick change, forcing the Zimbabwean Government to collapse of the and relieving the Zimbabwean people from suffering (Skelemani 2009). Several opposition politicians called upon the South African Government to impose sanctions (James 2009, Mubu 2009, Trollip 2010b), substantiating this demand with the argument that the power-sharing agreement had not brought any change to Zimbabwe. This argument was also proposed by the EU: sanctions could not be lifted because of the continued blocking of the implementation of power-sharing (EU 2009).

This heterogeneity notwithstanding, the persistence of the SADC heads of state in opposing the international sanction regime is remarkable. 'Sanctions' functioned as a stabilised Other, allowing the official representatives of the regional organisation to re-imagine 'the region' as a collective subject position that was unitedly withstanding Western imperialism – a signification also

138 *Regional forces in Zimbabwe*

proposed by the ZANU-PF government. Yet, other regional forces undermined this alleged regional homogeneity instead, being remarkably persistent in their endorsement of sanctions as a means to enact change. Ultimately the signifier 'sanctions' was a floating signifier. Depending on the filling, very different regional interveners could be imagined.

'Region' as a floating signifier

During the intervention in Zimbabwe, 'region' was a floating signifier torn between incompatible projections. As I will demonstrate in the following, the signifier 'region' was a site of a struggle over fixing the collective subjectivity. The discursive struggle followed the constantly moving frontier between the rather local logic of land and liberation and the global logic of liberal peace. This is not to suggest that the incompatible projections upon the region always manifested themselves in these terms. Describing the frontier thus is rather an approximation. In the following I will reconstruct the incompatibility in the significations of the 'region' in greater detail. In many statements the South African Government accentuated the sovereignty of Zimbabwe (Mbeki 2003b, 2006a, 2007b, 2008a, SACP 2004, Zuma 2010), which led to the articulation of a very limited regional agency: 'We ... believe that as neighbours, we have a responsibility to encourage and assist them to find solutions' (South African Parliament 2007, p. 4). The regional subjectivity was conceptualised as a force that could 'persuade' (Mbeki 2002c), 'encourage' (Pahad 2007a), and 'create conditions' (Mufamadi 2008a). These statements positioned the regional subject within the complexity of Zimbabwean politics. They explicitly did not attribute to the region the agency to reshape Zimbabwe from scratch. Instead these statements envisioned the regional interveners as *the* external force in the hegemonic struggle within Zimbabwe. As the following quote will illustrate, the region was not envisaged as being one intervener among many.

> We are constantly made aware of messages regarding Zimbabwe that come from regional groups such as the European Union, as well as from individual countries. The difference between their position and ours relates to geography. The only thing that separates us in South Africa from Zimbabwe is the Limpopo River, whereas many of the messages we hear come from far further afield. We in South Africa, as neighbours, will carry the consequences of anything that happens in Zimbabwe, and this fact is fundamental to our approach.
>
> (South African Parliament 2007, p. 5)

This statement is interesting in many regards. The South African Deputy Minister of Foreign Affairs reflected on the difference between regional and other interveners like the EU, arguing that this difference is best encapsulated in geographic terms. At the end of the statement, she specified that geographic distance bears upon the intervener's entanglement with the society under intervention. The statement implied that more entanglement with the society under intervention would bring about more suitable politics of intervention. In other words, this statement rationalised why the region should be the *only* external agent of (limited) change regarding Zimbabwe. Through chains of equivalence, the 'region' was closely entangled with the Zimbabwean land and liberation crisis. The representatives of the region were thus well aware of the complexities of this crisis. According to the rationale, as proposed in the various statements, their knowledge about the crisis legitimised their violation of Zimbabwean sovereignty and their role as the hegemonic agent of external change. It also delegitimised the distant sanctioners that could not immerse themselves in the particularistic logic of Zimbabwean politics well enough.

This depiction of regional subjectivity did not go undisputed. Many regional forces projected a different subjectivity upon the signifier 'region'. According to a South African parliamentarian, 'it is time for SADC to show the resolve and moral courage to deal with the crisis that threatens to topple one of its key members and to destabilise the whole region' (South African Parliament 2001, p. 97). Here the regional subjectivity is envisioned as an acting and determined force that would interpose itself in the name of universalised norms like rule of law and democracy. A parliamentarian referred to the rule of law and democracy provisions as codified in the SADC Treaty that, according to him, could function as the basis for such regional subjectivity (South African Parliament 2001, p. 82, see also p. 125, 2003, p. 77). Article 4 in the SADC Treaty stipulates that the member states should act in accordance with human rights, democracy, and the rule of law (SADC 1992, Art. 4c). However, the parliamentarian omitted that the same article called for sovereign equality and solidarity of all member states (SADC 1992, Art. 4a, b). The treaty thus allowed for multiple projections upon the signifier 'region' to flourish. One of the possible regional subjectivities was an agent acting in the name of universalised norms like rule of law and democracy. The treaty even allowed for sanctioning a member state that undermined 'the principles and objectives of SADC' (Art. 33, pt. 1). These statements and provisions thus envisage an assertive regional intervener, enforcing universalised norms at the expense of deviant local politics. This regional intervener was very different from the regional facilitator who respects local complexity.

With the passing of the SADC 'Principles and Guidelines Governing Democratic Elections' in 2004, those forces hoping for this universalised regional subjectivity felt strengthened – initially at least.[16] But shortly before SADC officially enacted the guidelines, the Zimbabwean Government announced a reform of its electoral provisions (ICG 2004b, p. 13). In this way the Zimbabwean Government was able to represent itself as being the first regional state to comply with the SADC electoral guidelines. Whereas many scholars have 'dismissed these changes as cosmetic and essentially a ploy to hoodwink the international community' (Kagwanja 2005, p. 6), SADC (2004) acknowledged that 'the government of Zimbabwe has drafted electoral legislation consistent with the newly adopted SADC Principles and Guidelines Governing Democratic Elections'.

This self-presentation as the 'first complier' with the SADC guidelines resonated among SADC constituencies. In the aftermath of the 2005 elections, SADC officials working at the headquarters in Gaborone were quoted as saying that Zimbabwe 'made an important contribution by becoming the first member state to attempt to incorporate them [the guidelines] into its laws and procedures' (ICG 2005, p. 19). In this sense, the SADC guidelines immediately became a floating element in the struggle over regional subjectivity. That the guidelines were subject to incompatible projections is also conveyed in the following statement. The Tanzanian President rejected the interpretation that the guidelines marked a change in the regional subjectivity: 'Contrary to what is often portrayed in the media, these principles are not directed at anyone, or any group of countries' (IRIN 2004). The official representative of SADC was thus very careful not to help craft a regional subjectivity that intervened in the name of universalised principles (or regional guidelines). Despite this rejection of a liberal subjectivity that championed universalised rules instead of hybrid peace, the SADC guidelines nevertheless began to function as a reference point. Prior to the 2008 elections the South African Government called for the strict observance of the guidelines (Pahad 2008a). In the election's aftermath, COSATU (2008e) concluded that 'the SADC protocols governing the conduct of elections were clearly breached in Zimbabwe' (see also ZCTU and COSATU 2009). And the then Botswanan President Khama (2008) reminded his regional colleagues that 'it is important for all SADC member states to uphold the regional standards they have collectively and voluntarily adopted'. In October 2008, COSATU campaigned for 'a SADC transformation project' that would allow societal groups to participate in the SADC decision-making process in order to enforce compliance amongst member states with the norms agreed upon in treaties and protocols (COSATU 2008h). It shows that many regional forces were at odds with the performance of regional subjectivity. In contradistinction to the entangled regional subjectivity articulated by the South African Government, many regional forces wanted a regional organisation that rose above the complexity on the ground, changing the course of events according to non-negotiable standards.

But the regional entanglements rendered void the hopes of a different regional subjectivity. In October 2007, the white Zimbabwean farmer Mike Campbell filed a case at the SADC Tribunal, challenging the fast-track land reform and more specifically the legal clause allowing land expropriation without compensation.[17] This verdict could have inspired those wanting to craft a regional subjectivity that acted on the basis of non-negotiable standards. And initially it seemed that the regional court would perform this function. A year later the Tribunal ruled that the clause was in breach of the SADC Treaty. Expropriations should be stopped and, when already executed, the Zimbabwean Government should compensate the farmers.[18] When the Zimbabwean Government however refused to comply, the SADC heads of state decided to suspend the Tribunal for a year in order to undertake 'a review of the role functions and terms of reference of the SADC Tribunal' (SADC 2010). In May 2011, the review process was extended for another year (SADC 2011b). Within South Africa, the opposition party harshly criticised SADC for having sided with Mugabe in violating the rule of law (Trollip 2011). The opposition leader concluded that 'it is hugely significant that SADC appears to have willingly dismantled its most respected structure to protect a rogue member state' (Trollip 2010d). With respect to the tribunal, SADC representatives did not perform according to the standards of the region but produced an entangled subjectivity.

The signifier 'region' thus remained a floating signifier throughout the intervention. It was claimed by two incompatible discourses that pictured almost antithetic regional interveners. Even though many voices from within the region imagined a regional subjectivity speaking in the name of universalised standards, this filling did not prevail. The other filling of the signifier was hegemonic. The 'region' became visible as entangled. Through chains of equivalence that tied South Africa and the region to Zimbabwe (and vice versa), the regional space was part of the complexities of the crisis of land and liberation. Along these chains, antagonisms travelled, not just speaking of the divisions within Zimbabwe, but also of similar divisions within the entire region – as I will detail in the next section. These entanglements did not allow for a regional intervener who rose above these complexities. In pointed terms: *instead of SADC rules and institutions shaping the regional interveners, Zimbabwe shaped the regional subjectivity.*

Dictators, stooges and imperialists: reconstructing antagonisms and regional divisions

The societal divisions criss-crossing Zimbabwe thus travelled beyond its borders along the chains linking the discursive order of Zimbabwe to the discursive order of its neighbourhood. In this last section, these divisions become visible as antagonisms that sustained the respective position on the regional intervention.

Mugabe 2000–2008: a larger-than-life political figure[19]

Many people ascribed the economic and political meltdown to the deeds of one man. A biographer of the 'freedom fighter who became a tyrant' wrote, that at some point in history his 'audacious ideas were to become synonymous with Zimbabwe' (Holland 2008, p. xii). Others heavily criticised 'Mugabe-centrism' on the grounds that an exclusive focus on one man would disguise broader historical and contemporary structuring (Ndlovu-Gatsheni 2012, pp. 317–318). How did the regional forces represent Mugabe? And how was this representation of Mugabe related to the subjectivity of the regional interveners? In the following I argue that, from 2000 to 2008, the regional forces were radically divided in their signification of Mugabe. The question *What's your take on Mugabe?* could also count as a synonym for a question about one's perspective on regional intervention politics. Mugabe embodied the rifts criss-crossing the region. The South African opposition was sure from the very beginning that the crisis in Zimbabwe was in fact attributable to one man: driven by his 'megalomania', the 'tyrant' created a multiplicity of crisis in order to stay in power (South African

Parliament 2001, p. 116). Zimbabweans were 'consumed by the fire and ire of the tyrant' (South African Parliament 2003, p. 201, see also 2007, p. 22). In pointed terms, 'the problem is not Zimbabwe and the problem is not the Zimbabweans either; the problem is the president of Zimbabwe, Mr Robert Mugabe, himself' (South African Parliament 2007, p. 20). In all of these statements, Mugabe was an omnipotent figure shaping the politics of Zimbabwe. He was not a representative of popular demands (for land, for example) but an evil person detached from society. He was not the most visible figure of a state structurally sponsoring large-scale violence since colonial times but an individual who stayed in power at all costs (for a critique on the over-determination of agency, see South African Parliament 2001, p. 122). This signification of Mugabe radically reduced the complexity of the Zimbabwean crisis that suddenly did not seem too difficult to solve: The solution *Mugabe must go!* was already being fabricated.

Initially the South African opposition called for the isolation of Mugabe (Leon 2000). A member of parliament argued that a tyrant like Mugabe must be removed at the ballot box and, if he would not accept the outcome of the election, he 'must be forced to accept the results' (South African Parliament 2001, p. 99). The parliamentarian however did not further specify the means of forcing Mugabe into acceptance. The South African President interpreted these statements as following:

> And when people say: Do something, we say to them: Do what? And nobody gives an answer, because they know that when they say: Do something, what they mean is march across the Limpopo and overthrow the government of President Mugabe, which we are not going to do.
>
> (Mbeki 2002c)

The South African President drew these conclusions at a time when the US Government was planning its intervention in Iraq. Around that time, the signifier 'regime change' emerged as a nodal point in foreign policy making. On the African continent many governments were alarmed (Raftopoulos 2010, p. 710). In this discursive environment the South African President began to articulate links between those regional forces reducing the crisis to the deeds of one man and the US regime-change policy: 'The notion that South Africa can walk across the Limpopo and remove that government – do what President Bush calls regime change in Zimbabwe – this is not going to happen' (Mbeki 2002c). Mbeki thus linked the South African opposition to the US regime-change policy, therewith putting strain on the position represented by the South African opposition. At that time no US politician explicitly advocated regime change in Zimbabwe. However, when the US Congress enacted the Zimbabwe Democracy and Economic Recovery Act in 2001, it mandated the US Government 'to support the people of Zimbabwe in their struggle to effect peaceful, democratic change' (US Congress 2001, sec. 2). The act testified of a US liberal peace policy vis-à-vis Zimbabwe, which was however not yet hyper-conservative – that is, openly advocating force as a means to enact liberal change (cf. Richmond 2006). Only in 2005, the then US Foreign Minister Condoleezza Rice called Zimbabwe one of the 'outposts of tyranny', linking it to the 'axis of evil'. Mbeki thus built upon the US regime-change policy to delegitimise the signification of Mugabe as the principle obstacle to peace. Those forces perpetuating this signification became advocates of 'Iraq-style' regime change.

Some regional forces considered it necessary to maintain a distance from regime-change policies: 'regime change should not be the goal of any war' (South African Parliament 2003, p. 107). The South African parliamentarian continued:

> the people themselves should get rid of the tyrant, however difficult that may be. He added: 'The protest marches in the streets of Harare indicate that the people of Zimbabwe are also finally prepared to take on the responsibility of regime change and it is obvious that Mugabe's days are numbered'.
> (South African Parliament 2003, p. 107)

It is remarkable how the globalised image of regime change haunted those signifying Mugabe as the biggest obstacle. In this statement, internal protest became overdetermined as a sign of approaching regime change rather than as a sign of a protracted societal conflict. This statement articulated a sentiment shared by many, namely that Mugabe's presidency was just about to end. There has been continuous guesswork about his internal 'heir', with many potential heirs coming and going, as well as rumours about his fading health throughout the Zimbabwean crisis.

The pictures of the Zimbabwean opposition leader Tsvangirai beaten up by the police after a rally in March 2007 disrupted the normality of the regional discourse. After the picture circulated on the internet many regional forces including SADC explicitly or implicitly said: We need to do something! (see above) Those wishing Mugabe to be removed from presidency multiplied, as became obvious during a parliamentary debate at the end of March 2007: 'The problem is, Mr Mugabe: Go home!' (South African Parliament 2007, p. 21); 'it is time for him to leave' (South African Parliament 2007, p. 26). 'While waiting for the departure of the Mugabe regime ...' (South African Parliament 2007, p. 32). 'If [Mugabe] does not abdicate, he should be removed forcibly', a South African parliamentarian further specified (South African Parliament 2007, p. 18). In the South African Parliament, it thus became normal to wait for his removal. The COSATU Secretary-General also agreed: 'We [South Africa] should have given him very, very stern indications some time ago that we must act like democrats ... or else we will have to teach you a lesson' (Vavi 2007). After the March 2008 general elections, regional voices calling for the end of Mugabe's presidency became even louder. COSATU (2008d) refused to recognise 'a regime that is determined to cling to power by stealing the elections and imposing its will through violence'. The South African Tripartite Alliance member prompted his ANC partner to reject Mugabe as an illegal, illegitimate despot (see also COSATU 2008f). The Botswanan Government equally positioned itself against Mugabe (Khama 2009a, Skelemani 2009) and leaked information suggesting that, in private, the former Zambian President Levy Mwanawasa[20] came out strongly against Mugabe (Khama 2009b, Skelemani 2009). Additionally, the Tanzanian President reported after a visit to Europe that 'they [the EU] see President Mugabe as some kind of devil, somebody who shouldn't have been there, and they think that we in Africa should have done something to have him removed' (Kikwete 2007a). The understanding that Mugabe constituted the single most important obstacle to Zimbabwe's political and economic betterment thus gained momentum among regional forces but also among the international community at large.

Constituting Mugabe as an obstacle created a clear target for intervention. In the terminology of political discourse theory, the polyphonic call of 'Mugabe must go' can be reconstructed as the (temporal) stabilisation of an antagonism. This antagonism reduced complexity such as to guide the (potential) interveners in what to do. It has to be recalled that an antagonism is not an objective presence. In the words of Laclau and Mouffe (2001 [1985], p. 125), 'its objective being is a symbol of my non-being'. The antagonising force (in this ontic case Mugabe) does not have an objective presence but, by functioning as the antagonising force, it *ex negativo* signifies the being of those antagonising it. Those demanding Mugabe's removal reinvented themselves as external interveners confronting a ruthless dictator. They became the international voices of 'the Zimbabwean people' who could not speak for themselves. The previous sections would tell a different story if the antagonism against Mugabe had become normalised and sedimented. Prior to the stabilisation of the antagonism against Mugabe, the then South African President Mbeki accused those perpetuating the antagonism of being racist:

> The white minority in South Africa had worked itself into a frenzy of fear about and hatred of Mugabe ... in much the same way that it had educated itself to fear and loathe an ANC composed of 'terrorists and communists'.
> (Mbeki 2001e)

By equating the then ongoing securitisation of Mugabe with the apartheid-regime's defamation of the ANC, the antagonism became a misguided and ultimately racist reading of Zimbabwe. However, this counter-representation lost plausibility when more and more regional forces perpetuated the antagonism. After the protest rally in March 2007, a South African Government official tried to counter the emerging stabilisation of the antagonism by repeating the justification propagated by the Zimbabwean Government, namely that external and internal 'regime changers' orchestrated the protest. The South African Government official added: 'I do not say that I accept this view, but this is a strong view held by senior government officials in Zimbabwe' (Pahad 2007a). Despite the note of caution, this statement tried to delegitimise those protesting as 'regime changers'. Such a reading could build upon a previous articulation enunciated by the president himself:

> It is clear that some within Zimbabwe and elsewhere in the world, including our country, are following the example set by 'Reagan and his advisers', to

'treat human rights as a tool' for overthrowing the government of Zimbabwe and rebuilding Zimbabwe as they wish. In modern parlance, this is called regime change.

(Mbeki 2003a)

This statement not only rejects external regime changes (as frequently practised by the US Government) but equated the illegitimate, external practice with internal anti-regime protest. Rather than conceptualising the latter as a practice of legitimate resistance against an authoritarian government, the internal anti-regime protesters became the extension of external forces. Additionally, SADC (2007) publicly reaffirmed its solidarity with the Zimbabwean Government under Mugabe. The Tanzanian President stressed that SADC would not remove Mugabe from office. Change could only be enacted through elections (Kikwete 2007a). A former Zambian President even argued that 'one shouldn't ignore history when judging Mugabe today', referring to the huge personal commitment for fighting for independence: 'We shouldn't demonize Mugabe. He went through hell' (Kaunda 2007a, see also 2007b). It shows how influential regional voices undermined the stabilisation of the antagonism that the figure of Mugabe seemed to embody.

The temporarily stabilised antagonism divided those reproducing it from those undermining it. How people felt about Mugabe said a lot about the regional subjectivity they hoped for. Constituting Mugabe as *the* problem allowed the possibility of a strong regional intervener, directing the intervention towards the correction of the problem. By rejecting this reductive antagonism, however, the regional interveners could no longer function as an agent of change. Instead SADC was thrown into a situation too complex to be controlled.

The Zimbabwean opposition and the region: hitting a glass ceiling

In 1999, members of the constitutional reform movement and the Zimbabwe Congress of Trade Unions founded the Movement of Democratic Change.[21] As the name suggests, the then new Zimbabwean opposition party rallied around the call for change. As an almost empty container able to accommodate shifting politics, the signifier 'change' signalled a departure from the post-independence status quo. The signifier 'change' provided the ground for temporally uniting heterogeneous forces, yet delaying the emergence of a more specific policy profile of the opposition. The clarification of the profile became further postponed once the crisis gathered pace in 2000 (Dansereau 2003, p. 186, Laakso 2003, p. 129, Maroleng 2004, p. 2). How did the regional forces make sense of the emergence of an opposition? And did the representation of the opposition structure their understanding of themselves? In the following I will analyse how the opposition's rallying cry – change! – never gripped official regional intervention. SADC and the South African Government were very careful not to openly constitute the MDC as a problem, though they were frequently accused of antagonising the Zimbabwean opposition in practice. By analysing the text corpus, it was possible to trace the contours of this antagonism. However, this antagonism became manifest especially through what SADC and the South African Government *did not* say (or do). For instance, the South African opposition criticised the South African Government for not openly expressing its support for the MDC (South African Parliament 2001, pp. 95, 98, 113, 2003, p. 79). The leader of the South African opposition contrasted how the South African Government frequently met Mugabe and other government officials while at the same time 'avoiding' Tsvangirai and other MDC officials (Leon 2003). In his autobiography he also recalled how he had approached the then South African Foreign Minister, reporting about the human rights violations he had witnessed in Zimbabwe.

> She [the then South African foreign minister] listened in largely polite silence, took no notes, and the meeting was unwitnessed by any departmental official. I left the meeting dismayed, if not altogether surprised. It was clear that little would be done to deter Mugabe from proceeding down the road to tyranny
>
> (Leon 2008, p. 359).

Here the antagonism was detected in a bureaucratic machinery that did not process information the way it was expected. Further above it was a government that did not exchange handshakes with the Zimbabwean opposition with the same frequency as with its Zimbabwean counterparts. These were practices of omission that were read as the manifestations of an antagonism that separated official regional intervention from the Zimbabwean opposition. It is difficult to capture such an antagonism. Those making it visible could only describe traces that are more disputable than tangible. But on closer inspection more tangible traces than these omissions can be found.

The South African Government often signified the MDC as an obstacle to any solution – though in a subtle way. For instance, after the 2002 presidential elections the South African Government together with its Nigerian counterpart initiated a first round of facilitation. But the MDC also filed a lawsuit about the elections, which they had lost officially. After that, the Zimbabwean Government refused to continue the facilitation, arguing that the court had to decide first.[22] The regional interveners accepted this, explaining that regional intervention cannot proceed 'until this court matter has been addressed' (Mbeki 2003b). The lawsuit became the obstacle for the continuation of the regional intervention.[23] In this sense, the MDC became a typical figure in the intervention scene, namely somebody who was obstructing the quest for peace. This figure has often served as a means of substantiating the intervener as a force of the greater good. In this statement the MDC – even if subtly – becomes this figure, even though many other people regarded them as the good guys. In 2003 the Zimbabwean opposition leader Tsvangirai published an article in the *South African Journal of International Affairs* accusing the South Africa Government of antagonising them:

> The Movement of Democratic Change accepted the offer [of facilitation] in good faith and in line with its commitment to peaceful resolution of political

disputes. However, the party now realises that the offer was nothing but a cynical act of deception. The real strategy of [the South Africa and Nigerian Governments] was simply to give Zimbabweans a false sense of hope and thereby buy time for Mugabe to make good his bloody electoral fraud and consolidate his dictatorship.

(Tsvangirai 2003, pp. 131–132)

The antagonism that separated the official regional intervention from the Zimbabwean opposition was subtle, like a glass ceiling, limiting the possibilities of the MDC. The empirical manifestation of this antagonism facilitated an intervention that contrasted with the policy inspired by antagonism to Mugabe. The antagonism did not suggest removing the MDC but ignoring it. Until that moment it was just not necessary to openly represent the Zimbabwean opposition as not capable of governing the country – as was later argued.

With the start of the official SADC mediation in March 2007, some SADC officials denied that such antagonism had existed (Kikwete 2007a, Pahad 2007b). However, soon, the antagonism separating the regional elites from the Zimbabwean opposition became more openly articulated than even before. The former Zambian President publicly admitted: 'It is not that I [don't] think Tsvangirai can make a good leader' (Kaunda 2007b). After the 2008 general elections, the SADC facilitation responded to a critique articulated by Tsvangirai, describing him as somebody 'who may have opinions that are not based on sufficient appreciation of what is going on' (Mufamadi 2008b). The member of the facilitation team added: 'When people are unable to find their way out of the problem they look for somebody to blame' (Mufamadi 2008b, see also Pahad 2008d, Chikane 2009). In these statements, Tsvangirai is seen as a bad leader who had not (yet) learnt the art of politics. A scholar and activist reported that the South African presidency had serious doubts about the MDC's capacity to form a stable government that would be able to gain the confidence of the armed forces (Raftopoulos 2007, p. 142). In these statements, official representatives of the regional intervention dared to openly declare the MDC a problem for the future of Zimbabwea for the first time. The official regional interveners represented the MDC as not capable of governing the country at a moment when their becoming the next government seemed a real possibility.

The most serious and insightful marker of antagonism was however enunciated by Mbeki in a private letter at the end of 2008 that was eventually leaked to the public. Preceding the letter, ZANU-PF and MDC strongly disagreed on who should head the Ministry of Home Affairs (the ministry that controls the police and supervises the elections). As a compromise, SADC (2008) decided that the ministry should be co-managed. The MDC, however, opposed this decision, arguing that without the full control over this powerful ministry they could not lay the foundations for a more democratic state (ICG 2008, p. 1). Tsvangirai explained the MDC's decision in a private letter addressed to Mbeki, who responded with the following:

The pain your country [Zimbabwe] bears is a pain that is transferred to the masses of our people.... This particular burden is not carried by the countries of Western Europe and North America.... I say this humbly to advise that it does not help Zimbabwe, nor will it help you as prime minister of Zimbabwe, that the MDC (T) contemptuously repudiates very serious decisions of our region ... describing them as *'a nullity'*.

(Mbeki 2008b, emphasis in original)

The letter is a very interesting testimony to the politics of scale underlying the regional intervention. In it Tsvangirai is represented as resisting regional intervention and subjecting himself to Western politics instead. The South African President criticised the MDC under Tsvangirai for not accepting regional/African authority in the Zimbabwean field of intervention, as also became visible in the afterthought: 'All of us will find it strange and insulting that ... you choose to describe us in a manner that is most offensive in terms of African culture, and therefore offend our sense of dignity as Africans' (Mbeki 2008b). The MDC is represented as not conforming to African-ness. It is constituted as undermining the regional subjectivity (the variant performed by the official regional interveners). The then Zambian President was even more blunt when he announced that he would not stop ZANU-PF from abandoning the government of national unity. He added: 'We don't know the policies of Morgan [Tsvangirai] – he has other people speaking for him rather than speaking for himself' (Sata 2012), indirectly calling him a Western stooge. In the terminology of political discourse theory, and in pointed terms, the MDC ultimately became a placeholder for a force undermining the regional authority in the world – as will be further reconstructed in the next section.

The ultimate antagonist of regional authority: counter-hegemony in the Zimbabwean field of intervention

Compared with the initial years of the Regional Peace Initiative on Burundi in the mid-1990s, by the end of the millennium regional interveners were already somewhat established. There was no need to invent a new subjectivity, building on a radical differentiation from something already existing in order to become an intervener. Yet, subjectivity is performative and, as we will see in this section, the difference separating 'the region' from 'the West' was even deeper and especially more stable than in the Burundian field of intervention.

From the beginning of the intervention in 2000, part of the regional forces clearly and strongly antagonised 'the West' and its associated forces. 'Colonialism' did not function as a signifier referring to a relatively distant past but the Zimbabwean crisis was directly related to British-colonial entanglements, as detailed at the beginning of this chapter. The South African Government constituted what was going on in Zimbabwe as a 'land crisis' that was caused by the British failure to live up to their financial commitments given at the Lancaster House negotiations in 1979. Therefore, initially, the British

Government was blamed with failing independent Zimbabwe. Regional statements referring to Britain's outstanding obligation to pay for land redistribution however did not openly antagonise Britain. They did not depict Britain, for example, as a pathological case of failure – as places under intervention are often imagined (e.g. Hughes and Pupavac 2005). However, some regional interveners classified British media reporting on the land occupations in 2000 (cf. Willems 2005) as pathological. In this signification, British media reporting testified to persistent racism that structured their appreciation of politics in (southern) Africa. When the British media did not stop reporting about the fate of white farmers, SADC (2001a) 'appealed to the international community to be objective in their portrayal of events in Zimbabwe'. Throughout the regional intervention, regional forces accused the British discourse on Zimbabwe – certainly without making visible the heterogeneity of this discourse – as being racist. COSATU, otherwise reproachful of the official regional intervention, criticised

> Britain, as the former colonial power is partly responsible for the continuing crisis in these countries [Zimbabwe and Swaziland.] [It] cannot just play an innocent angel or honest opinion-maker.... In fact, Britain ... plays double standards, outrightly condemning Zimbabwe, but doing all it can to protect the Swazi monarchy in Swaziland.
> (COSATU 2008a)

A similar remark was also voiced by Zuma, then still not president:

> Many in Africa believe that there is a racist aspect to European and American criticism of Mugabe. Millions of blacks died in Angola, the Republic of Congo and Rwanda. A few whites lost their lives in Zimbabwe, unfortunately, and already the West is bent out of shape.
> (Zuma 2006)

In Chapter 2, I argued that the signification of violence is indeterminate, but even the most unsettling instance of violence becomes re-integrated into discourse, rendering it meaningful. The violence might for instance signify a distant problem rather unrelated to my own being. Zuma, especially, incriminated the West for signifying violence in Angola, Congo, and Rwanda in this way. From a Western point of view these countries were distant places, largely inhabited by the Other with little relation to themselves. Despite being geographically even more distant, the violence in Zimbabwe was signified differently. In the Western and especially British discourse, Zimbabwe was related to the Self. I reconstructed the Zimbabwe/South Africa relation in terms of chains of equivalence that constitute closeness between the one place and the other. Those accusing 'the West' or 'the British' of racism also referred to such (sedimented) chains of equivalence, letting the horror of the violence travel from distant Zimbabwe to the trains in England. As a journalist explained:

As the farm invasions continued through 2000 – they were, I mean, they were extraordinary and it was a very good international story. The story was, rarely, very important in the UK, because of the colonial links. And also the white farmers had the same surnames as the people on the trains in England reading the paper. But it was really a story driven by the British newspapers and the British television. The numbers of dead were really quite small. But it caused fear.

(Interview with journalist, 30 August 2012)

By drawing (conscious or unconscious) analogies between here and there, the horror of violence was able to defeat the more than 7,000 miles, separating the one from the other. The analogy between family names helping to constitute the meaning of violence in Zimbabwe among the British newspaper readers was understood as racism by many regional forces. Racism, despite helping to overcome the indifference normally afflicting Western perspectives of African crises, thus tinted Western knowledge about and understanding of the crisis in Zimbabwe – according to the understanding of many regional forces. It is not hard to imagine that many of the regional interveners strongly rejected racism. Racism thus functioned as a clear marker of an antagonism that separated the regional forces from the West. This antagonism helped them to imagine the region as the better intervener, whose apprehension of Zimbabwe was not built upon sedimented, racist stereotypes.

According to some regional voices, the Western understanding was not only tinted by racism but also by geographical distance. 'SADC hasn't got the luxury of walking away from Zimbabwe. It is a country in our region so we have to deal with it until we find a solution' (Dlamini-Zuma and Salomão 2008). The South African President added that the 'burden [of hosting large numbers of Zimbabwean migrants] is not carried by the countries of Western Europe and North America, which have benefited especially from the migration of skilled and professional Zimbabweans to the north'[24] (Mbeki 2008b). The West thus embodied a place that was only able to transcend distance by racism, otherwise remaining detached from the Zimbabwean crisis.

From this constitution of the West as a racist and detached subject, it was not difficult to position the regional interveners as its opposite. Official representatives of the region criticised the Western interventions (for example, sanctions) as not helpful (Mbeki 2006b, 2008a), harmful (Mbeki 2007a, Pahad 2007a), and ineffective (Kikwete 2007a, 2007b). The SADC initiative 'offers the only realistic way out of the current crisis', argued a South African foreign affairs official, 'and the international community must back it' (Pahad 2007c). Citing an ICG report, the same official added: 'Western sanctions have proven "largely symbolic" ... and British and American condemnations of President Robert Mugabe are, "if anything, counterproductive"'. Referring to the US intervention in Iraq, Zuma asked: 'Are the Americans even qualified to criticize Mugabe?' (Zuma 2006). In these statements, the regional intervention was imagined as a counter-hegemony to Western approaches. All of these statements imply that regional solutions – in contrast to Western intervention – were helpful, effective, and legitimate. By antagonising international solutions, the regional authority became stabilised. Remarkably, this counter-hegemonic momentum was even perpetuated by the then Zambian President Mwanawasa (2007), otherwise critical of Mugabe, who argued that 'the Zambian government excludes [categorically] the direct or indirect involvement of any foreign state, which is not a SADC member'. His statement indicates that the antagonistic frontier was widely shared by the SADC governments.

However, other regional forces undermined this antagonism. In these statements the Western intervention was constituted as right and good. The South African opposition leader called upon the EU 'to be the Good Samaritan'; he added: 'Do not pass southern Africa by on the other side of the road' (Leon 2000). It is interesting that an EU intervention was signified as an act of benevolence, thereby totally neglecting global politics. Yet, it was not only the former opposition leader who undermined the antagonism established by SADC officials but also the then Botswanan President. The latter described his country as being powerless regarding Zimbabwe's 'drought of good governance', as he called it: 'We try to engage them: We are not the UK, we are not the US, we are not the EU. We are just their neighbour. There are 14m of them; there are less than two million of us' (Mogae 2002). The official SADC representative thus countered the self-presentation of the regional interveners as more effective and, hence, more helpful. The voices trying to destabilise the antagonism were however rare in comparison with those voices perpetuating it.

In Chapter 2, I differentiated between ontological antagonism and its empirical filling. Political discourse theory contends that it is impossible to move beyond ontological antagonisms as they constitute our being. However, as Mouffe (2005, 2013) contended, antagonisms can be filled so that the antagonising force is not imagined as an enemy but an adversary whose politics we oppose but whose existence we do not challenge. In the above statements the signifier 'West' is imagined as such an opponent, whose intervention politics are deemed inadequate, without however questioning its being as such. Traces of this agonistic rather than antagonistic filling also became visible in the desire to articulate a common approach towards Zimbabwe, as voiced by the then South African Deputy Foreign Minister (Pahad 2007a). Yet the irreconcilable sense-makings of the crisis in Zimbabwe, as I have reconstructed them throughout this chapter, rendered the gap separating the one from the other impossible to bridge. The Global Political Agreement might have functioned as a shared nodal point and, hence, as a starting point, from which to develop a common intervention. But the US and the EU only lukewarmly received the agreement as it did not remove the principle obstacle to progress: Mugabe (Raftopoulos 2010, p. 715, 2013, p. 16). Accordingly, neither the EU nor the US suspended the sanctions. Disappointed the South African President concluded:

If we are in the shoes of the big countries I would have said here is an agreement we are in support of this agreement and lifting sanctions, even conditionally, even for six months to a year, to give a chance for this agreement. That would have been support for the agreement.

(Zuma 2010)

Thus, the antagonistic frontier that constituted the interveners as specifically *regional* was rather stable, lasting throughout the intervention.

Notes

1 Designating these events as land occupations is controversial, as the designation already suggests a particular interpretation of the violence. These events have also been called land demonstrations (cf. Chaumba, Scoones, and Wollmer 2004, p. 543, Moyo 2001, p. 320). It seems impossible to use a designation that is not politically charged. In the following I will refer to these events as land occupations as it has become the more common and hegemonic designation.
2 This is not to say that previously people had not demanded to be ruled democratically. On the contrary, the Zimbabwean liberation struggle emerging at the beginning of the twentieth century was not only a quest for the right to rule but partially also for political equality and broad participation (Moore 2001, p. 166). For an impressive account on how radical democratic tendencies were suppressed in the Zimbabwean liberation movement, see Moore 1995.
3 The Lancaster House Constitution was a product of British facilitation between the (white) Rhodesian Government and the (black) liberation movements. Therefore, it lacked popular participation and, according to the scholar Lloyd Sachikonye (2004, p. 175), broad legitimacy. A clause ensured that the constitution could not be substantially changed during the first decade of post-independence Zimbabwe: that is, during the 1980s. The parliament was, however, allowed to amend the constitution and, over time, the ruling party centralised power in the executive. In 1997, the constitutional reform movement was founded, drawing its membership from labour, religious, business, human rights, women, and student organisations (Kagoro 2004, p. 241). In the beginning, its objective was limited to constitutional reform but some members saw the movement as a first step to building a real (in the sense of really challenging) opposition. Others, however, felt uncomfortable with becoming too political. The latter faction sought to enable constitutional reform via dialogue and cooperation with the government (LeBas 2006, p. 425). In this sense, the constitutional reform movement was heterogeneous as well.
4 This clause played with the ignorance of the voters, as the Zimbabwean Government was certainly not in the position to *oblige* the British Government to pay for the land reform.
5 The practices of the land occupiers varied from locality to locality. For a nuanced account, see Moyo 2001, 324–325.
6 In the first post-apartheid legislative period from 1994 to 1999, the parliament was a place of vibrant debate. Many prominent anti-apartheid activists were elected MPs. They were committed to diligently exercising their duty as a democratic watchdog and their prominence enabled them to wield enormous political authority within the ANC. Yet, after the first post-apartheid legislative period, many of the prominent MPs were recruited to cabinet positions. Upon their departure, the parliament became increasingly less able to control the government (Calland and Oxtoby 2010, p. 101, Klug 2010, pp. 174–180). The decreased possibilities reveal themselves with respect to the situation in Zimbabwe, which was not an official item on the agenda until

February 2001 (South African Parliament 2001, pp. 73–133). In April 2000, MPs used the agenda item 'Our roles in making the 21st century the African century' to make 'Zimbabwe' a subject of parliamentary debate. The opposition leader therefore complained: 'We cannot even have a proper parliamentary debate on the subject of Zimbabwe' (South African Parliament 2000a, p. 152).
7 Scholars differ in their opinions of how far the land occupations after the 2000 referendum reflected a longstanding popular demand for land. Jocelyn Alexander (2003) argued that land occupations in the year 2000 were both popular but also managed. The popular demand for land was one constant throughout post-independence Zimbabwe, not just originating from historical injustices but also the pressures of a faltering economy. In 2000 politicians attended to this popular demand as they were in need of a constituency. Sam Moyo (2001) emphasised how the demand for land grew stronger during the 1990s. In contradistinction to urban constituencies that began to claim political rights, the opposition movement marginalised demands for economic redistribution: The opposition movements 'have made some valid demands for democratisation, within a liberal electoral and human rights framework, but no wider demands for redistribution of resources or economic restructuring' (Moyo 2001, p. 316). In this political context of political negligence, according to Moyo, the ruling party ZANU-PF reactivated its historic, rural constituency by appropriating the demand for land and redistribution.
8 In a review of the Mbeki Mugabe Paper, David Moore (2010) argued that the National Democratic Revolution as an approach to socio-economic transformations was critical for Mbeki's understanding of Zimbabwe. Based on this ideology, he came to the conclusion that the economic liberation of southern Africa was still outstanding (see also Gevisser 2009).
9 The Commonwealth Observer Group (2003, p. 44) for example determined the election as 'not adequately allow[ing] for a free expression of will by the electorate'. Not only non-regional forces came to such conclusion but also two South African judges who were appointed by then President Mbeki:

> Having regard to all the circumstances, and in particular the cumulative substantial departures from international standards of free and fair elections found in Zimbabwe during the pre-election period, these elections, in our view, cannot be considered to be free and fair.
> (Khampepe and Moseneke 2002, para. 99)

The report was not released to the public until after a years-long legal struggle by the South African daily *Mail and Guardian* with the South African Government.
10 The common position identified by the regional interveners contrasted with the continuing discord within Zimbabwe. Before the Global Political Agreement, the regional discourse in one way or another reproduced the schisms within Zimbabwe. With respect to the post-Global Political Agreement constitution-making process, however, these schisms stayed in Zimbabwe, no longer being reflected in the regional discourse. According to the scholar Gwinyayi Dzinesa (2012, p. 4), the Zimbabwean ZANU-PF and MDC 'turned the constitution-drafting process into a battleground' (see also Sachikonye 2013). Some of the Zimbabwean civil society organisations disputed that the constitution-making process was people-driven, launching a No campaign as soon as the draft was put to the vote: 'It is not about what people wanted or said but about the selfish and personal interests of politicians. We need a constitution that will survive the test of time and not a deal for current politicians' (NCA 2013). Unlike during the 2000 constitutional referendum, the No campaign had little backing from the MDC. In March 2013 the electorate endorsed the draft with 94.49 per cent, paving the way for the July elections that re-affirmed Mugabe as president and hence marked the end of the regional intervention politics.

11 For a more complex reflection on the 'common' past, see SACP 2004.
12 After Malema's return from Zimbabwe, the ANC Youth League qualified Malema's call to copy Zimbabwe. A press statement announced: 'We, as the youth of South Africa, are greatly inspired and will encourage as many young people as possible to participate in productive and commercial agriculture to avoid almost total reliance on white farmers for food production' (ANC Youth League 2010).
13 According to executive order 13288 (issued March 2003) seventy-seven members of the ruling elite including Mugabe 'constitute an unusual and extraordinary threat to the foreign policy of the United States'. Their assets that at this point were under US control were subsequently frozen. As the Zimbabwe Democracy and Economic Recovery Act had already announced such measures, those targeted by the sanctions however had plenty of time to transfer their assets to 'safer' places (Stübig 2007, p. 4).
14 The EU member states were reportedly divided on the question of how to respond to Zimbabwe. Whereas Britain, the Scandinavian countries, and the Netherlands supported sanctions, France and Belgium preferred to facilitate change through the political consultations as institutionalised in the Cotonou Agreement (Grebe 2010, p. 13). The discord among the EU members openly surfaced regarding the EU–Africa Summit 2007. In 2007, the host country Portugal – wanting to prevent a repetition of 2003 when several African heads of state had boycotted the summit because Mugabe was not invited – pushed for an exemption from Mugabe's travel ban. This exemption led to the boycott by the then British Prime Minister Gordon Brown (cf. EU 2002).
15 The movement nevertheless made sure that the campaign was crafted by forces from within SADC, so as to avoid being accused as stooges of imperialism (Larmer 2008, p. 489).
16 The AU Declaration on the 'Principles Governing Democratic Elections in Africa' enacted in 2002 reportedly functioned as the primary inspirational source in the crafting of the SADC guidelines (Matlosa 2004, p. 12, Kagwanja 2005, p. 12). But the SADC guidelines also profited from the previous work of regional civil society organisations like an initiative of SADC parliamentarians as well as from the Electoral Institute of Southern Africa that had already articulated norms and standards for elections (Matlosa 2004, p. 12).
17 The case was made accessible for a wider public by the documentary 'Mugabe and the White African' of 2009.
18 For the judgement, see www.saflii.org/cgi-bin/disp.pl?file=sa/cases/SADCT/2008/2.html&query=cambell (accessed 20 December 2013)
19 In a review of published books on Zimbabwe, the reviewer criticised many scholars for mainly attributing the crisis to Mugabe: they tend to

> hold Mugabe responsible for destroying the economy and authorizing state violence on citizens. Thus Mugabe emerges in most of the recent literature as this *larger-than-life political figure* who was midwife to the birth of the nation before becoming its undertaker.
>
> (Ndlovu-Gatsheni 2012, p. 316, emphasis mine)

20 He died suddenly in office in August 2008.
21 Prior to the formation of the MDC the Zimbabwe Congress of Trade Unions was part of the Zimbabwean liberation movement. In post-independence Zimbabwe, however, the Zimbabwe Congress of Trade Unions was gradually alienated from the alliance partner ZANU-PF: labour issues were treated as less important than rural concerns. Once workers suffered more from the structural adjustment programme imposed upon Zimbabwe by the international financial institutions, the Zimbabwe Congress of Trade Unions began to openly oppose its former liberation partner (Dansereau 2003, pp. 175–176). In the mid-1990s, the union organised a number of strikes and soon articulated demands beyond labour relations, aiming at reforming state institutions.

22 The Zimbabwean Government is said to have understood the lawsuit as 'a ploy to use the inter-party talks to overturn the 2002 presidential election results' (ICG 2006, p. 4). By contrast, the MDC argued that ZANU-PF opportunistically used the court case to unilaterally withdraw from the facilitation (DIRCO 2002b).
23 In the end, the court case challenging the presidential elections of 2002 was hardly dealt with. The first hearing on legal and constitutional aspects of the elections was first delayed and then dismissed. The hearing on violence, intimidation and other forms of rigging never took place. In 2005, the MDC called instead upon the Supreme Court, but the petition also remained pending (Compagnon 2011, p. 160).
24 This statement should also be read against the backdrop of the violent murder of more than 60 people and the wounding of many more in May 2008 in South Africa. South African citizens, especially from informal settlements and townships in and around Johannesburg, turned on their neighbours, mostly migrants coming from other parts of Africa, including Zimbabwe. This xenophobic violence seemed to contradict the post-apartheid constitution that put itself into the service of human rights. Yet, as Landau (2010, p. 216) argued, the violence can be seen as a demon, 'living within a society to turn on itself to exorcise those it sees as denying the promise of post-Apartheid power and prosperity'. Based on a long history of violently suppressing native foreigners within, the sedimented forms of exclusions were projected upon others. When Mbeki drew the line between the distant West and the near neighbours, he had certainly in mind how the crisis in Zimbabwe, in multiple ways, shaped the societies of the neighbourhood (for xenophobia in Botswana, see Morapedi 2007).

References

Alden, C., and Anseeuw, W., 2009. *Land, liberation and compromise in southern Africa*. Basingstoke: Palgrave Macmillan.

Alexander, J., 2003. 'Squatters', veterans and the state in Zimbabwe. In: A. Hammar, B. Raftopoulos, and S. Jensen, eds., *Zimbabwe's unfinished business: Rethinking land, state and nation in the context of crisis*. Harare: Weaver Press, 83–117.

ANC [African National Congress] 2000. Press release of 15 May. Available from: www.anc.org.za/content/statement-delegation-zimbabwe (accessed 1 November 2013).

ANC Youth League 2010. Press release of 8 April. Available from: www.politicsweb.co.za/party/we-must-follow-zimbabwe-model-ancyl (accessed 6 January 2014).

Anseeuw, W., and Alden, C., 2011. *From freedom charter to cautious land reform: The politics of land in South Africa*. Pretoria: University of Pretoria.

Booysen, S., 2011. *The African National Congress and the regeneration of political power*. Johannesburg: Wits University Press.

British Commonwealth 2001. Conclusions of 6 September. Abuja: Committee of Commonwealth foreign ministers.

British Commonwealth 2002. Statement on Zimbabwe of 4 March. Coolum: Commonwealth heads of government.

Calland, R., and Oxtoby, C., 2010. Machiavelli meets the constitution. In: D. Glaser, ed., *Mbeki and after*. Johannesburg: Wits University Press, 71–102.

Chandler, D., 2014. Beyond good and evil: Ethics in a world of complexity. *International Politics*, 51 (4), 441–457.

Chaumba, J., Scoones, I., and Wollmer, W., 2004. From jambanja to planning: The reassertion of technocracy in land reform in south-eastern Zimbabwe? *Journal of Modern African Studies*, 41 (4), 533–554.

Chikane, F., 2009. *Transcript of the Southern African Development Community agreement on Zimbabwe briefing* of 28 January, Pretoria: Presidency. Available from: www.gov.za/f-chikane-transcript-southern-african-development-community-sadc-agreement-zimbabwe-briefing (accessed 21 November 2013).

Commonwealth Observer Group 2003. *Zimbabwe presidential election 9–11 March 2002*. London: Commonwealth Secretariat.

Compagnon, D., 2011. *A predictable tragedy: Robert Mugabe and the collapse of Zimbabwe*. Philadelphia: University of Pennsylvania Press.

COSATU [Congress of South African Trade Unions] 2007a. Press release of 3 April. Available from: www.cosatu.org.za/show.php?ID=1154 (accessed 19 November 2013).

COSATU 2007b. Press release of 27 August. Available from: www.cosatu.org.za/show.php?ID=1187 (accessed 19 November 2013).

COSATU 2008a. Press release of 4 March. Available from: www.cosatu.org.za/show.php?ID=1647 (accessed 7 November 2013).

COSATU 2008b. Press release of 18 April. Available from: www.cosatu.org.za/show.php?ID=1490 (accessed 13 November 2013).

COSATU 2008c. Press release of 21 April. Available from: www.cosatu.org.za/show.php?ID=1492 (accessed 13 November 2013).

COSATU 2008d. Press release of 22 April. Available from: www.cosatu.org.za/show.php?ID=1494 (accessed 13 November 2013).

COSATU 2008e. Press release of 24 June. Available from: www.cosatu.org.za/show.php?ID=1594 (accessed 19 November 2013).

COSATU 2008f. Press release of 29 June. Available from: www.cosatu.org.za/show.php?ID=1600 (accessed 27 November 2013).

COSATU 2008g. Press release of 15 September. Available from: www.cosatu.org.za/show.php?ID=1698 (accessed 19 November 2013).

COSATU 2008h. Press release of 2 October. Available from: www.cosatu.org.za/show.php?ID=1722 (accessed 19 November 2013).

COSATU, Zimbabwe Congress of Trade Unions, Zimbabwe Solidarity Forum, Revolutionary Youth of Zimbabwe, Zimbabwe Exiles, Crisis in Zimbabwe Coalition, Peoples United Democratic Movement of Swaziland, Swaziland United Democratic Front, Swaziland Federation of Trade Unions, Swaziland Federation of Labour, Swaziland Youth Congress, Federation of Unions of South Africa, Treatment Action Campaign, and Anti-privatisation Forum 2008. *Memorandum to SADC summit on Zimbabwe and Swaziland* of 16 August. Johannesburg. Available from: www.cosatu.org.za/show.php?ID=1518 (accessed 6 November 2013).

Cousins, B., and Scoones, I., 2010. Contested paradigms of 'viability' in redistributive land reform: Perspectives from southern Africa. *Journal of Peasant Studies*, 37 (1), 31–66.

Dansereau, S., 2003. Liberation and opposition in Zimbabwe. *Journal of Contemporary African Studies*, 21 (2), 173–191.

Davidson, I., 2012. Press release of 5 March. Democratic Alliance. Available from: www.polity.org.za/article/da-statement-by-ian-davidson-democratic-alliance-shadow-minister-of-international-relations-and-cooperation-on-zimbabwes-democracy-05032012-2012-03-05 (accessed 3 December 2013).

DIRCO [South African Department of International Relations and Cooperation] 2002a. Press release of 18 February. Pretoria. Available from: www.dirco.gov.za/docs/2002/zimb0218.htm (accessed 13 November 2013).

DIRCO 2002b. Press release of 8 April. Pretoria. Available from: www.dirco.gov.za/docs/2002/zimb0517.htm (accessed 17 November 2013).

Dlamini-Zuma, N., and Salomão, T., 2008. Media briefing of 13 August. Johannesburg: South African Department of International Relations and Cooperation.
Dzinesa, G.A., 2012. *Zimbabwe's tortuous road to a new constitution and elections.* Pretoria: Institute for Security Studies.
Edkins, J., 2002. Forget trauma? Responses to September 11. *International Relations*, 16 (2), 243–256.
Eriksson, M., 2011. *Targeting peace: Understanding UN and EU targeted sanctions.* Farnham: Ashgate.
EU 2002. Council common position concerning restrictive measures against Zimbabwe of 18 February, 2002/145/CFSP.
EU 2009. Council common position renewing restrictive measures against Zimbabwe of 26 January, 2009/68/CFSP.
Fassin, D., and Pandolfi, M., 2010. Introduction: Military and humanitarian government in the age of intervention. In: D. Fassin and M. Pandolfi, eds., *Contemporary states of emergency.* New York: Zone Books, 9–25.
Fransman, M.L., 2011. Media briefing of 1 March. Available from: www.dirco.gov.za/docs/speeches/2011/frans0301.html (accessed 28 November 2013).
Gevisser, M., 2009. *A Legacy of liberation: Thabo Mbeki and the future of the South African dream.* New York: Palgrave Macmillan.
Gibb, R., 1998. Southern Africa in transition: Prospects and problems facing regional integration. *Journal of Modern African Studies*, 36 (2), 287–306.
Glendinning, L., and Jones, A., 2008. Tsvangirai pulls out of 'sham' Zimbabwe election. *Guardian*, 22 June.
Global Political Agreement 2008. *Agreement between the Zimbabwe African National Union Patriotic Front (Zanu-PF) and the two Movement for Democratic Change (MDC) Formations, on resolving the challenges facing Zimbabwe.* Available from: www.ru.ac.za/media/rhodesuniversity/content/zimsoc/documents/power_sharing_agreement.pdf (accessed 1 November 2016).
Grebe, J., 2010. And they are still targeting: Assessing the effectiveness of targeted sanctions against Zimbabwe. *Africa Spectrum*, 45 (1), 3–29.
Gumede, W., 2007. *Thabo Mbeki and the battle for the soul of the ANC.* London: Zed Books.
Gumede, W., 2008. Briefing: South Africa: Jacob Zuma and the difficulties of consolidating South Africa's democracy. *African Affairs*, 107 (427), 261–271.
Habib, A., 2009. South Africa's foreign policy: Hegemonic aspirations, neoliberal orientations and global transformation. *South African Journal of International Affairs*, 16 (2), 143–159.
Hall, R., 2004. A political economy of land reform in South Africa. *Review of African Political Economy*, 31 (100), 213–227.
Holland, H., 2008. *Dinner with Mugabe: The untold story of a freedom fighter who became a tyrant.* Johannesburg: Penguin Books.
Hughes, C., and Pupavac, V., 2005. Framing post-conflict societies: International pathologisation of Cambodia and the post-Yugoslav states. *Third World Quarterly*, 26 (6), 873–889.
ICG [International Crisis Group] 2004a. Blood and soil: Land, politics and conflict prevention in Zimbabwe and South Africa. *Africa Report*, no. 85.
ICG 2004b. Zimbabwe: Another election chance. *Africa Report*, no. 86.
ICG 2005. Post-election Zimbabwe: What next? *Africa Report*, no. 93.
ICG 2006. Zimbabwe's continuing self-destruction. *Africa Briefing*, no. 38.

ICG 2007. Zimbabwe: A regional solution? *Africa Report*, no. 132.
ICG 2008. Ending Zimbabwe's nightmare: A possible way forward. *Africa Briefing*, no. 56.
IRIN [Integrated Regional Information Networks] 2004. SADC leaders to adopt election guidelines, 16 August.
James, W., 2009. Press release of 23 September. Democratic Alliance. Available from: www.polity.org.za/article/da-statement-by-wilmot-james-democratic-alliance-representative-to-the-southern-african-development-communitys-parliamentary-forum-on-mugabe-23092009-2009-09-23 (accessed 11 November 2013).
Kagoro, B., 2004. Constitutional reform as social movement: A critical narrative of the constitution-making debate in Zimbabwe, 1997–2000. In: B. Raftopoulos and T. Savage, eds., *Zimbabwe. Injustice and political reconciliation*. Cape Town: Institute for Justice and Reconciliation, 236–256.
Kagwanja, P., 2005. Zimbabwe's March 2005 elections: Dangers and opportunities. *African Security Review*, 14 (3), 5–18.
Kagwanja, P., 2006. Power and peace: South Africa and the refurbishing of Africa's multilateral capacity for peacemaking. In: R. Southall, ed., *South Africa's role in conflict resolution and peacemaking in Africa: Conference proceedings*. Cape Town: Human Sciences Research Council Press, 27–58.
Kaunda, K., 2007a. Africa has huge problems. *Der Spiegel*, 20 April.
Kaunda, K., 2007b. Viewpoint: Kaunda on Mugabe. *BBC*, 12 June.
Khama, I., 2008. State of the nation address of 3 November. Gaborone: Botswanan Parliament.
Khama, I., 2009a. Interview. *Financial Times*, 8 March.
Khama, I., 2009b. Interview. *Africa Report*, 27 July.
Khampepe, S., and Moseneke, D., 2002. '*Khampepe report*' on the 2002 presidential elections of Zimbabwe. Available from: http://cdn.mg.co.za/content/documents/2014/11/14/reportonthe2002presidentialelectionsofzimbabwe.pdf (accessed 13 February 2015).
Kikwete, J., 2007a. SADC cannot abandon Zimbabwe. *The New African*, 30 March.
Kikwete, J., 2007b. Interview. *Financial Times*, 6 November.
Kikwete, J., 2009. Statement of 3 February. Addis Ababa: African Union Summit of the Heads of State and Government.
Klug, H., 2010. *The constitution of South Africa: A contextual analysis*. Oxford: Hart Publishing.
Laakso, L., 2003. Opposition politics in independent Zimbabwe. *African Studies Quarterly*, 7 (2–3), 119–137.
Laclau, E., 1990. *New reflections on the revolution of our time*. London: Verso.
Laclau, E., 2007 [1996]. *Emancipation(s)*. London: Verso.
Laclau, E., and Mouffe, C., 2001 [1985]. *Hegemony and socialist strategy*. 2nd edn., London: Verso.
Lahiff, E., and Cousins, B., 2001. The land crisis in Zimbabwe viewed from south of the Limpopo. *Journal of Agrarian Change*, 1 (4), 652–666.
Landau, L., 2010. Loving the alien? Citizenship, law, and the future in South Africa's demonic society. *African Affairs*, 109 (435), 213–230.
Landsberg, C., 2000. Promoting democracy: The Mandela-Mbeki doctrine. *Journal of Democracy*, 11 (3), 107–121.
Larmer, M., 2008. The Zimbabwe arms shipment campaign. *Review of African Political Economy*, 35 (117), 486–493.
LeBas, A., 2006. Polarization as craft: Party formation and state violence in Zimbabwe. *Comparative Politics*, 38 (4), 419–438.

Leon, T., 2000. Address to European Parliament of 3 May. Available from: http://supportservices.ufs.ac.za/dl/userfiles_workflow/Documents/00006/4005_eng.pdf (accessed 1 November 2013).

Leon, T., 2001. South Africa's defining moment. *Time*, 23 August.

Leon, T., 2003. *Road map to democracy in Zimbabwe* of 2 December. Johannesburg: South African Institute of International Affairs. Available from: www.polity.org.za/article/leon-roadmap-to-democracy-in-zimbabwe-02122003-2003-12-02 (accessed 11 November 2013).

Leon, T., 2004a. Press release of 17 March. Democratic Alliance. Available from: www.polity.org.za/article/leon-mdladlanas-attack-on-da-economic-policy-lacks-credibility-17032004-2004-03-17 (accessed 6 November 2013).

Leon, T., 2004b. Press release of 21 March. Democratic Alliance. Available form: www.polity.org.za/article/leon-we-have-rights-on-paper-but-not-in-practice-21032004-2004-03-21 (accessed 13 November 2013).

Leon, T., 2005. Press release of 15 February. Democratic Alliance. Available from: www.polity.org.za/article/leon-we-must-choose-an-open-opportunity-society-150205-2005-02-15 (accessed 5 November 2013).

Leon, T., 2008. *On the contrary: Leading the opposition in a democratic South Africa.* Johannesburg: Jonathan Ball Publishers.

Maclean, S.J., 1999. Peacebuilding and the new regionalism in southern Africa. *Third World Quarterly*, 20 (5), 943–956.

Malan, M., 1998. *Regional power politics under cover of SADC: Running amok with a mythical organ.* Institute for Security Studies, Occasional Paper no. 35. Pretoria: Institute for Security Studies.

Mandela, N., 1993. South Africa's future foreign policy. *Foreign Affairs*, 72 (5), 86–97.

Maroleng, C., 2004. *Zimbabwe's Movement for Democratic Change: Briefing notes.* Institute for Security Studies, Situation Report, 3 May. Pretoria: Institute for Security Studies.

Matlosa, K., 2002. Election monitoring and observation in Zimbabwe: Hegemony versus sovereignty. *African Journal of Political Science*, 7 (1), 129–154.

Matlosa, K., 2004. *Managing democracy: A review of SADC principles and guidelines governing democratic elections.* Johannesburg: Electoral Institute for Sustainable Democracy in Africa.

Matombo, L., and Sachikonye, L.M., 2010. The labour movement and democratisation in Zimbabwe. In: B. Beckman, S. Buhlungu, and L.M. Sachikonye, eds., *Trade unions and party politics: Labour movements in Africa.* Cape Town: Human Sciences Research Council Press, 109–130.

Mbeki, T., 2000a. Interview. *World Association of Newspapers*, 3 May. Available from: www.thepresidency.gov.za/pebble.asp?relid=1965 (accessed 1 November 2013).

Mbeki, T., 2000b. State of the nation address of 4 May. Cape Town: South African Parliament.

Mbeki, T., 2000c. Speech in Bulawayo, Zimbabwe, of 5 May. Available from: www.unisa.ac.za/contents/colleges/docs/tm2000/tm050500.pdf (accessed 1 November 2013).

Mbeki, T., 2001a. *The Mbeki–Mugabe papers.* Available from: http://archive.kubatana.net/docs/demgg/mbeki_mugabe_papers_010831.pdf (accessed 5 December 2013).

Mbeki, T., 2001b. Interview. *South African e.tv*, 24 April. Available from: www.thepresidency.gov.za/pebble.asp?relid=1944 (accessed 7 November 2013).

Mbeki, T., 2001c. Interview. *Independent Television News*, 3 May. Available from: www.thepresidency.gov.za/pebble.asp?relid=1958 (accessed 7 November 2013).

Mbeki, T., 2001d. Interview. *BBC*, 6 August. Available form: www.thepresidency.gov.za/pebble.asp?relid=1939 (accessed 7 November 2013).

Mbeki, T., 2001e. Clamour over Zimbabwe reveals continuing racial prejudice in South Africa. *ANC Today*, 1 (9).

Mbeki, T., 2002a. State of the nation address of 8 February. Cape Town: South African Parliament.

Mbeki, T., 2002b. Zimbabwe: 'Two blacks and one white'. *ANC Today*, 2 (10).

Mbeki, T., 2002c. Interview. *South African Sunday Times*, 8 October.

Mbeki, T., 2003a. We will resist the upside-down view of Africa. *ANC Today*, 3 (49).

Mbeki, T., 2003b. Interview. *South African Broadcasting Cooperation TV2*, 16 February. Available from: www.thepresidency.gov.za/pebble.asp?relid=1911 (accessed 26 February 2013).

Mbeki, T., 2006a. Interview. *South African Broadcasting Cooperation TV2*, 5 February. Available from: www.dirco.gov.za/docs/speeches/2006/mbek0205.htm (accessed 29 November 2013).

Mbeki, T., 2006b. Interview. *BBC*, 24 May. Available from: www.gov.za/t-mbeki-interview-bbc (accessed 13 November 2013).

Mbeki, T., 2007a. Interview. *Financial Times*, 3 April.

Mbeki, T., 2007b. Interview. *South African Broadcasting Cooperation*, 17 August. Available from: www.gov.za/t-mbeki-transcript-media-briefing-and-sabc-interview-following-sadc-summit (accessed 2 December 2013).

Mbeki, T., 2008a. Interview. *Al Jazeera*, 8 May. Available from: www.thepresidency.gov.za/pebble.asp?relid=1863 (accessed 28 November 2013).

Mbeki, T., 2008b. Letter to Morgan Tsvangirai of 22 November. Available from: www.flickr.com/photos/sokwanele/3065872812/in/photostream/ (accessed 20 November 2013).

Mogae, F., 2002. Drought of good governance is the real problem. *African Business*, 281 (Nov), 26.

Moore, D., 1995. Democracy, violence, and identity in the Zimbabwean war of national liberation: Reflections from the realms of dissent. *Canadian Journal of African Studies*, 29 (3), 375–402.

Moore, D., 2001. Commentary: Democracy is coming to Zimbabwe. *Australian Journal of Political Science*, 36 (1), 163–169.

Moore, D., 2010. A decade of disquieting diplomacy: South Africa, Zimbabwe and the ideology of the National Democratic Revolution, 1999–2009. *History Compass*, 8 (8), 752–767.

Morapedi, W.G., 2007. Post-liberation xenophobia in southern Africa: The case of the influx of undocumented Zimbabwean immigrants into Botswana, c.1995–2004. *Journal of Contemporary African Studies*, 25 (2), 229–250.

Motlanthe, K., 2008. Media briefing of 17 December. Pretoria: South African Department of International Relations and Cooperation. Available from: www.dirco.gov.za/docs/speeches/2008/motl1217.html (accessed 27 November 2013).

Motlanthe, K., 2009. Speech on the occasion of the swearing-in of cabinet ministers in Harare of 13 February. Available from: www.dirco.gov.za/docs/speeches/2009/motl0216.html (accessed 9 December 2013).

Mouffe, C., 2005. *The democratic paradox*. London: Verso.

Mouffe, C., 2013. *Agonistics: Thinking the world politically*. London: Verso.

Moyo, S., 2000. The political economy of land acquisition and redistribution in Zimbabwe, 1990–1999. *Journal of Southern African Studies*, 26 (1), 5–28.

Moyo, S., 2001. The land occupation movement and democratisation in Zimbabwe: Contradictions of neoliberalism. *Millennium: Journal of International Studies*, 30 (2), 311–330.

Mubu, K., 2009. Press release of 4 September. Democratic Alliance. Available from: http://m.polity.org.za/article/da-statement-by-kenneth-mubu-democratic-alliance-mp-shadow-minister-of-international-relations-and-cooperation-on-zuma-failing-in-zimbabwe-04092009-2009-09-04 (accessed 14 November 2013).

Mubu, K., 2011. Press release of 17 August. Democratic Alliance. Available from: www.polity.org.za/article/da-statement-by-kenneth-mubu-democratic-alliance-shadow-minister-of-international-relations-and-cooperation-calling-on-zuma-to-hold-mugabe-to-account-during-sadc-meeting-17082011-2011-08-17 (accessed 28 November 2013).

Mufamadi, S., 2008a. Media briefing of 15 April. Pretoria: South African Department of International Relations and Cooperation. Available from: www.politicsweb.co.za/iservice/transcript-of-mufamadis-briefing-on-zimbabwe (accessed 27 February 2013).

Mufamadi, S., 2008b. Interview. *South African Broadcasting Cooperation*, 28 April.

Mwanawasa, L., 2007. Speech of 22 March. Available from: http://maravi.blogspot.de/2007/03/levy-mwanawasa-dinner-speech.html (accessed 13 January 2014).

Nathan, L., 2006. SADC's uncommon approach to common security, 1992–2003. *Journal of Southern African Studies*, 32 (3), 605–622.

NCA [National Constitutional Assembly] 2008. Press release of 7 July. Available from: www.thezimbabwean.co/2008/07/nca-position-on-june-27-elections-run-off/ (accessed 3 December 2013).

NCA 2013. *Take charge: Vote NO in the referendum*. Available from: http://takecharge-179489.blogspot.de/2013/02/take-charge-vote-no-in-referendum.html (accessed 3 December 2013).

Ndlovu-Gatsheni, S.J., 2011. *Reconstructing the implications of liberation struggle history on SADC mediation in Zimbabwe*. South African Institute of International Affairs, Occasional Paper no. 92 Johannesburg: South African of Institute International Affairs.

Ndlovu-Gatsheni, S.J., 2012. Beyond Mugabe-centric narratives of the Zimbabwe crisis. *African Affairs*, 111 (443), 315–323.

Ntsaluba, A., 2009a. Media briefing of 8 April. Pretoria: South African Department of International Relations and Cooperation. Available from: www.dirco.gov.za/docs/speeches/2009/ntsa0408.html (accessed 10 December 2013).

Ntsaluba, A., 2009b. Media briefing of 10 November. Pretoria: South African Department of International Relations and Cooperation. Available from: www.dirco.gov.za/docs/speeches/2009/ntsa1110.html (accessed 10 December 2013).

Ntsaluba, A., 2009c. Media briefing of 21 April. Pretoria: South African Department of International Relations and Cooperation. Available from: www.dirco.gov.za/docs/speeches/2009/ntsa0423.html (accessed 10 December 2013).

Ophir, A., 2010. The politics of catastrophization: Emergency and exception. In: D. Fassin and M. Pandolfi, eds., *Contemporary states of emergency: The politics of military and humanitarian interventions*. New York: Zone Books, 59–88.

Pahad, A., 2000. Speech of 13 June. Cape Town: South African Parliament. Available from: www.dirco.gov.za/docs/speeches/2000/paha0613.htm (accessed 1 November 2013).

Pahad, A., 2007a. Media briefing of 23 March. Pretoria: South African Department of International Relations and Cooperation. Available from: www.dirco.gov.za/docs/speeches/2007/pahad0326.htm (accessed 27 November 2013).

Pahad, A., 2007b. Media briefing of 17 April. Pretoria: South African Department of International Relations and Cooperation. Available from: www.dirco.gov.za/docs/speeches/2007/paha0417.htm (accessed 20 November 2013).

Pahad, A., 2007c. Media briefing of 19 September. Pretoria: South African Department of International Relations and Cooperation. Available from: www.dirco.gov.za/docs/speeches/2007/paha0919.htm (accessed 20 November 2013).

Pahad, A., 2008a. Media briefing of 10 April. Pretoria: South African Department of International Relations and Cooperation. Available from: www.dirco.gov.za/docs/speeches/2008/paha0410.html (accessed 20 November 2013).

Pahad, A., 2008b. Media briefing of 14 May. Cape Town: South African Department of International Relations and Cooperation. Available from: www.dirco.gov.za/docs/speeches/2008/paha0515.html (accessed 6 December 2013).

Pahad, A., 2008c. Media briefing of 13 June. Pretoria: South African Department of International Relations and Cooperation. Available from: www.dirco.gov.za/docs/speeches/2008/paha0613.html (accessed 6 December 2013).

Pahad, A., 2008d. Media briefing of 15 July. Pretoria: South African Department of International Relations and Cooperation. Available from: www.dirco.gov.za/docs/speeches/2008/paha0715.html (accessed 26 February 2013).

Palmer, R., 1990. Land reform in Zimbabwe, 1980–1990. *African Affairs*, 89 (355), 163–181.

Petretto, K., 2007. *Fallstricke und Chancen in Simbabwe: Entwickelt sich eine neue Dynamik zur Lösung des politischen Konflikts?*, SWP-Aktuell no. 52. Berlin: Stiftung für Wissenschaft und Politik.

Pleming, S., 2007. Rice demands release of opposition in Zimbabwe. *Reuters*, 13 March.

Poku, N., 2001. *Regionalization and security in southern Africa*. Basingstoke: Palgrave Macmillan.

Raftopoulos, B., 2007. Reflections on the opposition in Zimbabwe: The politics of the Movement for Democratic Change. In: R. Primorac and S. Chan, eds., *Zimbabwe in crisis: The international response and the space of silence*. Abingdon: Routledge, 125–148.

Raftopoulos, B., 2010. The Global Political Agreement as a 'passive revolution': Notes on contemporary politics in Zimbabwe. *Round Table*, 99 (411), 705–718.

Raftopoulos, B., 2013. An overview of the politics of the Global Political Agreement: National conflict, regional agony, international dilemma. In: B. Raftopoulos, ed., *The hard road to reform: The politics of Zimbabwe's Global Political Agreement*. Harare: Weaver Press, 1–38.

Ranger, T., 1985. *Consciousness and guerrilla war in Zimbabwe: A comparative study*. London: James Currey.

Richmond, O., 2006. The problem of peace: Understanding the 'liberal peace'. *Conflict, Security and Development*, 6 (3), 291–314.

Richmond, O., and Tellidis, I., 2014. Emerging actors in international peacebuilding and statebuilding: Status quo or critical states? *Global Governance*, 20 (4), 563–584.

Sachikonye, L.M., 2003. From 'growth with equity' to 'fast-track' reform: Zimbabwe's land question. *Review of African Political Economy*, 30 (96), 227–240.

Sachikonye, L.M., 2004. Constitutionalism, the electoral system and challenges for governance and stability in Zimbabwe. *African Journal on Conflict Resolution*, 4 (2), 171–195.

Sachikonye, L.M., 2005. South Africa's quiet diplomacy: The case of Zimbabwe. In: J. Daniel, R. Southall, and J. Lutchman, eds., *State of the nation: South Africa 2004–2005*. Cape Town: Human Sciences Research Council Press, 569–585.

Sachikonye, L.M., 2013. Briefing: Continuity or reform in Zimbabwean politics? An overview of the 2013 referendum. *Journal of African Elections*, 12 (1), 178–185.

SACP [South African Communist Party] 2004. Zimbabwe: Let's keep focused. *Usembenzi Online* 3 (21). Available from: http://archive.kubatana.net/html/archive/demgg/041103umsebenzi.asp?sector=ELEC&year=2004&range_start=1 (accessed 6 November 2013).

SADC [Southern African Development Community] 1992. *Declaration and Treaty of the Southern African Development Community* of 17 August, Windhoek.
SADC 2000. Communiqué of 7 August. Windhoek: SADC Summit.
SADC 2001a. Communiqué of 11 September. Harare: SADC Ministerial Task Force on Developments on Zimbabwe.
SADC 2001b. Communiqué of 11 December. Harare: SADC Ministerial Task Force on Developments in Zimbabwe.
SADC 2003a. Communiqué of 3 April. Harare: SADC Organ on Politics, Defence and Security Cooperation.
SADC 2003b. Communiqué of 26 August. Dar es Salaam: SADC Summit.
SADC 2004. Communiqué of 16 August. Grand Baie: SADC Summit.
SADC 2007. Communiqué of 29 March. Dar es Salaam: SADC Summit.
SADC 2008. Communiqué of 9 November. Johannesburg: SADC Summit.
SADC 2009a. Communiqué of 30 March. Swaziland: SADC Summit.
SADC 2009b. Communiqué of 8 September. Kinshasa: SADC Summit.
SADC 2009c. Communiqué of 5 November. Maputo: SADC Organ on Politics, Defence and Security Cooperation.
SADC 2010. Communiqué of 19 August. Windhoek: SADC Summit.
SADC 2011a. Communiqué of 1 April. Livingstone: SADC Organ on Politics, Defence and Security Cooperation.
SADC 2011b. Communiqué of 20 May. Windhoek: SADC Summit.
SADC 2011c. Communiqué of 29 May. Johannesburg: SADC Summit.
SADC 2012a. Communiqué of 1 June. Luanda: SADC Summit.
SADC 2012b. Communiqué of 18 August. Maputo: SADC Summit.
SADC 2012c. Communiqué of 8 December. Dar es Salaam: SADC Summit.
SADC 2013. Communiqué of 11 January. Dar es Salaam: SADC Organ on Politics, Defence and Security Cooperation.
Sata, M., 2012. Interview. *Telegraph*, 22 January.
SATAWU [South African Transport and Allied Workers' Union] 2008. Press release of 17 April. Available from: www.etf-europe.org/etf-press-area.cfm/pressdetail/1918/region/2/section/0/order/1 (accessed 13 November 2013).
Short, C., 2007. One bad letter with long-lasting consequences. *The New African*, 462 (May).
Skelemani, P., 2009. Interview. *SW Radio*, 29 January. Available from: www.mmegi.bw/index.php?sid=1&aid=8&dir=2009/January/Thursday29 (accessed 21 November 2013).
Smith, D., 2010. Eugene Terre'Blanche's death stirs up fear and anger in South Africa. *Guardian*, 5 April.
Smith-Höhn, J., 2010. *Zimbabwe: Are targeted sanctions smart enough? On the efficacy of international restrictive measures*. Institute for Security Studies, Situation Report, 4 June. Johannesburg: Institute for Security Studies.
South African Observer Mission 2002. Interim statement to the Zimbabwean presidential elections of 9 and 10 March 2002. Harare. Available from: www.dirco.gov.za/docs/2002/zimb1303.htm (accessed 20 June 2016).
South African Parliament 2000a. Proceedings of 11 April. Cape Town: National assembly.
South African Parliament 2000b. Proceedings of 23 May. Cape Town: National assembly.
South African Parliament 2001. Proceedings of 27 February. Cape Town: National assembly.
South African Parliament 2003. Proceedings of 25 March. Cape Town: National assembly.
South African Parliament 2007. Proceedings of 28 March. Cape Town: National assembly.
South African Parliament 2008. Proceedings of 25 June. Cape Town: National assembly.

Southall, R., 2009. Understanding the 'Zuma tsunami'. *Review of African Political Economy*, 36 (121), 317–333.
Stübig, S., 2007. Wirkungsloser Druck: 'Pariastaat' Simbabwe zwischen westlichen Sanktionen und regionaler Solidarität. *GIGA Focus*, no. 5.
Taylor, I., 2011. South African 'imperialism' in a region lacking regionalism: A critique. *Third World Quarterly*, 32 (7), 1233–1253.
Tendi, B.-M., 2010. *Making history in Mugabe's Zimbabwe: Politics, intellectuals and the media*. Bern: Peter Lang.
Trollip, A., 2010a. Press release of 1 February. Democratic Alliance. Available from: www.polity.org.za/article/da-statement-by-atholl-trollip-democratic-alliance-parliamentary-leader-calling-on-jacob-zuma-to-take-a-decisive-stand-on-zimbabwe-at-uk-talks-01022010-2010-03-01 (accessed 6 November 2013).
Trollip, A., 2010b. Press release of 5 April. Democratic Alliance. Available from: www.polity.org.za/article/da-statement-by-athol-trollip-democratic-alliance-parliamentary-leader-on-zimbabwe-05042010-2010-04-05 (accessed 6 November 2013).
Trollip, A., 2010c. Press release of 3 March. Democratic Alliance. Available from: http://m.polity.org.za/article/da-statement-by-athol-trollip-democratic-alliance-parliamentary-leader-on-zimbabwe-03032010-2010-03-03 (accessed 11 November 2013).
Trollip, A., 2010d. Press release of 20 August. Democratic Alliance. Available from: www.polity.org.za/article/da-statement-by-athol-trollip-democratic-alliance-parliamentary-leader-accusing-zuma-being-complicit-in-the-effective-disbandment-of-the-sadc-tribunal-20082010-2010-08-20 (accessed 18 December 2013).
Trollip, A., 2011. Press release of 27 June. Democratic Alliance. Available from: www.polity.org.za/article/da-statement-by-athol-trollip-democratic-alliance-parliamentary-leader-calling-in-president-zuma-to-ensure-tougher-sadc-stance-on-zimbabwe-is-maintained-27062011-2011-06-27 (accessed 28 November 2013).
Tsvangirai, M., 2003. Zimbabwe's deepening crisis. *South African Journal of International Affairs*, 10 (1), 131–137.
US Congress 2001. Zimbabwe democracy and economic recovery act. Washington DC.
US President 2003. Blocking property of persons undermining democracy processes or institutions in Zimbabwe. Executive order 13288 of 6 March. Washington DC.
Vavi, Z., 2004. *We are not quiet diplomats*. Available from: http://archive.kubatana.net/html/archive/opin/041105cosatu.asp?sector=lab&year=2004&range_start=1 (accessed 19 November 2013).
Vavi, Z., 2007. Interview. *Financial Times*, 12 December.
Willems, W., 2005. Remnants of empire? British media reporting on Zimbabwe. *Westminster Papers in Communication and Culture*, October, 91–108.
WOZA [Women of Zimbabwe Arise!] 2008. *Freedom in a fortnight? A view from the trenches*. Available from: http://wozazimbabwe.org/?p=240 (accessed 3 December 2013).
ZCTU [Zimbabwe Congress of Trade Unions] and COSATU 2009. Statement of 3 February. Available from: www.cosatu.org.za/show.php?ID=167 (accessed 19 November 2013).
Žižek, S., 2000. Da capo senza fine. In: J. Butler, E. Laclau, and S. Žižek, eds., *Contingency, hegemony, universality: Contemporary dialogues on the left*. London: Verso, 213–262.
ZLHR [Zimbabwe Lawyers for Human Rights] 2008. Statement of 15 July.
Zondi, S., and Bhengu, Z., 2011. *The SADC facilitation and democratic transition in Zimbabwe*. Johannesburg: Institute of Global Dialogue.
Zulu, L., 2010. Interview. *SW Radio*, 17 June. Available from: http://nehandaradio.com/2010/06/22/sa-mediator-lindiwe-zulu-speaks-to-bth/ (accessed 27 February 2013).
Zuma, J., 2006. The West is bent out of shape. *The Spiegel*, 20 December.

Zuma, J., 2009a. Speech of 27 August. Harare. Available from: www.dirco.gov.za/docs/speeches/2009/jzum0827.html (accessed 10 December 2013).
Zuma, J., 2009b. Speech of 28 August. Harare. Available from: www.gov.za/statement-president-jacob-zuma-conclusion-his-official-working-visit-zimbabwe-read-minister (accessed 11 November 2013).
Zuma, J., 2009c. Speech of 7 September. Kinshasa. Available from: www.dirco.gov.za/docs/speeches/2009/jzum0907.html (accessed 10 December 2013).
Zuma, J., 2010. Interview. *Financial Times*, 24 February.
Zuma, J., 2011. Zimbabwe Report of 31 March. Livingstone: Southern African Development Community. Available from: http://nehandaradio.com/2011/06/17/zumas-controversial-report-on-zimbabwe/ (accessed 10 December 2013).

6 Regional interventions in Africa and beyond

This book aims to contribute to theorising a phenomenon that has not received much attention from critical intervention scholarship yet, despite being very topical. *Regional* forces seem to perform interventions as much as the wider international community does. This book has conceptualised regional interventions as a discrete set of discourses and practices, without however essentialising this difference to a universalised peace, generally conceived of in terms of liberal peace. Based on the re-reading of previous research on interventions with political discourse theory, it was possible to reconstruct the fragility and elusiveness of the differences in the Burundian and Zimbabwean fields of intervention. The book started with a question: How did the intervention shape the regional interveners? The main argument I developed throughout the book revolves around the rise and fall of regional authority in two fields of intervention. The crises in Burundi and Zimbabwe functioned as discursive surfaces that modified the collective subjectivity of the respective neighbourhoods. The book is an analysis of how regional politics towards these crises shaped regional agency in international relations.

In this concluding chapter, I will first give an answer to the guiding question of this book. This section will summarise the findings from the two empirical cases of the regional interventions into Burundi and Zimbabwe. It will become clear that both interventions altered the ways in which the regional forces comprehended themselves. However, the emerging regional subjectivities were contrary to each other, as I will explain in detail below. Based on this answer to the guiding question, I will then discuss how this book contributes to our better understanding of regional interventions more generally.

How the interventions shaped the regional interveners

Suturing dislocations: the constitution of Burundi and Zimbabwe as objects of regional intervention

In Chapter 2, I conceptualised interveners as aiming at externally suturing a dislocated place. In the contemporary world, mass violence is widely considered as a sign of dislocation. By implication, many interventions are justified to contain mass violence and heal a dislocated society. Burundi can be considered as a paradigmatic example of such reasoning. By 1995, both regional and international forces feared 'another Rwanda', that is, mass violence on a genocidal scale. In the light of deepening violence, calls to urgently do something appeared almost natural. By contrast, the Zimbabwe of 2000 was a significantly less violent place that nevertheless became an object of international intervention. The last case highlights the contingency of constituting a place as dislocated. Diagnosing a dislocation is thus already an act of signification, providing a foundation for a future intervention.

The emerging regional interveners in Burundi and Zimbabwe constituted the dislocation quite differently. In the case of Burundi, the texture of the crisis seemed quite clear. The violence was widely seen as the result of an historic antagonism that divided the Burundian polity into a majority and a minority. Although regional interveners like Mandela, Mkapa, Museveni, and Nyerere initially tried to articulate a counter-position to this hegemonic signification of the violence in Burundi, it was impossible to escape these categorisations. Understanding the Burundian polity as ethnically divided was a deeply sedimented representation that emerged throughout history and gripped most of the forces in the field of intervention. The above-mentioned figures could re-signify the crisis, but the sedimented representations imposed themselves onto their statements and speeches as well. Despite this reductionist signification of the Burundian dislocation, the constitution of the problem as being attributable to a demographically defined antagonism between a majority and a minority functioned as a shared foundation for the regional interveners. In the light of the deepening dislocations in Burundi the emerging regional intervention could constitute itself as preventing the worst of all dislocations, namely genocide.

The dislocation in Zimbabwe was far from clear. Initially the South African Government denied the existence of such a dislocation, whereas the opposition was already speaking of a multidimensional crisis that had set Zimbabwe on a tragic course. Depending on the position of the speaker, the dislocation in Zimbabwe looked quite different and was ascribed to different origins. The official regional intervention initially constituted the dislocation as a land crisis that originated from the land dispossessions during British colonialism. In this signification an antagonism similar to the one in South Africa divided the Zimbabwean polity, rendering land reform a necessary policy. Enacting the crisis as related to a particular policy demanded a careful approach to facilitating reform. A fundamental external transformation of the politics – as demanded by those seeing Mugabe plunging Zimbabwe into the abyss – seemed misplaced from this point of view, at least initially. Over time, it became more difficult to constitute Zimbabwe in terms of limited crisis. Most regional forces could no longer escape from signifying the dislocation as resulting from a political antagonism between an increasingly authoritarian ruling party on the one hand and the opposition on the other. So, between 2000 to 2007, the meaning of the dislocation was fiercely contested, constituting Zimbabwe as an arena of regional disagreement rather than unity.

168 *Regional interventions in Africa and beyond*

The difference in signifying the respective dislocation had an effect on how the intervention shaped the regional interveners. To recapitulate, interveners imagine themselves suturing a dislocated polity, which itself has lost its ability to do so. By refusing to constitute Zimbabwe as such a dislocated place, the official regional interveners in southern Africa could not imagine themselves in the same way as their eastern African counterparts, as I will elaborate in the following.

Inducing external closure: liberal peace and its alternatives

Using political discourse theory, I conceptualised regional intervention as being subjected under the modi of hegemony and counter-hegemony. As soon as a strong dislocation in need of external closure is attested, a field of intervention is emerging, in which – almost by definition – a multitude of significations of a future yet to come circulate. It is a field which is not yet ordered: that is, a field in which no particular future has emerged as a shared horizon of change. This assertion of a particular future as a shared horizon of change is what Laclau theorised as a discursive hegemony. It so happens that no field of intervention is a completely unstructured terrain that is open for any future to assert itself as the horizon of change. On the contrary, liberal peace had long functioned as the international standard order vis-à-vis the many possible futures that a crisis might expose. At the time the Regional Peace Initiative on Burundi was established, liberal peace functioned as an empty signifier structuring the global thinking about interventions. Even though some might have expected that the regional intervention would give rise to a *different* empty signifier (cf. Tickner and Blaney 2012, p. 3), the regional intervention into Burundi did not escape from this hegemonic mode of conceptualising external closure. Instead of being *essentially* different from other forms of intervention, the difference is in the detail – as became visible in Zimbabwe. Here the official regional intervention identified 'redistribution', a different signifier to 'liberal peace', as potentially suturing the dislocation.

The Burundian field of intervention was a crowded terrain in which there was however a basic agreement about the dislocation, as summarised in the preceding paragraph. The emerging ordering of the field could thus build on this common signification but also on a history of suturing this dislocation. In preceding years, power-sharing had already functioned as a device to destabilise said antagonism in Burundi. Even though initially the regional interveners denied hegemonising a particular order, in the light of the deepening violence, the Regional Initiative soon bounded its own existence to the establishment of 'democracy and security for all' – a circumscription of power-sharing. Power-sharing thus asserted itself as a horizon of change that was empty enough to be acceptable to heterogeneous forces. The Burundian power-sharing as codified in the Arusha Peace and Reconciliation Agreement reflected the emerging global hegemony of liberal statebuilding as the standard device to effect external closure. The intervention into Burundi thus seems to confirm the diagnosis that regional interveners have not yet yielded a different peace (Mac Ginty 2008, p. 143, Richmond and Tellidis 2014, p. 578).

The official regional intervention into Zimbabwe, however, refused to constitute the country as a terra incognita whose structure needed to be radically recast externally. Rather than thinking of their intervention in globalised liberal statebuilding terminology, the official regional interveners integrated the Zimbabwean dislocations into the logics of settler colonialism and liberation. Accordingly, they imagined their function as helping to address historical injustices as well as facilitating the continuation of the liberation. It is striking that much of the alternative filling of the intervention was not articulated in public but in internal discussion documents that were leaked years later. The official regional intervention was careful not to position itself against liberal peace. Rather, structural signifiers like 'democracy' and 'power-sharing' were filled differently, rendering the difference from hegemonic peacebuilding less obvious.

These cases illustrate the difficulties in articulating a counter-hegemony to liberal peacebuilding. It would be misguided to expect 'African solutions to African problems' to signal a radical alternative to hegemonic peace. But the regional intervention in Zimbabwe was also a testament to the possibility of articulating traces of difference to liberal peacebuilding. The regional intervention was not able to openly propose the continuation of the revolution as the horizon of change for Zimbabwe. Such potentially counter-hegemonic terminology no longer signalled a prosperous future in global politics, but a past. Yet the regional intervention was able to utilise accepted terminology, filling it differently. Other cases on the African continent, like Libya in 2011, seem to testify to this limited difference as well. When Western government officials and media still constituted Libya as the rerun of the Tunisian uprisings, African forces under the auspices of the African Union saw not just a popular uprising but also features familiar from other African civil wars. But the African Union could not convince the US, UK, and French Governments of their signification nor was anybody else prepared to listen (De Waal 2013). Sedimented ideas about politics on the African continent being deviant prevented such traces of difference being seen. In this sense, 'African solutions to African problems' can also be read as an invitation to listen to a little difference.

The constitution of regional interveners

As the guiding question of this book I asked how interventions shaped regional interveners. Very few studies explicitly focus on the subjectivity of the interveners and their transformation. Yet, as many post-structuralists argued well before the publication of this book, subjectivity is performative (Butler 1997), being formed and altered through our discursive practices. In this sense, the conclusion that in both cases, the practice of intervention altered how the regional forces comprehended themselves is not very surprising. But, as I tried to reconstruct throughout Chapters 4 and 5, the discursive practice of intervening transformed the regional interveners in very different ways. It is even possible to argue that the emerging subjectivities were contrary to each other: Once discursively enacted as a subject, the Regional Peace Initiative on Burundi distanced itself from its position of implementing policies crafted elsewhere and reinvented itself as a progressive region that was capable of action. Southern Africa, previously constituted as a group of political subjects able to manage their own affairs, became visible as a divided place reflecting upon itself while discussing Zimbabwe. This entangled regional subjectivity was not able to rise above the complexity and achieve closure from outside. In the following, I will compare the two subjectivities that emerged during the interventions, before discussing how the two cases help us to better understand other instances of regional intervention.

I approach the difference in the constitution of the regional interveners by recapitulating the first paragraph on dislocation. Based on rather sedimented discourses, the crisis in Burundi presented itself as relatively clear. The mass violence and the potential genocide demanded an urgent intervention, even from forces not having any experience in intervening. By constituting Burundi as a strongly dislocated society in need of external closure, the new interveners could imagine themselves as being sound. In Chapter 4, I reconstructed how the regional forces constituted Burundi and its representatives as an aberration to an otherwise progressive region. Although the antagonism was never completely stabilised and although it took different shapes, this frontier between intervener and intervened upon helped the regional forces to embrace a subjectivity typical for interveners but not for eastern Africa. Instead of remaining a recipient of external help or an extension of Western policies, the Regional Initiative claimed the ability to enact change. They tried to emancipate themselves from the oppressive positioning as passive subjects that barred them from shaping international relations.

The regional discourse on Zimbabwe was, by contrast, divided in constituting Zimbabwe as an object of intervention. The dislocations remained subject to antagonistic projections that criss-crossed the entire regional space. In Chapter 5, I reconstructed how the regional discourse did not establish a frontier separating the interveners from the intervened upon, but divided both the interveners and the society under intervention. The empirical manifestation of the antagonism remained fluid but the signifiers 'liberation' and 'liberalism' had at one point functioned as nodal points of the respective sides. Analogies between Zimbabwe and South Africa undermined the sovereign separation, otherwise being constitutive for external interventions (cf. Weber 1992). These chains of equivalence linking the intervener to the intervened upon prevented the regional interveners from reinventing themselves at the expense of Zimbabwe. They could not imagine themselves as being different from their neighbours but asked themselves self-reflectively: Will we become like Zimbabwe?

These two contrary subjectivities also had an effect on the policies identified by the regional interveners. Given the chains of equivalence linking the society under intervention to its neighbours, the regional discourse was not able to understand Zimbabwe as an unstructured terrain that the interveners could remodel from scratch. The official regional intervention could not imagine Zimbabwe as a body politic changed by them. The Regional Peace Initiative on Burundi, however, considered itself as remodelling state institutions so as to end the domination of an ethnically defined minority. Their relative subjective distance from Burundi enabled them to reduce complexity, to imagine solutions without immediately encountering their antithesis.

Given these contrasting subjectivities, what makes these interveners distinguishable regionally? First of all, both discourses delineate the regional performance from Western interventions, yet to a different degree. The regional interveners in southern Africa discovered agency especially in opposing Western-imposed sanctions. Throughout the intervention, SADC and other political representatives of this regional space did not get tired of demanding an end to sanctions. In these statements, 'the region' is enacted as a united space in opposition to the ignorant and deaf West, whose claim to represent the universal spoiled their ability to listen to local and regional voices. The regional agency thus began to become visible primarily by opposing Western intervention policies, thereby positioning their subjectivity in opposition to the West. The antagonistic frontier was remarkably stable throughout the intervention. On Burundi the antagonism was less pronounced, maybe given the dependence on donors financing the peace talks. The gap separating the regional from the international opened up, especially during the regional imposition of sanctions between 1996 and 1999, the period in which the regional interveners reinvented themselves as agents of change. Thereafter, the differentiation between scales became less rigid, also due to the South African Government becoming more involved. In these two discourses, regional agency was imagined as counter-agency, against a West that did not accept the regional signification of the crisis.

Yet, it would be too short-sighted to reduce their regional difference to this antagonistic frontier. Rather, in both cases, 'the region' functioned as a shared political space that would outlast the intervention. The interveners and the intervened upon would remain bounded beyond these extraordinary politics of intervention. While intervening in Burundi, the Tanzanian and Ugandan Governments, together with Kenya, revived the East African Community, which Burundi (and Rwanda) joined in 2007. Although Burundi functioned as an Other in the regional discourse, it was an internal Other – a regional aberration that could be rectified. Zimbabwe has all along been an integral part of the collective Self. Its crisis paralysed the Self, hampering the reinvention as a vanguard in the politics of African Renaissance. After the 2013 general elections in Zimbabwe, in which Mugabe was re-elected, the SADC heads of state were yearning to declare the end of the regional intervention, nominating Mugabe as the next SADC chairperson. In the words of current chairperson of the AU Commission: 'SADC hasn't got the luxury of walking away from Zimbabwe. It is a country in our region so we have to deal with it until we find a solution' (Dlamini-Zuma and Salomão 2008). Thus, 'the region' functions as a rather sedimented and, hence, stable shared space for the interveners and the intervened upon, rendering regional interveners different from the international community.

Researching other regional interventions

In this section, I will discuss how this book helps us to better appreciate other instances of regional intervention. As argued at the outset, critical intervention research has not yet conceptualised regional interventions as a different set of practices. Throughout the book I reconstructed how the regional interventions into Burundi and Zimbabwe eluded the liberal peace framework. The differences, albeit limited, from other instances of intervention would not have become visible if I had exclusively engaged with already established heuristics in this field of study. However, by engaging with a theoretical perspective that acknowledges difference, 'the region' became visible as a marker of difference. In this sense, the analytical appreciation of *regional* interventions might help to acknowledge global diversity, without dissolving difference into Western hegemony (Hobson 2007) or essentialising difference as statically given. It might help to acknowledge agency beyond the usual suspects, however without denying the limits of such agency.

It is possible to give many examples of interventions that could be subsumed under the category of regional intervention. Certainly the best researched case of regional intervention (without calling it such) is the EU's interventions in its neighbourhood. Recently the regional dimension of the war in Syria has attracted much public attention as well. Non-deniably, these cases are very different. However, as I will argue here, apprehending them as cases of regional interventions can enhance our understanding of these practices. This does not mean that such an analytical heuristic can fully capture the complexity of each case. Yet, as has been prominently demanded with respect to Europe, it can help to provincialise these interventions (Chakrabarty 2000). I contend that the logics disclosed with respect to Burundi and Zimbabwe and the analytical grammar developed here can also be transferred to other instances of regional intervention beyond the African continent. As argued in the previous section, the regional interventions into Burundi and Zimbabwe can be comprehended as contrarian cases of subject formation. So can the EU interventions and the regional engagement in Syria.

The subsumption of the EU under the signifier 'regional intervener' does certainly engender objections. After all the EU, itself representing a regional space, has not only intervened in their neighbourhood but its interventions have been directed towards dislocated places elsewhere. Yet, in many of these interventions, 'the region' has functioned as a nodal point. Research has often drawn attention to the EU's use of regional integration or association as a politics of intervention. By offering an EU membership or association perspective the latter has aimed at transforming and changing the respective field of intervention. EU membership and to a lesser degree EU association has been conditioned upon the fulfilment of the Copenhagen criteria, thereby offering a horizon of change. As research has shown, this policy of external change has been rarely successful and only under certain conditions (cf. Diez, Stetter, and Albert 2006), rendering it a crucial element of a potential European amendment or alternative to the liberal peace (Richmond, Björkdahl, and Kappler 2011). Understanding the EU's interventions into its neighbourhood as cases of regional intervention can set the EU's difference into perspective. Instead of considering the EU as a unique intervener, a comparison with other regional interventions would make visible the diverse functions of 'the region' in the respective politics of intervention.

If the EU's practices seem to burst the heuristic of regional interventions, the Syrian war does so all the more. The Syrian war stands out in its complexity, emerging as an arena of global, regional, national, and local politics since the uprisings in 2011. The diverse interventions do not even give the impression of operating in the name of a universalised peace. Rather differences in external closures have openly surfaced. This violent complexity of the field of intervention hardly bears any similarity to the cases discussed in this book – maybe most to the Second Congo War, during which numerous African armies and non-state armed groups operated on Congo's territory. Despite these limits, the heuristic might nevertheless have some added value. For instance, comparably to Zimbabwe, the regional forces seem to be deeply divided in how to signify the dislocations in Syria. Instead of being able to establish a clear frontier between them and the intervened upon, they are separated by chains of equivalence and, hence, antagonisms criss-crossing the regional space. In this sense, regional practices referring to Syria have not only shaped the Syrian war but also the regional politics in the Middle East and, considering the presence of Russia and the relative absence of the United States, also much beyond.

The theoretical grammar proposed here is receptive to the contingencies structuring other cases of regional intervention as diverse as the EU interventions in its neighbourhood and the regional interventions in the Syrian war. After all, discourse theory is a formal theory, outlining the ontologies of the political instead of making statements about empirical politics such as regional interventions. Discourse theory is thus not without language vis-à-vis the different relationality between what counts as normal peacebuilding and counter-hegemonic interventions. It would be a straw man if I had assumed a clearly definable hegemony from which regional interventions could differ. What counts as normal has changed in the last two and a half decades and is changing at the moment. A hegemonic discourse is thus a moving target, never standing still but fully performative. In this sense regional interventions cannot per se be considered as a stable, fixed counter-hegemony. It would be misleading, romanticising, and essentialising to set regional interventions as resisting Western peace-making (cf. Wodrig and Grauvogel 2016, pp. 276–277). Rather, the terminology of hegemony and counter-hegemony allows for analysis of the fragile processes between discursive formations that are constantly rearticulated, sometimes merging, sometimes diverging. Against this background, political discourse theory is able to provide an analytical heuristic to reconstruct the shifting relations of difference that are so eminently important in and characteristic of the field of intervention as they structure the possibilities for transformation.

References

Butler, J., 1997. *The psychic life of power: Theories in subjection*. Stanford: Stanford University Press.
Chakrabarty, D., 2000. *Provincializing Europe: Postcolonial thought and historical difference*. Princeton University Press.
De Waal, A., 2013. African roles in the Libyan conflict of 2011. *International Affairs*, 89 (2), 365–379.
Diez, T., Stetter, S., and Albert, M., 2006. The European Union and border conflicts: The transformative power of integration. *International Organization*, 60 (3), 563–593.
Dlamini-Zuma, N., and Salomão, T., 2008. Media briefing of 13 August. Johannesburg: South African Department of International Relations and Cooperation. Available from: www.polity.org.za/article/sa-dlamini-zuma-transcript-of-southern-african-development-community-summit-media-briefing-13082008-2008-08-14 (accessed 26 February 2013).
Hobson, J., 2007. Is critical theory always for the white West and for Western imperialism? Beyond Westphilian towards a post-racist critical IR. *Review of International Studies*, 33, 91–116.
Mac Ginty, R., 2008. Indigenous peace-making versus the liberal peace. *Cooperation and Conflict*, 43 (2), 139–163.
Richmond, O., Björkdahl, A., and Kappler, S., 2011. The emerging EU peacebuilding framework: Confirming or transcending liberal peacebuilding? *Cambridge Review of International Affairs*, 24 (3), 449–469.
Richmond, O., and Tellidis, I., 2014. Emerging actors in international peacebuilding and statebuilding: Status quo or critical states? *Global Governance*, 20, 563–584.
Tickner, A.B., and Blaney, D.L., 2012. Introduction: Thinking difference. In: A.B. Tickner and D.L. Blaney, eds., *Thinking international relations differently*. London and New York: Routledge, 1–24.
Weber, C., 1992. Reconsidering statehood: Examining the sovereignty/intervention boundary. *Review of International Studies*, 18 (3), 199–216.
Wodrig, S. and Grauvogel, J., 2016. Talking past each other: Regional and domestic resistance in the Burundian intervention scene. *Cooperation and Conflict*, 51 (3), 272–290.

Index

African peace and security architecture 2, 64, 94
African Renaissance 80, 95n13, 125, 171
African solutions to African problems 1, 21, 74, 81, 91–2, 94, 169
agency: African 78–82; interveners as the embodiment of agency 1, 4, 26–7, 66, 72, 82, 125; regional interveners' 5, 8–9, 52, 63, 67, 72–4, 79, 82–4, 87, 91–3, 125, 134–8, 166, 170–2; Western 106, 134
agonism 25, 90, 151
alternative concepts of peace: inequality 2, 9, 22, 106–7, 111–13, 128, 152n2; liberation *see* liberation; redistribution *see* land redistribution; Mbeki Mugabe Paper *see* Mbeki Mugabe Paper; revolution *see* revolution (*see also* liberal peace)
analogy 1, 56, 75–8, 82, 108, 127–30, 132, 150
ANC (African National Congress) 42–3, 46n9, 77, 109–11, 114, 118–19, 126–7, 130–2, 144, 152–3n6; Youth League 43, 130, 154n12
antagonism(s): concept of 3, 5–7, 13, 18, 21, 23–5, 27–8, 35–6, 45 (*see also* friction); in the Burundian field of intervention 54–5, 57–8, 60, 85–90, 92–3, 167–8, 170–1; in the Zimbabwean field of intervention 108, 144–7, 150–1, 167, 170–1 (*see also* MDC and Mugabe, Robert)
apartheid 8, 52, 75–8, 110, 125–8, 131, 133, 152–3n6, 155n24
Aradau, Claudia 34, 37
articulation: concept of 22, 34, 36, 39, 45; in the Burundian field of intervention 54, 60, 69, 71–3, 75, 78–9, 82–4, 86–8, 90, 93–4; in the Zimbabwean field of intervention 105, 113, 116, 126, 131–2, 138, 142, 144, 151, 167
Arusha Agreement (Arusha Peace and Reconciliation Agreement) 51, 61–2, 81–3, 87–8, 91, 168
AU (African Union) 1–3, 62, 75, 80–4, 154n16, 171 (*see also* OAU)
Autesserre, Séverine 3, 12
authority *see* agency

Bah, Mamadou 62
Barkawi, Tarak 15–16
Bentley, Kristina 56, 76, 78, 81, 94n2, 96n25
Bilgin, Pinar 21
Bliesemann de Guevara, Berit 1, 4, 15, 26, 29n1
BRICS (Brazil, Russia, India, China, and South Africa) 20–1, 113
Britain: land reform/outstanding promise 105, 107, 112–13, 148–9, 152n4; press 108, 149–50
Burundi: 'another Rwanda' 1, 50, 62–3, 85, 167; coups d'état 51, 53–4, 58–60, 64, 66–7, 73, 82, 87, 94n7; genocide 54, 56, 61–3, 67, 72, 78, 85, 167, 170; 'glimmer of hope in an instable region' 79; 'model for the rest of Africa' 53, 79, 84–5; 'regional aberration' 84, 87, 171
Butler, Judith 26, 72, 169
Buyoya, Pierre 51, 58–61, 67, 69–70, 77, 82–8, 95n18–21

chain(s) of equivalence: concept of 20; in the Burundian field of intervention 56, 60, 77–8; in the Zimbabwean field of intervention 113, 126–32, 134–5, 139, 141, 149, 170, 173 (*see also* analogy)

176   Index

Chandler, David 16, 19, 21, 72, 87, 132
change, horizon of 14, 53, 62–3, 115, 123, 168–9, 172
Chrétien, Jean-Pierre 56
CNDD-FDD (Conseil national pour la défense de la démocratie–Forces pour la défense de la démocratie) 59, 83–4, 89–90, 95n16–17, 95–6n22
coding: compatibility with political discourse theory 38–9, 46n13 (*see also* grounded theory); method of 35, 37–9; scheme 35, 44–5 (*see also* potential key signifiers and sensitising concepts)
colonialism 21, 74, 85, 91, 93–4, 105, 108, 111, 126, 142, 148–50, 167, 169
COMESA (Common Market for Eastern and Southern Africa) 70
Commission of Inquiry *see* UN Commission of Inquiry
Commonwealth 75, 106, 109, 134, 153n9
Congo, Democratic Republic 12, 16, 133, 149; Congo wars 50, 74, 78–9, 83, 90
Convention of Government 58, 64
corpus 7–8, 37, 39–44, 46n11, 72, 145
COSATU (Congress of South African Trade Unions) 42–3, 119–21, 124, 131–2, 136, 140, 143, 149 (*see also Tripartite Alliance*)
Cousins, Ben 127–8
counter-hegemony *see* hegemony
creativity 34, 36, 38–9
crisis: concept of 3–4, 15–17, 168 (*see also* dislocation); in the Burundian field of intervention 54, 64, 76, 82, 91, 167, 170; in the Zimbabwean field of intervention 9, 105–11, 114, 116–18, 120–3, 125–6, 129, 133–5, 139, 141–3, 145, 148–51, 154n19, 155n24, 167, 171 (*see also land crisis*)
critical intervention studies 3–4, 7–8, 12, 14, 19–20, 23, 25–6, 34, 166, 172

DA (Democratic Alliance) 43, 111 (*see also* Leon, Tony)
Daley, Patricia 53, 61
democracy 8, 22, 39, 44–5; in the Burundian field of intervention 50, 52–3, 55, 57–8–63, 77–8, 80, 84–5, 94n3, 168; in the Zimbabwean field of intervention 106–10, 113–16, 119, 123, 133–4, 139, 142, 169 (*see also* Mbeki Mugabe Paper)
Derrida, Jacques 5
difference: concept of 3, 5, 8, 15, 20–3, 25, 27, 34, 37, 44, 166, 171–3 (*see also* alternative concepts of peace, antagonism(s), hegemony, post-Western IR, and subjectivity); in the Burundian field of intervention 51, 60–3, 74–6, 79, 82–5, 87–8, 90–2, 168–9, 171; in the Zimbabwean field of intervention 107–8, 110–13, 115–16, 120–1, 124, 128–30, 132, 134, 138–9, 148, 168–9, 171
dislocation(s): concept of 13, 15, 17–18, 27–8, 166–8 (*see also* crisis and violence); in the Burundian field of intervention 53–4, 56, 61–3, 70, 73, 78, 81, 83–4, 167–8, 170; in the Zimbabwean field of intervention 108–9, 116–18, 120, 123–4, 126, 133, 167–70; other cases of regional interventions 172–3
distance 1, 12, 16, 67, 73, 78, 89, 91, 108, 110, 115, 129, 138–9, 143, 148–50, 155n24, 170–1 (*see also* chain(s) of equivalence and difference)

EAC (East African Community) 8, 51, 65, 69, 73–4, 95–6n10–11, 171
emancipation 5, 8, 20, 23, 52, 73, 82, 137, 170
emergency 13, 15, 67 (*see also* dislocation(s))
empty shell 19 (*see also* terra incognita)
empty signifier: concept of 18–20, 22, 39 (*see also* liberal peace); in the Burundian field of intervention 51–3, 57, 61–3, 168; in the Zimbabwean field of intervention 117, 121–2, 124 (*see also* power-sharing and change)
ethnicity 45, 54–8, 60–1, 87, 94n6, 167, 171
EU (European Union) 45n1, 92, 94, 96n24, 106, 134–8, 144, 151, 154n14, 172–3
external closure 13, 18, 23, 53, 89–90, 109, 168–70 (*see also* crisis and dislocation)

Fassin, Didier 15, 108
Feyerabend, Paul 34
field of intervention: conceptualisation 3–7, 12–13, 16, 23–6, 28, 39, 168, 173; Burundian 51, 57, 62–6, 74, 76–8, 80–1, 84, 86, 90, 93, 167–8; Zimbabwean 113, 115–18, 122, 134, 137, 148; other cases of regional intervention 172–3
floating signifier(s): concept of 5, 22–3, 27–8; in the Burundian field of intervention 69, 71, 73, 79, 83; in the

Zimbabwean field of intervention 124, 138, 140–1
friction(s) 2–3, 23–5, 27, 87 (*see also* antagonism)
Frodebu (Front pour la démocratie au Burundi) 53, 59, 70, 83, 95n20

Glaser, Barney 38
Global Political Agreement 106, 121–4, 136, 151, 153n10
government of national unity 116, 118–22, 124, 148
Gramsci, Antonio 5
grounded theory 38, 44 (*see also* coding)

hegemony (incl. counter-h.): concept of 3, 5, 8, 13, 18–25, 27–8, 34, 168–9, 172–3 (*see also* liberal peace); in the Burundian field of intervention 51, 54–5, 57, 62–3, 66–9, 71–5, 81, 83–4, 88, 90–4, 167–8; in the Zimbabwean field of intervention 105, 110–11, 113, 116, 121–2, 124–5, 131, 138–9, 141, 148, 150–1, 152n1, 169
Hegemony and socialist strategy 5, 36
human rights 45, 61, 109–10, 120–1, 133, 139, 145–6, 152n3, 153n7, 155n24
Huysman, Jef *see* Aradau

international community 14–15, 26, 44–5, 54, 63, 66–8, 72, 74, 77, 81, 84–5, 91–4, 112, 137, 139, 144, 149–50, 166, 171
interviews 7, 44–5, 45n2, 46n14

judgement 39

Kagame, Paul 40, 89, 91
Kappler, Stefanie 3, 12, 25–6, 28, 173
Khama, Ian 46n10, 122, 140, 143–4
Kikwete, Jakaya 40, 46n10, 89, 121, 137, 144–5, 147, 150
Koddenbrock, Kai 15–16, 19, 29n1, 29n3, 87

Laclau, Ernesto 4–8, 12–13, 15, 17, 19–20, 22–4, 26–8, 34–6, 46n11, 60, 66, 69, 87, 90, 117–18, 120, 137, 144, 168
Lahiff, Edward *see* Cousins, Ben
Lancaster House Constitution 107, 152n3
land: crisis 109–11, 148, 167; demonstrations 152n1; occupations 105, 107, 111, 115, 127–8, 149, 152n1, 152n5, 153n7; property rights 111–12, 129; question 108–10, 127–30, 135; redistribution 9, 106–7, 109, 111–13, 127–8, 149, 153n7, 168; reform 105, 107–10, 112–13, 127–9, 140, 152n4, 167; unfulfilled demand 107–8, 111–12, 153n7; willing seller/willing buyer 112, 127–8
Lemay-Hébert, Nicholas 4, 19, 29n1, 57
Leon, Tony 109, 111–12, 129–30, 136, 142, 146, 151 (*see also* DA)
lessons learnt 75, 78
liberal peace 4, 13–14, 18–24, 44, 52, 57, 62, 90, 110–11, 113, 115, 124–5, 138, 142, 166, 168–9, 172–3 (*see also* alternative concepts of peace)
liberation 107, 110–12, 114–15, 126–7, 130–2, 135, 138–9, 141, 152n2–3, 153n8, 154n21, 169–70
local ownership 26, 90
local turn 13, 19, 91

Mac Ginty, Roger 4, 19–21, 28, 29n7, 91, 169
Malema, Julius 43, 130, 154n12 (*see also* ANC Youth League)
Mandela, Nelson 8, 40, 50–1, 55, 57, 61, 63, 74, 77–82, 87–9, 92–3, 94n2, 95n12, 95n15, 110, 127, 167
materiality 5, 13
Mbeki, Thabo 1, 40, 42, 62, 80, 89, 93, 95n13, 105–6, 108–10, 113–16, 120, 123, 125–9, 131–2, 134–5, 137–8, 142–8, 150, 153n8–9, 155n24
Mbeki Mugabe Paper 114–16, 153n8
MDC (Movement of Democratic Change) 106–8, 111, 116–17, 119–21, 135–6, 145–8, 153n10, 154n21, 155n22–3 (*see also* antagonism(s) in the Zimbabwean field of intervention)
metaphor(s): 2, 12, 14, 24, 29n1, 70, 80, 82, 91, 129–30
Mitchell, Audra 3, 18, 26, 72
Mkapa, Benjamin 1, 40, 54–5, 58–61, 63, 71–4, 84–7, 92–3, 95n15, 167
Mogae, Festus 46n10, 110, 151
Motlanthe, Kgalema 120–1, 136
Mouffe, Chantal 5, 7, 12–13, 15, 17, 20, 22, 24–6, 35–6, 46n11, 66, 69, 87, 144, 151
Moyo, Sam 111, 127, 152n1, 152n5, 153n7
Mthembu-Salter, Gregory 56–7, 60, 70, 88
Mugabe, Robert 45, 105, 112, 119–23, 126, 130, 141–7, 149–51, 153n10, 154n13–14, 154n17, 154n19, 167, 171 (*see also* antagonism(s) in the Zimbabwean field of intervention)

178 *Index*

Museveni, Yoweri 40, 52, 54–6, 61, 65, 73, 78–9, 81–2, 89, 91, 94n8, 95n15, 167
Mwalimu Nyerere Foundation 41, 50–1, 92
Mwanawasa, Levy 46n10, 117, 143, 151
myth 23, 62, 70, 120–4 (*see also* Arusha Agreement, power-sharing, region(al) unity, and government of national unity)

Nabers, Dirk 17, 35, 39
Ndadaye, Melchior 53–4, 62, 64, 84–6
Ndlovu-Gatsheni, Sabelo 126, 141, 154n19
negative forces 88–9
nodal point(s) 8, 52, 59–60, 63–6, 74, 77, 81, 83, 110–11, 116, 118–19, 122, 124, 142, 151, 170, 172
Nonhoff, Martin 18, 36–7, 40
Nqakula, Charles 8, 50–1, 62, 80–1, 90, 94
Nyerere, Julius 8, 40–1, 50–2, 54–7, 59–60, 63, 65–6, 68–9, 71–3, 75–7, 80–1, 83, 85, 87, 90–1, 94n2–3, 95n19, 96n24, 167

OAU (Organisation of African Unity) 1–2, 40, 63–8, 70–1, 74–5, 81–3, 85, 88, 92, 95n18, 95n21, 110 (*see also* AU and Salim, Salim Ahmed)
Ould-Abdallah, Ahmedou 54, 58, 64, 66 (*see also* UN special representative)

Palipehutu-FNL (Parti pour la liberation du peuple hutu–Forces nationales de liberation) 83–4, 89, 95n16–17, 95n22
Pan-Africanism 65, 74
Pandolfi, Mariella *see* Fassin, Didier
Paris, Roland 4, 14, 23, 57
Peirce, Charles Sander 36
political discourse theory *see* antagonism(s), articulation, chain(s) of equivalence, difference, discourse, dislocation(s), empty signifier, floating signifier(s), hegemony, sedimentation, subject position(s), and subjectivity
post-Western IR 8, 21–2
poststructuralism 5, 169
potential key signifiers 38–9, 44–5
power-sharing 8, 45, 51, 53, 57–63, 78, 86, 116–17, 119–24, 136–7, 168–9

quiet diplomacy 42, 106, 109, 133

racism 9, 45, 75, 106, 126, 129, 144, 149–50
Raftopoulos, Brian 120, 123, 136–7, 142, 147, 151

regime change 135, 142–3, 145
region 8–9, 44, 50, 52–3, 57, 60–1, 63, 65, 67–75, 78–81, 87, 131–9, 141, 145, 148, 150, 170–1
Regional Initiative (Regional Peace Initiative on Burundi) 2, 7–9, 40–2, 50–2, 54–5, 57–9, 64–75, 79–89, 91–4, 95n20, 125, 148, 168, 170–1
retroduction 7, 34, 36–8
revolution 114–16, 124, 131, 153n8, 169
Richmond, Oliver 4, 14–15, 18–21, 63, 91, 113, 142, 169, 173

Sabaratnam, Meera 22
SACP (South African Communist Party) 42, 110, 116–17, 131, 138, 154n11 (*see also Tripartite Alliance*)
SADC (Southern African Development Community) 2, 9, 42–3, 105–6, 108–10, 112, 117–19, 121–4, 133–7, 139–41, 143, 145–7, 149–51, 154n15, 171; Organ on Politics, Defence and Security Cooperation 105; Principles and Guidelines Governing Democratic Elections 139–40, 154n16; Task Force on Zimbabwe 105, 113; Treaty 139–40; Tribunal 140–1, 154n18
Salim, Salim Ahmed 64–6, 70 (*see also* OAU)
sanctions 45; in the Burundian field of intervention 8, 51–2, 59–61, 67–72, 76–7, 82–4, 86–7; in the Zimbabwean field of intervention 106, 110, 118, 134–9, 150–2, 154n13–14, 171 (*see also* Zimbabwe Democracy and Economic Recovery Act)
Sata, Michael 46n10, 148
Saussure, Ferdinand de 5
scientificity 37
sedimentation 3, 5–6, 9, 13, 26, 40, 45n2, 54–5, 57, 75, 92, 105–6, 129, 144, 149–50, 155n24, 167, 169–71
sensitising concept(s) 44
South Africa: civil society 9, 42–3, 46n12, 46n14, 106, 121, 124, 136; 'model for the rest of Africa' 76–7, 132 (*see also* lessons learnt); parliament 40–3, 62, 80, 88, 89, 95n13, 109, 111–15, 117–20, 125, 128, 130–1, 133, 135–6, 138–9, 142–3, 146, 152n6; presidents *see* Mandela, Mkapa, and Zuma; opposition *see* DA and Leon
Southall, Roger *see* Bentley, Kristina
sovereignty 2, 4, 21, 73–5, 94n10, 116, 129–30, 133, 138–9, 170

Index 179

statebuilding 4, 15, 21, 23, 113, 168–9
Strauss, Anselm 38, 44
subject position(s): concept of 6, 26–7, 40; 'interveners' 4, 6, 28; 'regional interveners' 27, 67, 71–5, 78–9, 82, 91, 93, 125, 132, 137 (*see also* subjectivity)
subjectivity: concept of 1, 4–6, 12–13, 25–8, 40, 166, 169; in the Burundian field of intervention 2, 45, 60, 63–4, 69, 73, 75, 78–81, 83–5, 170; in the Zimbabwean field of intervention 2, 125–6, 132–6, 138–42, 145, 148, 170–1 (*see also* subject position(s))

Tanzania: democracy 52–3, 57; local residents 40–1; presidents *see* Nyerere, Mkapa, and Kikwete; refugees 41
Tellidis, Ioannis 21, 63, 113, 169
terra incognita 4, 57, 169 (*see also* empty shell)
Torfing, Jacob 36
Tripartite Alliance 42–3, 131–2, 143
Tsvangirai, Morgan 117–19, 122, 143, 146–8

Uganda: armed forces 45n4; democracy 52, 57, 94n5; parliament 40–2, 45n4, 53, 62–3, 79, 84–5; president *see* Museveni
UN 6, 46n5–6, 57, 63–4, 66–8, 71, 81, 88–9; Commission of Inquiry 55, 85; Secretary General 64, 66; Security Council 16, 64–5, 67–8, 81–4, 88–9, 93, 95n15, 95n20; special representative 58, 60, 64, 66 (*see also* Ould-Abdallah, Ahmedou)
Uprona (Union pour le progrès national) 53, 70, 86
Vandeginste, Stef 53, 58

violence: conceptualisation 12–13, 15–18, 29n5, 166–7 (*see also* crisis, dislocation(s), and emergency); in the Burundian field of intervention 50, 53–7, 59, 61–4, 67, 72, 79, 82, 85–6, 89–90, 125, 167–70 (*see also* Burundi and ethnicity); in the Zimbabwean field of intervention 105, 107–8, 115, 120, 128, 130, 134, 142–3, 149–50, 152n1, 154n19, 155n23–4

Weber, Cynthia 2, 73, 170
West, the 3, 9, 15–16, 19, 21–3, 44–5, 52, 70, 77, 91, 110, 116, 134–5, 137, 148–51, 155n24, 169–73

ZANU-PF (Zimbabwe African National Union-Patriotic Front) 105–6, 110–11, 114–16, 119–22, 131–2, 138, 147–8, 153n7, 153n10, 154n21, 155n22
Zimbabwe Congress of Trade Unions 145, 154n21
Zimbabwe Democracy and Economic Recovery Act 106, 134, 142, 154n13
Zimbabwe: constitutional reform 105–7, 121, 123–4, 127–8, 145, 152n3, 153n10, 155n23; elections 105–6, 115–17, 119–24, 136, 140, 142–3, 145–7, 153n9–10, 155n22–3, 171; opposition *see* MDC and Tsvangirai; parties *see* MDC and ZANU-PF; president *see* Mugabe
Žižek, Slavoj 18, 27, 61, 121
Zuma, Jacob 8, 40, 42–3, 50–1, 62, 80–1, 83, 88–9, 93, 106, 122–4, 132, 136–8, 149–50, 152

Taylor & Francis eBooks

Helping you to choose the right eBooks for your Library

Add Routledge titles to your library's digital collection today. Taylor and Francis ebooks contains over 50,000 titles in the Humanities, Social Sciences, Behavioural Sciences, Built Environment and Law.

Choose from a range of subject packages or create your own!

Benefits for you
- » Free MARC records
- » COUNTER-compliant usage statistics
- » Flexible purchase and pricing options
- » All titles DRM-free.

Benefits for your user
- » Off-site, anytime access via Athens or referring URL
- » Print or copy pages or chapters
- » Full content search
- » Bookmark, highlight and annotate text
- » Access to thousands of pages of quality research at the click of a button.

 Free Trials Available
We offer free trials to qualifying academic, corporate and government customers.

eCollections – Choose from over 30 subject eCollections, including:

Archaeology	Language Learning
Architecture	Law
Asian Studies	Literature
Business & Management	Media & Communication
Classical Studies	Middle East Studies
Construction	Music
Creative & Media Arts	Philosophy
Criminology & Criminal Justice	Planning
Economics	Politics
Education	Psychology & Mental Health
Energy	Religion
Engineering	Security
English Language & Linguistics	Social Work
Environment & Sustainability	Sociology
Geography	Sport
Health Studies	Theatre & Performance
History	Tourism, Hospitality & Events

For more information, pricing enquiries or to order a free trial, please contact your local sales team:
www.tandfebooks.com/page/sales

 The home of Routledge books

www.tandfebooks.com